INSIDE THE BUREAUCRATIC JUNGLE

THE *UNOFFICIAL* EMPLOYEE HANDBOOK

WILLIAM B. PARKER

Library of Congress Control Number:		2006910093
ISBN:	Hardcover	978-1-4257-4364-2
	Softcover	978-1-4257-4363-5

This book was printed in the United States of America.

Notice: Known or suspected possession or use of this publication by unappointed
government employees could become grounds for extreme disciplinary sanctions,
up to and including dismissal.

No government funds were used in the direct production of this publication

To order additional copies of this book, contact:
Xlibris Corporation
1-888-795-4274
www.Xlibris.com
Orders@Xlibris.com
37522

THE AGENCY GAME:

INSIDE THE BUREAUCRATIC JUNGLE

CONTENTS

PREFACE

"It's great that you're writing your book, because it's important that

And despite increasing evidence that this is so, many citizens just don't care.

As living instruments of public policy, government employees become the natural focal point for public mistrust, ill-will, and resentment. It's easier to focus on a tangible presence, like people, than on an intangible one, like an agency or its policies and programs. So much as with lawyers, many of the public hate government workers—until they need one. This, I think, explains the dislike and mistrust government employees incur from the general public.

However, the feelings and perceptions of the public don't stop here: government employees are also misunderstood. The public denigrate government workers and calls\ them inefficient, which they sometimes are, and stupid and lazy. But this second criticism misses the mark. Government employees may be many things, but they are neither lazy nor stupid. Far from it! Having worked in the public and private sectors, I can attest that government workers can be just as hard working, and are just as talented and intelligent, as their private-sector counterparts. In fact, some of the brightest people I know work for the government. So why the misdirected skepticism and distrust?

My answer: government employees' best efforts often aim neither to help nor serve the public; instead, their finest efforts are expended just to enable themselves to survive and sometimes flourish at their jobs. It's these day-to-day actions that—with good reason—soak up much of their time and energy.

11

Why? Simple: their reward structure, their entire incentive system, demands this. In this curious, ironic twist, the public gets shortchanged because the incentive structure at government agencies won't let the employees do their real job—giving away money and other goodies—efficiently. Thus, the public is damned, curiously similar to the way William H. Vanderbilt meant when he uttered the immortal, unfortunate words by which he is remembered today—if he is remembered at all.* In both cases, "the public benefit" is a distraction, and an unneeded one at that.

This realization, that sucking the public teat means sucking hind teat, sifting through to increasing numbers of voters, prompted no less a personage than former Vice (but not quite) President Gore to inaugurate his much ballyhooed initiative to "reinvent government" (what does *that* mean, anyway?). This non-effort (insofar as I could determine, it resulted in nothing more than a few perfunctory buyouts and layoffs—to him and his colleagues, layoffs may be politically and philosophically new, but one needs an elastic imagination to call them technologically new) received much attention from a compliant, sympathetic media, and produced results in the same way that we "won" the Viet Nam War—we declared ourselves victorious and left. Mr. Gore was no more likely to improve, much less replace, the procedures that generations of faceless, anonymous agency employees have created, perfected, and employed to survive, even as they govern, than he was likely to invent a better shape for the wheel. Nothing has changed, much less been improved; *nothing* has been reinvented. Moreover, any change that actually gets implemented is likely to louse up a system that has over time evolved a symmetry and beauty of its own.

Rather than waste the reader's time with an alleged, naïve and fruitless attempt at reinvention, I have sought initially to dissect, describe and categorize the everyday behavior and phenomena which I have encountered and observed in thirteen years of government life. The next step, ambitious if inelegant, attempts to build a descriptive framework within which all (well, most) agency behavior can be readily understood. This is the first step, admittedly a crude one, in constructing a new science of government (not to be confused with political science): how

---

*   Least we forget, Vanderbilt was asked by reporters if he could run a first-class passenger train from New York to Chicago for a fare of $15—he couldn't, he responded, then he added that if it weren't for competitive pressures, he would abandon the train. His reply prompted a follow-up question that classically illustrates the ignorance and perfidy of the media, "Wasn't he running the railroad for the public benefit?" and Vanderbilt thundered his famous reply, "The public be damned!" He either neglected to follow this, or, more likely, if he did, it went conveniently unrecorded, with the point that he ran his enterprise for make money, not to give it away to the public.

government agencies act and, insofar as I can explain, why they behave that way. Not how civilians think they should act, or even want them to behave, but how they actually function. I hope these insights will explain the otherwise anomalous, aberrant, even destructive behavior of people and agencies alike.

My conclusion: it's a real jungle out there. Government employees are not Boy Scouts. They sometimes lie, cheat, and steal; they will not hesitate to stab you in the back—just like their private sector counterparts. And with good (i.e., valid) reason. If you don't believe me, just read the book—or ask Mr. Gore, who's no Boy Scout; better yet, ask his former boss.

But this handbook doesn't stop at describing: this is meant to be a jungle

rung he reached; to improve chances for the professional, who long ago achieved his terminal promotion, to reach retirement twenty years hence without suffering a reduction in pay, perks, power, or prestige along the way; and to enable the newly appointed agency head to secure his position and enjoy a pleasant tenure, as free from trouble or trauma or drama as possible. At its highest, most sublime level, this manual seeks to impart ways for staff at all levels to bend the agency and its processes to them and their aims . . . which to me, is the public sector equivalent of self-actualization. It covers behavior both at the individual level and at that of the agency. Finally, it seeks to help the practitioner understand not just how the agency acts, but also recognize the work climate and working relationships with other parties and institutions and how these affect behavior.

This handbook, I suspect, applies equally well to management employees in labor unions (now there's a contradiction in terms!), trade associations, non-profit organizations, and companies in closely regulated industries, all of them entities whose incentive systems generally parallel those of government agencies and which continuously interact with government agencies and employees.

A few words about what this handbook does not cover: "the public benefit." People deserve the government they get, and they get the government they deserve. Period. This is merely a survival manual for government employees, not a "quality control" or a "how to better serve the people" or even, finally, a "cater to the special interests" manual (besides, special interests need no special favors from this quarter: they buy their help from lobbyists, trade associations, other pressure groups, even politicians). If you want to make your agency more responsive to the public, fine. Just don't look for help here, because then you would confuse serving the public with surviving at work.

Nor is this about how to get elected—or re-elected. That involves an entirely different game—impressing, or fooling, the public—than this manual covers. This is not to say that elected officials, and especially their staff, might not learn something useful here.

If curious (or angry or horrified) members of the public don't like what they read, they should bear in mind that this manual isn't intended for them. Most people (the general public, the media, academics, even many elected politicians, agency heads, and senior staffers whom you'd think would know better) confuse how an agency actually functions with how its founders envisioned it would behave. As an agency matures, these two models increasingly and inexorably diverge. So if the public can figure out a better way to provide and administer government services (i.e., if they *can* reinvent government), and make it stick, given the inescapable constraints under which government agencies toil, more power to them: I cordially invite them to try. In fact, if they are successful, it would be my fondest hope to detail their innovations in a later edition. But if, in the meantime, the behavior described here seems uncongenial to civilians, they might consider that there is a cost to everything they do in life, including shucking responsibility, and this is it. In that sense, the public be damned!

I acknowledge freely and without reservation a huge debt to Robert Townsend, author of *Up the Organization* and *Further Up the Organization*, whose work I admire unabashedly and without apology. I have borrowed his layout—no pretense at reinvention here—with an alphabetical listing of topics. And like Townsend, I invite you to open the book and browse it at random.

Ironically, Townsend himself helped kindle the faint glimmerings of my own awareness that government agencies may be "different." These glimmerings came slowly; they began to filter through to a young staffer whose background (perhaps unusual) included, in chronological order, majoring in history in college, a two-and-a-half year active duty hitch in the Navy, five years with a Fortune 15 manufacturing giant, five years at a regional agency and seven with a temporary federal agency which was actually sunsetted. As an amateur student of management (a holdover from my abbreviated tenure in the corporate world), I had, just before starting my civilian hitch in government, read Townsend's *Up the Organization*, an extensive compendium of rules and bromides for running a Theory Y corporation.

To a wide-eyed agency neophyte, Townsend's rules and, especially, his management philosophy seemed entirely sensible and logical, and it was with increasing incredulity and disbelief that I observed managers, not just at the company where I worked, but far more frequently and blatantly at my first agency, not only ignore, but seemingly go out of their way to violate, and violate systematically, most of Townsend's ideas of good management.

To be sure, there was no protocol manual, no published book of procedures, no official employee handbook, to suggest otherwise, much less guide an agency newcomer. Nor did the actions of most staff appear at all congruent with the agency's putative mission statement (I say "putative mission statement" because it had none). Public service (read customer service) was simply an alien concept.

Could there be, I wondered, an unwritten body of rules, regulations and procedures, an unpublished code, a protocol that governed the behavior and actions of everyone who counted? But there had to be; everyone else seemed to

describe the best practices of leading practitioners of government, just as other observers purport to do for business. All of the practices described herein have been observed, most at first hand, others by trusted colleagues and friends. In that sense, nothing new is presented here. Because we consider an agency to be a living entity that depends on outside, as well as inside factors, not just to flourish but to merely exist, this handbook addresses itself not just to an agency's inner workings but to outside factors which also strongly affect life within it.

Topics of interest have been cross-referenced to let the practitioner understand the richness of the interplay between related subjects. By checking the cross-references, one may gain a deeper, hopefully richer understanding of a particular topic.

So far as my modest researches suggest, no other publication comes remotely close to doing this, so this work fills (or, at least, starts to fill) a gaping void in understanding the workings of an agency. My fondest hope is that this may constitute, or stimulate, the groundwork for creating a true science of agency behavior, a true science of government.

Had such wisdom been compiled and readily available when my government career began, it might (I say "might" because I can be exceedingly hardheaded) have saved me many lumps and bruises, and spared my nervous and digestive systems great strain. In that vein, I hope you find it instructive and helpful, and as sparing to your nerves and lower tract as it could have been to mine. And while it may not exactly seat you in the VIP seat of the chauffeured limousine of public service, it could help move you into, or help keep you firmly lodged in, the driver's seat, and in the process, make governing a suspicious, ungrateful nation more comprehensible and, thus, easier and more rewarding.

Finally, I am most anxious to enhance the usefulness of this handbook. I will welcome readers' comments and suggestions at **www.bureaucraticjungle.com**, as they will help me do so as efficiently and painlessly as possible.

William B. Parker
Washington, DC

ACKNOWLEDGMENTS

First and foremost, to Willis Wills, a wonderful teacher of English. Everything

sharing many ...., ..., ...

To Gene Gordon, whose positive support and encouragement were enormously comforting and reassuring early on.

To Susan, Ann, and Sharon for their contributions, and again for their thoughtful criticisms and insightful comments on the manuscript.

To Robbie Robinson, who generously lent me the use of his house, his word processor, his time, and most of all his patience, and without whose help this book would have come to anything more than a few illegible scribblings.

To Paul T. Hester, who helped me through the last stages of editing, to transform an amorphous blob into a finished manuscript.

To Marney, who helped me wade through the morass of proofreading.

And finally, to my darling wife Gudrun, without whose support this work would never have come to print.

To all of you, my most profound thanks and deepest gratitude.

Finally, all errors and mistakes are solely mine: no buck-passing here!

ACADEMICS

Academics, like the media, play an enormously valuable role in government: indoctrinating the populace. Indeed, their primary role is to indoctrinate future generations to look to their government for support, and to respect and uphold it in turn. Most academics directly inhabit government payrolls (as public school teachers, state university faculty, even staff at the service academies), and most of those who aren't (private and parochial school teachers and university faculty) are on government payrolls indirectly because the institution at which they teach is supported by tax-deductible contributions and government grants

A second, equally valuable function that academics perform is to conceive and develop cutting-edge solutions to real and imagined social problems, problems that require government-imposed solutions—or at least, solutions in which the government plays a leading role. The net effect of this is to expand the role of the agency in the life of the country—which means job security to its staff. In this endeavor, universities hold a comparative advantage over think tanks, mostly, I suspect, because they have broader, deeper faculty (faculty in the functional field interact with others from a much wider variety of disciplines than think tanks can support), and are less inbred—they harbor fewer political appointees waiting on the sidelines to get back into agency life. Then, too, think tank work tends to be oriented more to justify the actions of their appointees after they return to an agency.

My own sense is that undergraduates at the better colleges and universities learn theory and receive a really thorough dose of indoctrination. Rival institutions are derogated and debunked, and government is held up as the solution to pressing societal problems. By the time they reach graduate school, the student/indoctrinees believe pretty much without question in the efficacy and efficiency of the agency. The most favored among them become single-issue adherents, even committed zealots, who are ready to study applied solutions. In graduate school, the focus of their studies shifts to the nuts and bolts of programs—social service administration, transportation, public policy studies—run by various agencies.

Finally, academics serve admirably as "independent" advisors and consultants. The quintessential outside experts. Consulting contracts and the chance to supplement his *vitae* by advising one agency or another confers at least as much power and prestige on the institution that engages him as it does to the advisor himself. Even if the consulting contracts are not as lucrative as other forms of payoff, the boast that he advises, say, the National Science Foundation, cannot help but translate into added bucks in an academic's pocket. It must be added that agency purse strings tie a strong measure of control over his output.

One last point regarding academics and their views towards the agency: they actually believe what they tell their students.

over, and then and there I practically napp

in glowing terms how *my* agency, my employer, was solving the problems of the world (or, at least, the region); how, as we were blazing exciting new vistas in representation, revenue generation (taxes) and much more, we provided the prototypical organizational and fiscal model for future agencies similarly constituted . . .

By this time, I had spent six years on the payroll, the last three of which saw unmistakable signs of our evolution into the advanced life-cycle stages becoming apparent to all, even the general public. Naturally, the thesis of my seat-mate's reading matter came as something of a shock. At least, it produced cognitive dissonance.

Later it hit me. The author of her text, almost certainly her professor, had done some consulting work for the agency somewhere along the line, and the agency had hired some of his students. He returned the favor by telling the world, via his text, what a great job we were doing.

It occurred to me afterward that this implicit *quid pro quo* takes place often.

See also AGENCY LIFE-CYCLE, CITIZEN PARTICIPATION, GOVERNMENT EMPLOYEES, HERETICS, INDOCTRINATION, MARKETING, THE MEDIA, PICKING WINNERS, RADICAL THOUGHT, SOLE SOURCE PURCHASES, and THINK TANKS.

AGENCY

As it appears in this manual, the term *agency* means any generic unit of government with more than one employee. Thus, *agency* can refer, variously, to an office, a department, a bureau, a presidential or other elected administration, an entire state government, even the whole federal government.

It includes all units in all branches of government. Thus, it could include the physics department at a state university, the university's school of education, its administration, the university as a whole; also, the state's department of education, the US Department of Education, and individual offices therein.*

It is germane to add here two additional—and useful—definitions of agency:

- To the general public or special interest the agency was created to serve, the agency is a benevolent engine of grace and generosity, a purveyor of goodies, a creature to be managed and milked (if the benefactors are well organized) for their greater good.

- To elected politicians, an agency, or more accurately, its payroll, serves first as a place to reward friends who got them elected in the first place and as a convenient parking place for their relatives. Secondarily, the agency may serve as an oratorical punching bag to impress voters.

The second definition may prove more imminently meaningful.

---

* As will be demonstrated later, a strong argument can be made to include in this characterization private universities that receive government funding, though at a more distant remove.

See also ACADEMICS, ELECTED OFFICIALS, PATRONAGE, and PUBLICS.

AGENCY BEHAVIOR

At its start-up, a young agency focuses on performing its mandate as well

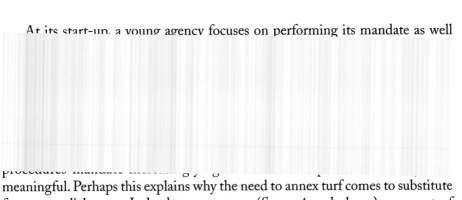

procedures mandate interacting by going meaningful. Perhaps this explains why the need to annex turf comes to substitute for accomplishment. Indeed, to a mature (Stage 4 and above) agency, turf annexation is accomplishment.

See also AGENCY LIFE-CYCLE, BLAME, and OPTIMIZATION.

AGENCY EMPLOYEES:
KNOW YOUR COLLEAGUES

I've found that (excluding appointed officials) most agency employees fall into three well-defined categories: committed idealists, hangers-on, and time-clock punchers. Each will be described in turn.

Imbued with messianic zeal, driven by burning conviction, *committed idealists* really believe that they (and only they) can solve all the great (and lesser) and pressing social problems that now afflict the world, or at least, our society. A credit to their teachers, they often harbor radical beliefs. Their views, if they were adopted, could be guaranteed to radicalize the agency's mission, which will only guarantee that when the other party gains control of the legislature, it will go out of its way to gut the agency. Committed idealists comprise many of the ambitious Young Turks who are on the make for promotion—otherwise, why not toil in the private sector where the monetary upside is higher? Many, perhaps most, are not just emotionally immature, but fated never to grow up. Often they display a one-dimensional outlook that borders on the unwholesome, which scares the hell out of me. A colleague who had once worked in a transit agency declared, in absolute seriousness, "I'd devote my life to transit." Whew!

I think he really needed to get laid.

Such people often lie, cheat, steal, and connive, and, like their counterparts with connections, rationalize or defend seemingly unethical behavior on the premise that the goodness of their cause justifies their actions. I trust committed idealists about as much as I trust a man who never drinks.

Hangers-on become that way when they suddenly realize that they are at best marginally competent and have maxed out with the Four Ps—Power, Pay, Perks, and Prestige. Painfully aware that no private sector job will pay them the salary and perks they now rate, they'll do almost anything to hang onto their job and title and all the perks that go with them. A hanger-on who feels threatened is among the most vicious people you'll ever encounter. They are threatened by capable employees, they value image over performance, they'll demand compliance with all the niggling, nitty-gritty rules, they won't let a scrap of paper go out under their signature without the proper signoffs; in short, they'll do everything can do to insulate themselves from blame.

Many hangers-on started out as committed idealists. But where idealists are above all cause-driven, hangers-on live a life of perpetual problem- and risk-aversion; their posture is quintessentially defensive. Hangers-on tend not to be overly aggressive in seeking additional turf to annex, but they'll defend their existing turf with every fiber of their being. For this reason, an idealist, especially an ambitious idealist, can drive a hanger-on bugs, and therefore will often receive severe sanctions. To a knowing onlooker, a battle between an idealist

... remarkably insignificant and self-revelatory candor, you don't become a clock puncher overnight; you aren't converted like Saul on the road to Damascus. Instead, becoming a puncher is a gradual evolutionary process. In his case, realization culminated with a friend telling him how much he'd changed over the years.

A time-clock puncher will do just about anything, no matter how ill-conceived or foolish, as long as someone else signs the authorization. Unlike hangers-on, punchers are seldom in danger of being demoted, because they are far enough removed from decision making (or avoidance) to be effectively insulated from their consequences—in fact, they are often the people who actually produce work. They tend to be unambitious; they will not challenge an up-and-coming idealist, which explains why ambitious young idealists seldom bother to stab them in the back—they almost never do anything blameworthy. Nor, for that matter, would a clock-puncher threaten a hanger-on.

Clock punchers sleep peacefully at night, hangers-on don't. Punchers are plodders; they will do their bit as long as they have to until they retire. If you ask their opinion, you probably won't get it—not a candid one, anyway. Everything about clock punchers is low, particularly their profile and energy, which explains why they appear more dead than alive. They constitute the faceless army of civil servants.

This covers most government employees, but there is a fourth category. Its members may be small in number, but they more than compensate for their relative scarcity by the savagery with which they go about amassing power. Just as Marxians characterize advancement and promotion in the private sector as climbing over the bodies one stabs to get ahead, then surely these are their agency counterparts (which I guess makes each of them a Marxian's Marxian).

om committed idealists in that they often haven't a shred
sion for the public their agency ostensibly serves, and they
having any.

dom let ethics stand in their way—they will connive, suck
and screw anyone below, level with or above them who
stands in their way or who presents them an opportunity to advance a rung up
the ladder of promotion and power. It is they who, once they grab the reins at
an agency, will force other agencies to run for cover. And despite their relatively
small numbers, it is they who set the competitive paradigm for agencies and
people in them.

Interestingly, power seekers may be neither particularly smart nor competent;
it's just that they determine with laser-like accuracy where the power is lodged
and whom to suck up to, and stab, stab, stab their way into the executive suites.
Once they arrive there, few (and then only rivals just like them) want to dislodge
them; maybe the others haven't the stomach to do so—or more likely, they just
don't care.

If you want to go a long way in public service before you become a hanger-on,
latch on to the coattails of a power seeker, preferably an able one, and enjoy
the ride. It helps to find one in an agency where few of this species exists. One
caution: if a power seeker is derailed along the road to greater power, the crash
may be spectacular—and may take you along with it.

See also COMPETITION, DECISION AVOIDANCE, ETHICS, BLAME-FREEDOM FROM, IMAGE,
PATRONAGE, POLITICAL APPOINTMENTS, and RADICALS.

AGENCY LIFE-CYCLE

form of this notion was applied to government agencies by Parkinson (Parkinson. *Parkinson's Law and Other Studies in Administration.* Boston, Heighten Mifflin, 1957), who describes the steady evolution of an agency from robust beginnings to the point that it can barely accomplish even the most basic, rudimentary tasks its founders intended (Parkinson terms this condition "Ingelitance").

Having worked in an agency at its start-up gives me a leg up on the academics, for I have experienced and seen first-hand the progression in agency evolution and maturation. My observations follow:

Stage 1: The Founding. The ink has barely dried on the agency's enabling legislation, and the electricity and excitement that can only accompany a pioneering effort crackle in the air. Morale soars. Everybody knows everybody, informality sets the tone, and no formal procedures have yet been created, much less implemented, to govern the way work gets done or even how the agency approaches its assigned tasks. Hard questions and beneficial suggestions are welcomed, and where appropriate, they are quickly implemented. Decision-making takes place on the spot by the people who must live with the consequences, so most things get done right and in a hurry. The work, which is actually challenging and fun, centers on determining how to carry out the agency's founding mandate; in other words, how to do the job the agency was created to carry out. Think of the early days of the Manhattan Project.

Funds, or more accurately access thereto and availability thereof, are plentiful; in fact, lenders fall all over themselves to set up the agency's finances and help it tap lines of credit. Spending the authorization poses a real problem; a financial surplus is the norm at the end of the first fiscal year.

There are no rivals to vie for its turf or duplicate the work it performs. In fact, as a by-product of start-up, the enabling legislation may well have expropriated turf from other agencies (too bad for them). Early hires are intelligent, aggressive, creative and competent. Many are consultants or contractors; few, if any, are politically appointed. Significant promotions go to younger, competent employees on the basis of their efforts to conceptualize and set up the program.

In a Stage 1 agency, how many employees does it take to change a light bulb? One. How long? Thirty seconds.

Stage 2: Establishing Procedures. Senior staff focuses on getting the work done. Internal procedures are being steadily developed and implemented, and the routinization of the agency's mission is taking place. Ditto for the organizational hierarchy: decisions start to get bucked up the chain of command for resolution. Though excitement no longer crackles in the air, staff remains sensitive and sympathetic to the needs of the specific public the agency was created to serve (the term *public* will be used uniformly to denote them throughout this chapter).

Flushed with the success of the founding, turf expansion becomes an explicit motivator for senior staff. More hires come aboard as the agency fleshes out its staff, among them career agency professionals and the first political placements, most of whom end up filling non-critical positions. The consultants and contractors either are absorbed onto the payroll, often to high-level positions, or they move on. If they haven't already been solved, the last of the problems relating to the discharge of the agency's founding mandate are being grappled with.

In a Stage 2 agency, how many employees does it take to change a light bulb? Two; one to change the bulb and one to ensure procedures are being complied with. How long does it take? Half a day.

Stage 3: Procedures Established. Fulfilling the agency's mandate no longer poses a vexing problem: it has been solved. And the agency's mission and internal procedures have been completely routinized and now absorb an increasing proportion of staff time and energy. Any unexpended surplus from the first couple of years disappears. Focus on programs begins to supersede focus on serving the public. Beneficial suggestions are good-naturedly accepted, but there's no longer any guarantee they'll be implemented, even if they are on target. Expansion and turf poaching explicitly and increasingly take place, often successfully, and begin to distract senior (and thus, the rest of the) staff from "mandate" work. Although work generally gets done reasonably well and on time, the need to defend new turf from other agencies crops up. Higher proportions of new hires are politically connected and increasingly take sensitive, responsible positions. Promotion becomes skewed toward the politically connected and yes-men. And the most capable of the early hires, those who conceptualized and implemented the agency's role and mission, begin to leave.

How many employees to change a light bulb? Three; one to requisition the bulb, one to change it, and one to ensure procedures are being complied with. How long? At least one day.

Stage 4: Full Maturity. Morale begins to flag. The work force unionizes. Routine and internal procedures begin to seriously curtail the ability of staff to perform

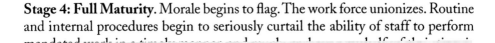

many run-of-the-mill openings are either patronage placements or have been chosen for their "reliability" by the general manager.

Year-end financial statements show a modest deficit, and the agency's bond rating falls a notch. The agency, if it enjoys taxing authority, jacks up the tax rate to compensate for the shortfall in operating funds.

How many employees does it take to change a light bulb now? Four; one to requisition the bulb, one to change it, one to ensure procedural compliance, and one to perform a safety inspection. By now, though, an official form requesting the change must be sent from the affected employee to his department head for signature, thence to the head of janitorial and maintenance services to document the need for a single light bulb. How long does it take? Four days.

Stage 5: Fragmentation and Decay. Things begin to unravel. Having become contemptuous of, even hostile to, the public, the staff can barely, if it's able to at all, keep up with its mandated work load. Important decisions are made at the very top of the organization, and then, only under outside threat. Much work simply goes undone. Worse, the agency begins to give cursory attention or leave unmet written or statutory commitments. If important work must get done, an informal network of competent employees, working outside normal channels, perform it—the other staff couldn't do it if their lives depended on it—and, depending on the quality (or lack thereof) of the inevitable review by senior staff prior to its release, the work may yet be perceived as a credible product by the public for whom it was intended. Board members routinely meddle in day to day agency business, bypassing (even ignoring) the agency head, and department heads who owe their position to individual board members take marching orders directly from their patron.

The bond rating falls another notch, and (if it is able) the agency raises taxes yet again. By now, senior staff has come to view all tax-paying entities, individuals and businesses alike, as cash cows to be milked. A few of these cash cattle, ungrateful and just a tad resentful, migrate to fresher pastures in a jurisdiction with lower taxes.

Morale hits rock bottom, only to sink lower still: professional and technical staff, who cannot believe any organization can get so screwed up as their agency, become increasingly embarrassed to even disclose their employment affiliation. Less fortunate colleagues view the lucky few who find jobs elsewhere in the same light as Devil's Island inmates viewed escapees: with awe and envy. Feelings of isolation and despair, of being trapped with no possible escape, come over the staff fated to remain. *Oh Jesus, I'll never get out of this goddamned place!* New hires comprise a menagerie of tired and worn-out staffers from elsewhere, down-and-outers and hard-luck folk who somehow earned a favor from their patron; dead-enders who can't hack it in the private sector. Promotion in menial positions, when it is not motivated by patronage, is based on seniority, not competence. Not surprisingly, despite fervent desires and frantic, ineffectual efforts to prevent it, turf is steadily being lost to competing agencies, and senior staff are grossly incapable of defending agency turf—much less recovering ground already lost.

How many employees are required to change a light bulb? Five. One to order the replacement bulb (none are on hand), one to requisition it from Stores, one to change it, one to ensure procedural compliance and one to perform a safety inspection. How long to get it changed? Seven to ten days—the fix-it order gets sent to the wrong department.

Stage 6: Dissolution and Dismemberment. The abyss from which there is no ascent. By now the agency has become a tackling dummy for the media. Worse, to the general public, it has become a widely recognized icon of inefficient futility. Stage 6 outfits aren't much fun to work in. It's silly even to mention morale: literally and figuratively, the subject is a dead issue. Gallows humor sets in with lower and mid-level employees, who have become so numbed to what goes on that they acquire the look of one ten years dead. But it's no more fun for senior officers, either; routinely pilloried in authorization hearings before the legislature and by the media, they feel besieged, and a bunker mentality sets in. Consistent with the behavior of the hangers-on they have become, outsiders and many insiders would term their actions (when they act at all) increasingly irrational. To ask a hard question or to offer a beneficial suggestion is to implicitly criticize the *status quo* and so could get you demoted or fired for heresy—doing so at this juncture would be unthinkable anyway. Besides, the agency would be incapable of acting on it even if it wanted to. Internally, a rictus sets in and seizes the agency. Vital and everyday decisions alike go unmade, and key work assignments get shuffled off to oblivion, with no follow-up to prod them along. So paralyzing is this rictus that run-of-the-mill ass-covering memos often go ignored or not acted upon—either nobody in a position to react cares enough or is capable of taking action, or there's no longer enough sense of accountability left to precipitate action (not that one should refrain from writing them: they may yet provide badly needed and welcome insurance to the writer if a Blue Ribbon panel is convened, or if someone tries to foist blame on him).

Year-end financial statements are awash in red ink, and the agency's bond rating plummets through the floor. In a frantic attempt to keep the agency

rival agency, or it is dissolved entirely.

How many men does it now take to change a light bulb? Eight or more. One orders the bulb, one requisitions it, a three-man gang (foreman, changer, and his assistant) changes it, a two-man team ensures procedural compliance, and, of course, there are one or more safety inspectors. How long to get the bulb changed? Maybe two weeks, because the gang is busy; maybe never, because they change the wrong bulb.

A classic example of a Stage 1 agency is George Washington's presidential administration. A more talented, capable, energetic group of achievers can scarce be imagined—anywhere. His cabinet included three future presidents (four including the veep, John Adams, plus Jefferson, Madison, and Monroe), and others (e.g. Hamilton) whose ability and accomplishments are proven and celebrated to this day—with Benjamin Franklin heading it up, even the Postal Service was competently run. The groundwork and accomplishments of these men stand unrivalled, and (Halberstam to the contrary) to these no other collection of cabinet personages comes even remotely close.

At the other end of the continuum, two examples, one municipal and one national, illustrate agencies which appear deeply mired in Stage 6: the District of Columbia City Government, and the US Postal Service. Both have become so dysfunctional and so unresponsive to the public that they serve as little more than welfare payment bureaus for their employees—except that their employees are generally compensated at substantially higher levels than their counterparts on welfare. The knowing observer follows developments at both with the same horrified, grisly fascination as one watches the explosion of the *Hindenburg*.

As with the creation of the universe, a lot happens early in the life of an agency: a new agency passes from Stages 1 through 3 quickly, generally in less than three years. The rest (i.e., most) of its life is taken up metamorphosing through the later stages, though, depending on who is selected to administer them, newly created departments may start life at Stage 4.

The natural evolutionary progression is from a lower numbered stage to a higher numbered stage. True, an occasional shakeup can push an agency in Stage 5 back to Stage 4, but seldom further: even the severest shakeup cannot turn the clock back too far, because the right people (performers) aren't around, and those who are, are too well entrenched and have too much invested in maintaining the *status quo*. Because of their smaller size, departments or offices can be set back a stage or (rarely) two, far more easily than an agency.

This evolution is as immutable as it is inexorable. It is also cross-cultural: the purges ordered by V. I. Lenin and the Red Guard crusades sanctioned by Mao Zhe Dong came about because each leader recognized that evolution had begun to drain his regime of revolutionary zeal (maybe Lenin and Mao believed they were reinventing government!). So the actions of many staffers were used as a pretext to have them exiled, imprisoned or executed. The great irony is that these purges only highlighted to the surviving staff (party members) that it was what you did, not what you didn't do, that could get you in deep trouble, and so even less ultimately got accomplished. The net effect of these well intended efforts was to push their governments into Stage 5.

As one might infer, not all agencies end up in Stage 6. Indeed, my observations suggest that the vast majority wind up wallowing along in Stage 4 or early 5. Structural impedances (to cite a few: legislators still need a place to park their friends; public apathy; and the likelihood that competing agencies may have advanced equally or further in their life cycle, thereby precluding their ability to snatch turf readily and insolently) preclude a speedy dissolution, no matter how short an agency falls in discharging its mandate. Nonetheless, once an agency has advanced into Stage 4, it is unlikely to blaze exciting new trails, to send a man to Mars, and its chance to "make a difference" is fast waning. When it reaches Stage 5, its chance of achieving even that modest aim can be written off. Certainly, achievement at the institutional level now becomes exceedingly difficult; accomplishment increasingly, nay, almost exclusively, devolves to individual initiative, which internal behavioral norms auger strongly against.

Rarely, after it becomes mired in Stage 6, does an entire agency disappear completely; however, offices, departments, even entire divisions (clusters of departments) may be dissolved or cease to exist. One sees them swallowed up, in whole or in part, with disturbing, and instructive, frequency. When this occurs, outsiders may ascribe it to internal reorganization, which, in a sense, it is. Insiders know better.

An exception to the "one-stage rule" involves war and the military. The sudden onset of WW II changed the US armed forces from a stodgy Stage 4 peacetime organization into a Stage 1 or 2 combat outfit. New people came in, risk takers supplanted peacetime paper shufflers, new units were created, new battle tactics and strategies were formulated and perfected, technologies which would only have brought censure to their proponents (e.g., Billy Mitchell) before the war were developed and rushed into the fray; in fact, the entire pace, level

work it was created to perform. The advent of overnight express service, which flourished because demand was high and the Postal Service made no effort to meet it until long after its competitors had become established commercially and politically, dealt the Service a blow from which it is unlikely to recover. Given the rise in the electronic transmission of the printed word and the payment of bills on-line, worse damage has been sustained. Moreover, its pricing decisions, its entire price structure, instead of being rendered by management in response to market conditions, must be reviewed by a congressional Postal Rate Commission, which is more strongly influenced by postal customers and competitors than by the Postal Service itself.

Similarly, the rise of competing modes of transportation—air, especially— undercut the preeminence of the Interstate Commerce Commission in transportation regulation. These technological changes did little to retard the agency in its march through its life-cycle. In fact, they almost certainly helped accelerate it toward Stage 6.

The progression described above is inevitable as death, as inexorable as the taxes that are collected to pay for it. The Life-Cycle Model affords the knowing observer a good indication where his agency, or department, stands in its evolution. Based on his talent and motivation, it also provides valuable clues as to whether to come aboard, remain, or move on.

If there's still demand for the services (read turf) a Stage 6 agency or department putatively performs when it is being broken up, these will be transferred to a surviving entity, always to one less advanced in its life cycle. Otherwise, the work simply lapses.

A few years ago the *Washington Post* editorially slammed a congressman who served on the House Sub-Committee on the District of Columbia, the District's congressional oversight body. Apparently frustrated, the congressman had just blistered the DC City Government in writing because it had not responded to his earlier written request to fill a particularly wide and deep pothole that his car had encountered more than once on a major city thoroughfare.

Aggrieved, a higher-up in DC City Government passed the letter to the *Post*, which responded by castigating the offending congressman and likening his action to a spoiled child throwing a tantrum.

Through its editorial treatment of this matter, the *Post* surely advances its own agenda. Mine differs: if the DC City Government can't even respond to a simple, reasonable request (the congressman, after all, did not demand the District supply him after-hours sexual favors) from a member of its congressional oversight sub-committee, just think how responsive it would be if the same request originated from an average citizen.

Clearly, an agency in the advanced throes of Stage 6.

In a last-ditch effort to stave off his impending replacement (he was being fired), an embattled agency chairman, who in three short years had adroitly grown his agency from Stage 1 to a mature Stage 5 outfit, summoned his Power Team, and a cadre of supporters and friends (perhaps a dozen people all told) for one last desperate weekend-long offensive effort.

The chairman and his merry band of camp followers cranked up the Xerox machine and proceeded to photocopy some twelve hundred pages of "accomplishments." These ranged from marketing flyers to speeches he'd made to mother's clubs—proof positive of all the great good things (and everything else: moral uprightness?) that his tenure as agency head had seen.

The resultant twelve-hundred page—I'm not sure what you'd call it: instrument, document, or tablet of paper?—was sent the following Monday morning to the leading elected officials who had appointed him in the first place and—who else?—the news media. Prehaps because the first rational impulse on receiving this massive communication was not to read but to pitch it—or maybe weigh it—all recipients were mercifully silent on this subject in print and on the air.

This effort was likened, neither lightly nor inaccurately, by an unsympathetic department head, who clearly lacked membership in the chairman's Power Team, to Hitler in the bunker. Veterans of the last days of the Nixon White House, I am sure, know this feeling all too well.

Recounting this sordid tale today only leaves me with the most profound sadness that it had to happen; a feeling I find curious in light of the gloating satisfaction I felt when, as an eager young staffer, I heard of the weekend adventure and, even more, when the chairman's departure was announced soon afterwards. Now that I'm older, I appreciate their motivation (desperation bordering on terror) far more completely, and knowing how puny, ineffectual, and hopeless was their last, final effort only heightens my sadness.

See also BUREAUCRACY, COMMITMENTS, COMPETITION, EXPEDITERS, ...

ALPHA DEPARTMENT

In the lives of wolves, the dominant, or Alpha, Male exerts disproportionate influence on the life of the pack. Similarly, in public agencies *Alpha Departments* often exert dominance over their lower status counterparts.

Just as one can easily tell an alpha male from a lower status, or beta male (alphas get first crack at kills and at females during mating season, and pee on three legs; betas settle for nutritional and sexual leftovers, pee on four legs, roll in an alpha male's urine and otherwise behave with unchallenging submissiveness in an alpha's presence), so, too, can one determine an alpha department. Its secretaries let you know by the tone in their voice that they are getting off by ordering you to jump (at the instigation of their boss) and knowing that you have no recourse except to comply; its staff demand—and without challenge get—your support for their efforts and funding and other meaty internal resources; and they call the shots on sexy, high visibility projects. Nobody challenges them, not directly, anyway. For all I know, their male employees all pee on one leg—though I cannot verify this; however, I have seen beta staffers all but roll in the urine of their alpha brethren. In short, in the eyes of senior staff, an alpha department can do no wrong.

Every professional staffer in the agency with the slightest bit of moxie and competence wishes he could work in the alpha department (everyone rallies behind, or at least flocks toward, a perceived winner—or shuns a loser), few internal barriers are thrown up to frustrate or stall alpha work, and the authority and credibility of the alpha department head go internally unchallenged.

How does one department separate itself from its run-of-the-mill peers to become dominant? I really can't say; I have observed alpha departments whose nominal responsibilities bore little resemblance to, or congruence with, the agency's mandate; on paper, an alpha department may hold secondary, even tertiary responsibilities.

Still, a couple of possibilities suggest themselves. One, the alpha department manager is able to establish the appearance of greater competence and credibility with the agency's senior hierarchy, its board and legislators on its oversight committee. Throughout the agency, he is considered first among equals. When he speaks, others listen. So when opportunity or crisis arises, he is given the responsibility and the authority to meet them. His authority carries with it the ability to summon up without challenge or limit people and resources from other departments.

The flip side of this is that the heads of the beta departments, in contrast to the alpha head, are mediocre in quality and credibility, and could not even hope to challenge him (though they may fight a perpetual tong war among themselves to become the Avis to his Hertz). Possibly, they know they could never fill their alpha counterpart's shoes, could not long withstand the spotlight which his higher profile confers on his position, so they are content to

See also LEADERSHIP, MOCK-ALPHA DEPARTMENT, and PUBLICS.

ASSISTANTS

A sure sign of a weak, insecure manager is the proliferation of assistants. Assistants act as buffers between a boss and his subordinates, so that he won't have to face them. Assistants make his decisions for him and otherwise usurp his authority and erode his power.

In many ways, an assistant is the ideal managerial position in government—it allows access to, and often confers on one, all of the power, but little of the responsibility and none of the accountability, of the boss or his office. A weak, insecure manager welcomes this, because he will gladly let someone else make his decisions for him. A boss who encourages and sanctions this practice will generally back his assistants and, thus, their decisions and actions. No matter how wrong-headed their policies may be, no matter how much ill-will they subject the agency to, the institutional cost he inflicts from their consequences is lower that the psychic cost he would incur from shouldering responsibility.

My observations suggest that assistants who flourished under this arrangement, when they are promoted into the boss's shoes, usually continue this practice (i.e., they find someone else to decide issues for them) because they are not used to, and thus shrink from, the accountability that their lofty new position confers on them.

If anyone questions an assistant or complains of his actions, he will always invoke the authority of the boss, saying that the boss wanted or ordered it. Be sure that (if he is weak) he will faithfully report any who oppose him for not being team players or, worse, brand them as heretics. Or (if he is strong) act against them with the full authority and backing of his boss. The latter are much more formidable, and thus riskier to oppose.

See also AGENCY EMPLOYEES and BARRIERS.

AUTHORITY

...... is ...... for granted by government employees the same way it is granted, which is to say yielded, by most of the population—pretty much without question.*

And there is the kicker, the excitement. Many, perhaps most, Americans seem to want (and certainly need) direction in their lives. Many, incapable of making their own decisions, will do just about anything if it is ordered or ordained by *duly constituted authority*, willingly (even unwillingly, it really doesn't matter).†　They'll spy on other countries, on fellow citizens and on each other, execute felons, slaughter the citizens of hostile nations *en masse*, deprive an adult of his right to

---

*   Why is this so? While I don't know for sure, I believe that many, perhaps most, of the populace subconsciously view government as a substitute deity. By inference, your word, your official, duly constituted, duly authorized word, becomes the Word of God.

†　 Most instructive is a mid-1950s psychology experiment conducted at Yale. An authority figure (clad in a white lab coat) directed student subjects to "administer" a shock to punish the supposed subject who did not respond as desired to questions (the shockee really didn't get shocked; he merely feigned being shocked). As the "voltage" increased with each unsatisfactory response, the shockee responded with increasing drama and violence to each successive jolt. Whatever else it proved, the experiment showed conclusively that most Americans (or Yale undergraduates, at least) will go a long way to harm their fellow citizens without questioning, without resisting, apparently without even considering the consequences of their act, as long as their orders come from a seemingly competent and therefore, accepted authority. I get chills thinking of this.

---

reproduce, of his right to earn a living, of access to his pets and his children, seize his property and worldly goods, and attach some or all of his current and future income—and they tell us slavery is dead!

To me, the limitless power—the power to control almost every aspect of citizens' lives, including their right thereto, the power of life and death, power over the quality of life—to me, this is the ultimate high, almost better than sex. I tingle all over just thinking about it.

If you don't get the same tingle, then you're probably not cut out to run an agency, much less set public policy.

See also GOVERNMENT AS RELIGION and SEX.

BACK UP THE NUMBERS

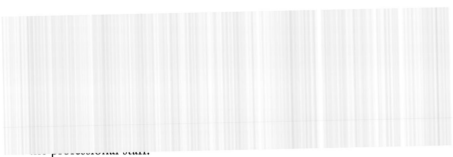

After the proofread copy had been sent off to the printer, an appointed checker came through the agency with a clipboard and a draft of the report. Starting with chapter one, he asked the person responsible for each section of the report to show him, literally, from where every cited number (above and beyond page numbers) came. The source, the derivation (Table X of the Bureau of Labor Statistics of such and such a date, column 2, line 3) of each figure was carefully noted, chapter and verse. I have never seen such care taken in a study, before or since.

This way, if any number, any data or source were questioned, no questioner, no attacker, could ever accuse us of fabricating numbers—and make it stick.

See also BLAME-FREEDOM FROM, COMPETITION, and SIGNOFFS.

BARRIERS, ERECTING

As agency (or department) head, your agency is your turf, your preserve. You neither need nor desire interference from outside meddlers and busybodies—not from the public, not from rival agencies, and definitely not from legislators or the media—or from any of the agency's other publics. With the help of your Power Team, your fiefdom is (or should be) yours to rule.

To preclude outside busybodies from obtaining access, you need to install barriers to keep them at bay. The barriers can be physical—keep 'em off the premises (chain link fences, watch dogs, security guards)—or procedural (restricted staff and media access, telephone systems where all calls must be either routed through a central switchboard, ostensibly to be returned, but are never taken directly, or better yet, routed into a grotesque automated voice mail loop with no provision for live human interaction, and so forth).

What outsiders can't see and don't know, won't hurt your agency or you.

See also ELECTED OFFICIALS, THE MEDIA-SOME THOUGHTS, POWER TEAM, PUBLICS, and TURF.

BEHAVIOR GAP:
TOTO, THIS AIN'T KANSAS!

Who says how agencies are supposed to function? The only people I know who so opine are non-participants like the general public, academics and the media, and the last two don't count because they're on the payroll. Elected officials? What do they know?

That's the whole point of this manual—how agencies really function. Reread the preface.

Yes, there is a gap, a wide gulf, between how the public believe government agencies function and how agencies really act—and there is little in common between the two. Think of the city of New Orleans after before, during and after Hurricane Katrina. The width of the gap depends on which stage in its life-cycle an agency finds itself, and as it advances, the gap turns into a yawning gulf (pun intended)

"And," as Walter Cronkite used to say, "That's the way it is . . ."

See also ACADEMICS, THE MEDIA-SOME THOUGHTS, THEORY OF THE AGENCY, and UNDERSTANDING THE GAME.

BELTWAY, INSIDE THE

As the focal point of government, Washington, DC has been a boom-town; the population of its metropolitan area quintupled between the 1930s and 1990. (Nor has growth in government by any means been limited to Washington, DC; state capitals such as Sacramento and Springfield, Harrisburg, Austin, and Albany have grown from small towns to major cities in their own right during this span.) Despite its celebrated inability to hang onto a major league baseball team during this period (since corrected), Washington DC truly evolved into an imperial city. Capital of the Free World and the First World (which amounts to the same thing). And knows it. Imperial Washington, I suspect, has much more in common with third century Rome, Bourbon Paris, and Victorian London, than with New York, Chicago, or Los Angeles. By this measure, Washington has a lot more in common with Sacramento, Springfield, Albany, and Harrisburg than it has with New York, Chicago, and Los Angeles.

When it comes to government, Imperial Washington is the National and American Leagues combined, and then some. And if Washington is the big leagues, then state government and big city halls (with a few exceptions) are the high minors, and all the rest—the other municipal and county governments and whatnot—the sandlots.

Thus it is to Washington where the most driven power seekers—the "best" legislators, the most persuasive politicians—are inevitably drawn. Ditto for the best bureaucrats. Hey, if a guy is really such a hot tamale, why's he working in Bangor? The federal corridors are filled with the most masterful agency operatives, the holders of numerous advanced degrees and black belts in bureaucracy. And the people who find their way here are the brightest and best, the most accomplished, the most highly educated, the upper case version of brethren in Pierre and Bangor and Salem and Santa Fe, from legislators and bureaucrats all the way down to the hangers-on. They aren't afraid to let others know it, either; a popular local bumper sticker a few years back read, "BUREAUCRAT AND PROUD OF IT!" Who better to do the job, to govern the ignorant and ungrateful, than they?

Some perceptive pundit noted that the people who actually run the country, those who really count, are surprisingly small in number: no fewer than two thousand, certainly no more than ten thousand. Their numbers include Congress and the White House and those who influence them—their respective spouses and lovers, handlers, image polishers and staff; the Supreme Court, its assistants and clerks; the cabinet and senior appointees; key career civil servants; the lawyers, lobbyists, and other interest group leaders who can get laws passed or blocked (both are equally important); and the leading news media and talking heads and consultants and think tankers whose influence on public policy goes unquestioned. In this sense, Washington is, indeed, a very small town. The preferred house organ is the *Washington Post*, though on occasion the *New York Times*, the *Wall Street*

talented underachievers, running on fewer than eight cylinders, is a sure-fire recipe for industrial strength emotional distress. Still, the frustrated have the background and education to do something about it. One good thing: their benefit package pays the tab . . .

As befits a center of empire, the largest industry in town outside the government is stroking: Imperial Washington boasts the greatest concentration of spin doctors, image creators and media manipulators this side of Hollywood. Nor does the comparison with Hollywood end here: many view Washington as Hollywood East, with its own cast of stars, glitz, and glamour. Except image plays a larger, more important role here than in Hollywood West, and notwithstanding the fact that a recent president was himself a Tinseltown transplant, the similarities between both cities have been noted by more than one observer.

But in Imperial Washington, star quality, or what passes locally for sex appeal, is measured in raw political power, not box-office draw, and it draws the power hungry like deprived addicts to a free fix. Like their Hollywood counterparts, they are inevitably pestered by squadrons of yes-men, rumor and gossip mongers, and assorted groupies and hangers-on, what G. B. Shaw terms "a host of parasites."

This makes Washington a city of front-runners. If you're Number One, everyone in town is your best friend. Until you become Number Two. God help you if you're a tail-ender: though if you are, you find out how many real friends you have. The Redskins, Washington's home-town professional football team for the culturally illiterate, provide a case in point. When they are enjoying a playoff season, everyone from the President down to the Third World embassy types is a devout 'Skins fan. When the team's fortunes fall, the locals constantly fill the sports talk airways with scapegoats to blame for the debacle. Too bad they haven't the clout to convene a Blue Ribbon panel to look into the matter further. Never mind . . . if they could, they would.

And in truth, the city provides a natural haven for all these and more. In no particular order, they include cause-driven dweebs (former Treasury Secretary William Simon declared that Washington DC harbors more idiots with IQs of 180 than any other locale on the face of this planet), and corporations which have much to gain (or lose) from government contracts or through congenial federal regulation. Far more fortunes are made in the nation's capital by transferring wealth than by creating it: many of the most accomplished fixers in the world swarm around. Ditto for lawyers of all stripes. Plus other assorted parties, the detritus of power.

Imperial Washington is *the* national center for the production—and dissemination—of news; and magnet for a host of non-profits, think-tanks, special interests, industry trade associations, and consumer groups, which, like Spanish Moss clinging to a live oak, somehow derive sustenance from the nearby ethereal presence of raw political power. Any number of consultants (aka Beltway Bandits) and other purveyors of expert wisdom cluster around to inform all those agencies how to do their jobs—and, the politicians, how to get reelected.

Mentioning Beltway Bandits brings up an aside: "Imperial Washington" refers to territory that lies mostly inside the Capital Beltway, a perpetually overcrowded, clogged, and often unmoving interstate highway, Interstates 95 and 495, to satisfy the literal-minded, that encircles the city (no doubt a critic would term it an apt metaphor for Congress). The locales thus circumscribed include the close-in Maryland and Virginia suburbs and one quadrant (of four) of the District of Columbia, all the turf which directly drains into the Potomac River.

Above all else, Imperial Washington is a state of mind, a city whose overwhelming objective function is to maximize power, not wealth. Imperious, insular, and curiously parochial, Washingtonians view with equal measures of distrust and disdain everyone outside the Beltway whose daily bread is earned by creating wealth. In pursuing profits, these outsiders, these *gaijin*, would imbue themselves with an alarming (to a Washingtonian's way of thinking) measure of independence, an open affront to the spirit of agency which permeates the city. Their natural "animal spirits" pose an element of discord in the natural, government-imposed order of life. Therefore, they sorely need to be governed, and their lives require, even cry out for, regulation under a *pax governmenta* that only the federal government (Washingtonians) can provide.

These *auslanders* are the same supplicants who come at once to Washington, hat in hand, to demand, beg, plead, whine, and grovel for the goodies that only their government can confer: outright handouts, such as price supports for their crops, subsidies for food, clothing, shelter, childcare, education, subsidies indeed for their very subsistence; and protection, protection from "evil empires" and

terrorists abroad, from crooks and violently inclined fellow citizens at home, protection for companies whose errant management has led their firm into deep or hot water, protection from "unfair" competition at home and abroad that's too intense for their unions, managements, companies and industries unless their government tilts the playing field steeply their way; protection, even, from
_____ f_____ d f___ _h_ddy goods and services that they are too

Naturally superior to (and suspicious of) the grubby, profit-seeking provincials who live and toil beyond the Beltway, Washingtonians view trips to the provinces—Maryland and Virginia suburbs exempted, of course—as they would trips to foreign countries, except that the states belong to them. Otherwise, the difference between, say, California and Baja California is more one of geography than of politics or diplomacy—except California has more votes.*

Imperial Washington glories in playing host to droves of tourists from Yuma and Petaluma, Osceola, Mineola, Arcola, Pensacola, and who cares where else; pilgrims come to worship at the temples and render homage in the shrines of highest government, to enjoy and experience and spend their hard-earned dollars in the wonderful "free" museums and cultural sites and steep themselves in their national mythology, even as their numbers render the streets impassable to the city's workers and residents (hence another curiously Washingtonian bumper sticker, "So Many Tourists And So Little Time!"), and renew their identification with an America they like to imagine. Ditto for the foreign tourists: Washington's (mostly) foreign-born hawkers and sidewalk vendors will take their money as gladly as anyone else's, whether they hail from Paris, Kentucky or Paris, France. (The extraordinary museums Washingtonians take for granted as "theirs" owe far more to the spending largesse of the federal government than to the beneficence of private donors, which forms the lifeblood of peer institutions in other U. S. cities. This distinction, to locals, is irrelevant: they take it as their due.)

---

* The narrowness of this distinction cannot be overstated. The apparent difference between these two locales diminished considerably when a federal appellate court ruling overturned California's Proposition 187, which would have denied state social services to illegal aliens residing in that state. At this rate, the right for illegal aliens to vote (hey, they pay taxes, don't they?) can't be far behind.

To the uninitiated and insider alike, Washington can be a tough, heartless town; it can chew up people, the high and mightily clouted as easily as the lowliest clerical functionary, and spit them out. The leading recreational sport of the governing class is zinging rivals—in other words, assigning blame. Except here the practice has been elevated to an art form, to a blood sport (think of Scooter Libby). The leading zinger delivery system is the *Washington Post*. At its highest and most sublime, the sport costs the good and the bad alike their reputation, the respect of their friends, their standing in the community, their job, their career, even their life—witness the suicides of White House aide Vincent Foster and Admiral Jeremy Boorda, the Navy's senior admiral. When a truly awesome zinger strikes home, insiders shake their heads (maybe a few friends bow their heads in sympathy), and life goes on.

Whether for the joy of playing or despite the obvious downside, Imperial Washington also plays a willing host to the "Potomac Fever" syndrome: once someone arrives from Dubuque and gets used to the big city lights, *la dolce vita*, the perks, the yes-men, and above all, the power, he doesn't want to return to Dubuque. Most don't.

I wouldn't, either.

And for Imperial Washington (to truly grasp the imperial aspect the city has taken on, visit the Diplomatic Reception Rooms at the State Department), the city has much to commend itself. All things considered, transferring wealth pays extremely well. The median income in suburban Fairfax County is reportedly the nation's highest. In the District's Northwest Quadrant, and the Maryland and Virginia suburbs, where the power elite and the lifetime civil servants and others of the "leadership class" and the better sort live and mingle, the schools range from good to outstanding, and the private and parochial and magnet public schools are among the best anywhere, indoctrinating and sometimes educating the *jugend* in the ways of their fathers (and, increasingly, their mothers). At the most elite private schools, the young inheritors learn that government is good and that blacks deserve equal treatment (unless they move next door or, God forbid, try to join the club to which their parents belong), and they steep themselves in the standard, smug, complacent attitudes and clichés that come only from growing up among a ruling elite.

The other social services are equally good and in plentiful supply, though happily, there's not too much demand for them here.

Still, Washingtonians can be forgiven for believing that because theirs is perforce the nation's, nay, the world's premier city (a few years ago, the District's leading bank unblushingly advertised itself as ". . . the most important bank in the most important city in the world . . ." and locals just lapped it up—well, no squawks were heard), they, its citizenry, therefore deserve more and better services—government provided, of course—than the colonials inhabiting the hinterlands outside the Beltway.

Because they govern the rest of the nation, they deserve museums and other cultural resources that are as good as or better than anywhere else—and the rest of the nation can and, by God, should pay for them. This is their entitlement. (Yes, America, some people *are more equal than others*.) Truly, Imperial Washington is a little different from New York, Chicago, or Los Angeles. This, pulling the levers and pushing the buttons, controlling the machine and not submitting to it, and getting everyone else to pay the tab, is true independence. Pure power. What holds for Imperial Washington holds also (though proportionally less)

inhabitants of the District of Columbia, which remains the lawfully designated Nation's Capitol, and most of them have little or nothing to do with the governance of their nation. So, like a vermiform appendix, they go largely ignored.

In these corners of town, all the urban ills a city can suffer the Distrik suffers in spades. Relics of the Jim Crow days of only four short decades past, they have been not only preserved and perpetuated, but systematically exacerbated by several decades of prevalent political and social thought, and the policies resulting therefrom. Collectively, they and their ills comprise an overwhelming triumph of the agency. Segregated, black, poor, crime—and drug-ridden, and best of all, highly agency-dependent (Distrik residents look to the government for their subsistence, or what passes for it—an agency's dream). Ironically though not unexpectedly, DC residents are exceptionally governed by a fund-less city government. Unlike Imperial Washington, the Distrik has a lot in common with New York, Chicago, and Los Angeles. Crime, poverty, etc.—conditions that require government intervention—flourish like plants in an equatorial rain forest, testimony to the pro-agency policies of the nation's self-described brightest and best.

So, too, does getting anything done at any level. Opening a store, building an office. In this, the Distrik has a great deal more in common with Tegucigalpa and Ouagadougou—and New Orleans—than with New York, Chicago, and Los Angeles: status here is measured solely by membership in or access to the governing class. Alas, this is strictly a Third World city. If Imperial Washington is the undisputed capital of the First World, it is less than certain that the Districk occupies anything like that position in the Third World. It could scarcely be termed "imperial."

One might argue fate has played a bitter joke on Distrik residents, because the DC City Government has become a metaphor for what all those ignorant, ungrateful money-grubbing provincials beyond the Beltway view as the downside of government. Stage 6 personified. Filled to the brim with functionaries, payrollers and other friends of the well-placed, few of whom seem to do much, DC City Hall struggles daily to supply the most basic municipal services—clean drinking water, trash removal, police and fire protection, and ambulance. There is plenty of demand for these public services, and despite all those City Hall payrollers, they seem perpetually in short supply. DC public schools are an unmitigated disaster, as bad as their affluent suburban and private counterparts are good. The most charitable thing that can be said of them is that they vie with public schools from the aforementioned peer cities for the dubious distinction of worst in the nation, meaning that they are not (yet) head and shoulders worse. Potholes perpetually challenge alike unfortunate motorists, who try to dodge them and sometimes succeed, and the DC Department of Public Works, which tries to keep some of them filled. Measured in programmatic largesse and agency employment, Distrik government is a model that New York, Chicago and Los Angeles can only envy but could never equal: the Distrik payroll is (at this writing) larger than Chicago's, a city whose population is five times larger than DC's. Perhaps it says something that those who govern the rest of the country provide so exquisite a role model for their own.

Whether because of this or despite this, Distrik residents have mounted a drive for statehood, no doubt thinking that this condition could pick up where self-governing cityhood stops. The current state (pun intended) of the DC City Government leaves it doubtful that statehood is in the cards. It seems about as achievable to DC City Government as keeping the potholes filled, and as the prospect of it functioning as a built-in lobby for government—for the institution, the agencies, the employees—fills me with expectant hope.

And it makes one wonder which of these, Washington-on-the-Potomac, the Imperial Washington that all those tourists from Dubuque come to see, or Washington-on-the-Anacostia, the Third World city where Dubuquers blunder only by accident even though most Washingtonians live there, which of these is the true Washington. Knowing that similar concentrations of disparity almost certainly contributed to the passing of empire from Rome and London, it also prompts one to wonder whether a national capital also has a life-cycle, and if so, what stage Imperial Washington has reached.

See also AGENCY, AGENCY LIFE-CYCLE, AUTHORITY, CAUSES, CODE WORDS, ELECTED OFFICIALS, GOVERNMENT AS RELIGION, IMAGE, THE JUDICIARY, LEGAL EAGLES, LOBBYISTS, THE MEDIA-SOME THOUGHTS, THE PUBLIC, SCAPEGOATS, and YES-MEN.

BLAME

_ _____. ___ with most

phenomena described herein, it applies both to individuals and organizations. But blame is more: it is the chief competitive weapon in the never-ending wars for turf. It is thus something to be avoided at all cost; something to be thrust, if at all possible, onto others.

No less prominent a chronicler of life in the nation's capital than the *Washington Post* characterizes the assignment of blame as "local blood sport." And many a prominent public service career has been built on doing just that, assigning and fixing blame.

The phenomena must be described more fully to be clearly understood—and appreciated. IN PUBLIC LIFE, BLAME IS A GREEN WEENIE TO BE AVOIDED AT ALL COST. Once it has been assigned, especially if it has been assigned in writing, it becomes a black mark, an all but inerasable blot on the permanent record. And the higher one ascends in an agency, the more enduring the stigma. For most staff, happiness is a blot-free (read blame-free) record.

Blame can be assigned two ways: directly and by innuendo. Direct blame is usually assigned when the general public is aware of the proximate cause of a well known problem or disaster, and (whenever possible) the allegedly culpable party cannot fight back. The Navy initially, and clumsily, tried to blame the 1992 gun turret explosion aboard the battleship USS *Iowa* on a sailor who died in the disaster (unfortunately, Naval investigators ignored the Two-Level Rule—see page 170). Nevertheless, the last condition cannot be overemphasized. Blue Ribbon panels tend to be peopled by agents whose charge is to assign direct blame ("This panel [never "we;" much too personal] finds the crash due entirely to human error . . .") when the problem is so well known that it can no longer be whitewashed or covered up.

Blame by innuendo involves fingering a victim without his knowledge. Therefore, it cannot be public, cannot be written. It is only verbal. A whispering campaign. Blame by innuendo is far more fun, far easier and less risky, and thus far more pervasive. It also is far more corrosive. It's far more fun because the blamee, unaware he is the object of blame, is not likely to retaliate. It can be seen at once that blame by innuendo is a low-risk strategy. It's also far more effective.

Since it is a low-risk strategy, and because it does not focus unwelcome *public* attention on the agency involved and on government in general, blame by innuendo takes place far more often than direct blame. Upon a little reflection, this makes sense. After all, when blame reaches the stage where it is publicly assigned, it becomes a blot on all of government, which by unspoken convention, all parties wish to avoid. Or it implies that a tragedy or disaster has already occurred. Blame by innuendo is most effectively accomplished as a long-term campaign, modeled after Chinese water torture—a drop at a time. One drop is no big deal, but cumulatively, it moves mountains and over a long term can destroy a man and his career. More than one or two major gotchas, since it conveys the impression of long-term, hopeless incompetence and, worst of all, weakness.

I know no better way than blaming to launch an offense against personal and organizational rivals. "Look how badly Social Services screwed up that program. "We should take it over," or, "Everything he touches turns sour. Give his assignments to me."

One can see why agency behavioral norms are explicitly designed to dampen the risk of blame, to shield the agency from blame, and insulate the heads of the agencies, departments, and offices from any blameworthy actions of their subordinates.

See also BLAME-FREEDOM FROM, BUREAUCRACY, COMPETITION, COVERING UP, CREDIT, HIERARCHY, *IPSE DIXIT*, THE MEDIA-SOME THOUGHTS, REVENGE, RULES AND PROCEDURES, and TURF.

BLAME,

commentator, Ken Beatrice, used to say "Offense fills the seats, but *defense wins the game* [emphasis added]."

Similarly, if offense (attempts to annex new turf) leads to more clout and influence, the foundation for individual or agency success in government begins with a stout defense, an impregnable shield against blame and criticism (merely another form of blame).

Organizational and individual behavior implicitly recognize this axiom. People and agencies alike go to incredible extremes to protect themselves. In fact, they'll go to far greater extremes to protect themselves than they'll go to accomplish meaningful work.

This ethos is deeply ingrained, almost instinctive. If agency work is flawed or criticized, the knee-jerk response is to find a scapegoat, a culprit—not necessarily *the* culprit—to blame. This gives rise to a subspecies of government worker whose power and influence, and therefore, whose station in the organization derive in large measure from fingering the blameworthy (often regardless of whether they are at fault). Most power seekers are masters of this tactic. Seldom, if ever, are mistakes corrected; instead, the culprit is blamed and loses points, the finger-pointer wins points for fingering the guilty party, and life goes on.

To say that this phenomenon merely distorts the intended *raison d'etre* of the agency grossly understates the case. And since most actions are accompanied by some risk, the path of least resistance for many staff and many departments is to do nothing, or at least, as little as can be gotten away with. Staff, departments, even entire agencies have tried this—and for a surprisingly long time have gotten by with it—some pursue this course, or non-course, even now. "Zero Output" is perhaps best understood as an extension of the "Zero Defects" philosophy to all work undertaken by the agency. The implied logic seems irrefutable: what doesn't go out the door can't be criticized or blamed. This behavior simply amounts to risk aversion to the nth degree.

However, producing nothing is at best a short- to medium-term expedient: over the long-run, rivals and critics are likely to notice a lack of output and use that to blame (there's that word again) the agency, or department, or person in question. So many, perhaps most, public agencies and government workers opt (subconsciously—I'm sure most would never characterize this strategy as conscious) to minimize risk by producing the lowest acceptable minimum to forestall blame for doing nothing or too little. Be assured that anything which actually gets accomplished under this strategy is unlikely to be either controversial or substantive.

In offices where this norm governs, deviations from it are about as welcome as a newly discovered case of genital warts, are viewed with all the seriousness of a malignant tumor . . . and are removed with the same urgency. Initiative, creativity, and willingness to take a risk are not desired, and anyone who exhibits these traits instantly becomes subject to numerous lumps. To cite an extreme example, a nearby community college serves a student body of whom 40 percent are non-native English speakers, and in which the average grade in an English literature class is reportedly an *A*. Not surprisingly, students have come to expect *A*s whether they did any work or not. An adjunct faculty member was summarily fired because one student complained about her teaching methods. By giving virtually every student an *A* and firing teachers whom students protested, the administration clearly sought to keep all its students happy—and itself blame-free.

One proven way to dampen blame is to obtain consensus. If a key project or letter is not approved by relevant department heads, it won't be undertaken or sent out. Across-the-board approval ensures that the initiator cannot be singled out for blame if the work is criticized; instead, it guarantees that any criticism can only be spread over the entire agency, or over many agencies, or even the entire process. In this way, collective action breeds individual security.

And helps diffuse blame—or keep the green weenie pointed elsewhere.

See also AGENCY EMPLOYEES, COMPETITION, PROCESS, SANCTIONS, SCAPEGOATS, and SIGNOFFS.

BLAME STRATEGIES

Books, 1984, a sometimes technical, but eminently readable, treatment of the topic), a few general guidelines and ideas regarding the shucking and casting of blame are presented instead.

Regarding the casting of blame, there are two constraints: blame must 1) be aimed at someone or someplace else, and 2) it must fall on a credible target, someone within or preferably outside, whose culpability seems plausible to the public.

Beyond that, it is most helpful if the party you seek to pin it on cannot shirk it and, more important, cannot retaliate. Someone who has died, moved on, or retired is made to order for this purpose.* An intriguing—though unproven—variation (attempted by a harassed official who, at this writing, is being skewered by a Blue Ribbon Panel): blame the computer, an inanimate adding machine which can't bite back. Another bet, almost as good: someone in trouble, who, because of his problem, has neither the time nor other resources to resist effectively. In other words, kick him while he's down. Still, this must be done with caution, even stealth, because this strategy also harbors a potential downside: if the blamee stages a comeback, bet that he will remember your act and be waiting for a chance to stick it to you in return.

There exist several ways, a hierarchy, really, of attaching blame. The best: if you must blame someone, do so in private. Even then, it's better to correct than blame, but if you must lay blame, criticize the action or work, not the person: "This work sucks!" not "You suck!" (However, as with much in this handbook, there is an exception: if you wish to get rid of someone and seek to make his life

---

* Once you've left, expect yourself to be blamed in absentia for anything and everything that went wrong, even work you barely touched. Since you are no longer around, there is little, if anything, you can do to prevent this.

---

as unpleasant as possible, then criticize the person, not his work. Then, do so only in public. In this way, you publicly humiliate him and cause him to lose face. If you do, he'd better be culpable, because if he can show he isn't, then you come across as an ass to your staff, few of whom wish to be party to a public dressing down, anyway. Worse, you lose leadership points with them.)

If, on the other hand, you seek to elude blame, then one time-tested way to cover any and all potentially blameworthy actions is in writing about them; in other words, by documenting. This precaution may not prevent someone from trying to blame you, but it sure makes it harder for his accusations to stick.

Another trick, really more a preventative (but then, a stitch in time . . .), involves how you assign work to a subordinate. Assign work so that he cannot involve you in any problem that develops: give him all the responsibility and authority he needs to complete his task properly. That way, if it goes wrong, he cannot credibly point the green weenie at you for giving him insufficient resources. But you can blame him if things sour.

If a blameworthy action or condition is not made public, then little is liable to come of it. Many managers successfully sit on blameworthy conditions until they leave. But there's a tradeoff in doing so: after they've departed, everything that goes amiss will be blamed on them because they're not present to defend themselves. If they ran a tight operation, fewer nasty revelations will come to light.

So, if you're handed a moldy doggerpillar, if possible, sit on it until you retire. On the other hand, you can only sit on some problems for so long, and if you can cover up no longer, quit while you're ahead—with your reputation intact. If you can swing it, move to an agency to which your current shop is beholden. Your presence at the new place of work poses an implicit threat to your former employer, and will quiet, or at least dampen, any external squawks about the can of worms you left behind. (One charming real-life solution: a county executive was elected governor of his state. Back at the county, few would risk, much less dare, publicly blaming him for hefty deficits that came to light after he moved on—for that matter, what appointed or elected county official would dare blame his governor for anything?) Moreover, if something is blamed on you after you've gone, you aren't around to take the hit.

With a little luck, a blameworthy event will remain undetected long enough into your successor's tenure that he dare not say anything about it, either ("You mean you've only discovered this now?"), because ownership of the problem has now passed on to him. A US Navy manual for newly frocked ship captains points out that no matter what salient problems existed when an incoming ship captain relieves another skipper, after three months, any that persist are now his. If your successor cannot correct your problem, he will ignore it (if he is smooth and can afford to) until it passes along to his successor. This tactic must be seen first hand to be fully appreciated.

See also CONTROL, CORRECT VERSUS BLAME, CREDIT STRATEGIES, FACE, IMAGE, INTIMIDATION, LEADERSHIP, LOCK THE DOOR, LONG-TERM, PUBLICS, PURGING, REVENGE, and SCAPEGOATS.

BRIBES

Bribes, some sage noted, provide the lubrication that keeps the wheels of government turning.

In many cultures, particularly in Third World Africa, Asia, and South America, *baksheesh* is an ancient and honorable—and integral—part of the daily business of government, as natural as tipping a waiter. If you expect results in those parts, you'd best grease a palm or two, or else forget receiving any government goodies or services.

In the United States, many citizens labor under the quaint notion that government should be clean and impartial; that it should serve all citizens equally, not the highest bidder.* No doubt this foolish idea goes back to our egalitarian roots. But it is also misguided: after all, a bribe is an equal-opportunity purchase, open to anyone. Hey, how could bribery ever be more All-American? And government itself employs bribes as part of day to day business—or at least it ought to. With a little luck, the large scale assimilation of newly minted citizens from countries where bribes constitute a daily part of government should swiftly erode this outdated notion. Thankfully.

———————

It goes without saying that those who enjoy bought favor should be treated as valued customers, which in a real sense they are. And if agency wheels turn a little slowly, it is OK by my lights for someone impatient to bestow, and for an agency employee to accept, a gratuity for expediting things, just as it's customary

———————

*   In theory and in high school textbooks this is great stuff. In real life, government in this country provides across-the-board services to few, and selectively to those who subscribe to a special interest that benefits them. If you work in government, chances are you owe your job to a special interest or, at least, to the clout it enjoys in Congress or State House or City Hall. So forget the notion that government serves all.

for the maitre'd at a busy restaurant to accord head-of-the-line privileges to a customer who slips him $40 up front. *Just don't get caught.*

An ex-Congressman acquaintance, whose California district was home to

forget in the heady atmosphere of Washington, DC, especially when home lies three thousand miles away. This process, in my view, amounts to much more than merely a nice job perk; in a city of fiercely competing interests, it offers a friendly, pointed reminder that folks back in the home district (some of them, anyway) expect you to use your influence in their behalf.

If you do choose this avenue to augment your salary, by all means resist the urge to display your excess wealth openly. Consume only with discretion . . . travel, for instance. If you drive a high-end late model Lexis or Mercedes, delete the need to take it to work if your chairman drives (or is chauffeured around in) a four-year-old Buick.

It was this that led to the fingering of Soviet spy Aldrich Ames—he vainly (and foolishly) drove his expensive new Jaguar to work at the CIA.

See also ACADEMICS, BELTWAY, INDOCTRINATION, and NEWSLEAKS.

BUCKPASSING

Quick now, what do you do when someone wants you to decide or take responsibility for an action you really don't want known as "yours?"

The answer should be almost reflexive, a no-brainer: *pass the buck*. Foist, force, or hand the responsibility off to someone else. Some staffers spend an entire career without making a decision or taking responsibility for an action. I've encountered a fair number along the way.

And the reason for doing so is clear: avoidance of blame. Buck passers would have you stand in for them at their own execution.

Passing the buck should not be confused with referring a difficult or technical question to a colleague whose training, background and functional expertise allow him to give a more accurate, highly informed answer.

Harry Truman (whose Oval Office desk was adorned with a sign proclaiming "THE BUCK STOPS HERE") notwithstanding, almost everyone I have encountered in public life quickly learns this ploy. Buck passing is an ancient and honorable rite, from elected officials (when one hears, "I speak/act for the people" means "if it turns sour, don't blame me") down to first level supervisors, even to non-supervisory staff.

As with assigning blame, there exists a preferential hierarchy of buck passing. The best option is the "Outward Buckpass": award the work to a consultant. Since you sign his paycheck, you exercise tight control over his output. If the work is in any way flawed or controversial, you can have him re-do it—or blame him. Why is this best? Because blame can be assigned outside the agency. Clearly, this ploy is made to order for a zero-output department.

A second option, almost as good and equally effective: Have your boss or (better yet) your boss's boss decide an issue (the "Upward Buckpass"). As a staffer, I like this best because if it entails associated action you must eventually take, then in taking it you only are carrying out your assigned duties; this can land you in trouble only if your assigned duties are on the order of gassing prisoners at Dachau. Also, in having someone farther up the ladder decide or act, you reaffirm your loyalty and reliability, and signal them that you would never undertake any act or decision on your own.

The next option: pass the hot potato along to another agency or department or peer (the "Sideways Buckpass"). Understand that this ploy is riskier than the Upward Buckpass; it may invite the other party to poach on your turf. Thus, I'd advise against it, unless the issue is especially tricky or sticky.

The final, and least desirable, option is the "Downward Buckpass": Ask, manipulate or bully a subordinate into acting

back passing. Aside from providing a telling commentary on the prevailing ethos at her agency, her assertion is incorrect: true delegation entails giving the delegate authority commensurate with his responsibility and accountability to accomplish the task he has been assigned. More often than not, this authority is held tightly, not delegated.

† The most creative working example of the Downward Buckpass I've encountered: assigning major projects (and, implicitly, the blame if they turn sour) to hourly temps. Incidentally, this example comes from the halls of state government.

See also BLAME-FREEDOM FROM, CONSULTANTS, CONTROL, TEMPS, and THEORY OF THE AGENCY.

BUDGETS: THREE THOUGHTS

1) To control an agency's budget is to control that agency—by the short hair.

2) If you've got budgeted funds, exhaust all avenues to spend them, lest next year you receive a smaller authorization to spend.

3) If you are responsible for managing a project, be sure that the blame for any schedule or cost overrun is attached to someone else, preferably an outsider.

See also DALEY and BLAME-FREEDOM FROM.

BUREAUCRACY

Bureaucracy describes all the *written* procedures and routines, and rules and regulations that these observers love to hate and rail against. In most agencies, they are pervasive; one can encounter procedures for everything from submitting time sheets to blowing your nose. And procedures are a nuisance. They seem only to get in the way, make work more difficult to perform and longer to finish, add to the payroll extra people whose role is to ensure all the rules and procedures are being fully complied with, thus increasing the agency's overhead costs and sapping staff morale. So why have them?

Perhaps one clue to their ubiquitous presence lies in the fact that written procedures have been around in one form or another since the beginning of recorded history, across every form of government that man has invented, through all cultures which have evolved. In other words, bureaucratic procedures form a universal, indispensable component of government life. Period.

But that doesn't explain why. Why have all these procedures? The answer is as basic as government itself: bureaucracy eliminates, or at least dampens, uncertainty. Rest assured that the mother of each and every procedure is an incident that led to the assignment of blame. When work is handled in accordance with set procedures, there's little or no chance that unfavorable outcomes (blame) will result.

Together with the hierarchical pyramid, bureaucracy forms the foundation on which all organizations rest. If the hierarchical pyramid organizes and rank-orders human resources (authority), then bureaucracy is its analog in ordering the actions and behavior of people and entire agencies.

But it is still more: bureaucracy provides the agency and its officers with the quintessential framework to live a blame-free existence. And because of that, it will remain a part of government life as long as governments remain instituted among men.

And it will be cursed by those whom it inconveniences, and by those who fail to understand why it exists.

The other day my ears pricked up at a radio news story.

The State of Illinois refused to license an automobile. Why? Well, Illinois statutes specify that for all vehicles to be duly licensed, each must pass a mandatory exhaust emissions test. But this one experimental car ran only on batteries, so it was exhaust-free; it emitted nothing. So it could not be tested for emissions and could not, perforce, pass the state's mandatory and (more important) statutory emissions test. And so it went unlicensed. Of course.

Hey! The system works. All the time. Regardless of, and indifferent to, the prevailing circumstances. And therein lies its genius.

Some fifteen months after the founding of my first agency, there appeared a two-month department head. He earned this title because that was how long he remained on the payroll before moving on. It was neither the brevity of his tenure nor his real title (director of security, I think) that were noteworthy, but what his brief tenure produced (his output, by the way, bore no relationship whatever to his title or his job description): The Official Agency Secretary's Manual.

Ostensibly twenty-odd pages of instructions for secretaries, the manual was so much more: it, or, more precisely, the procedures it tersely set forth, advanced the agency from early Stage 2 to mature Stage 4, in a single, discrete, easily identifiable step—two full stages in its life-cycle! Instantaneously—the moment it became effective. In observing the significance of this modest promulgation, I felt like Galileo discovering a new planet!

In no uncertain terms, the manual proscribed who was authorized to sign letters headed outside the agency (department heads and above), and who could send—and receive—inter-departmental memoranda (department head to department head within one division, division head to division head for interdivisional correspondence). No longer could a staffer pen a memo or note to his opposite number in a different department: now he had to draft a memo for his department head's signature that went to the department head of his opposite number.

Note where the authority became instantly—and officially—lodged.

As noted, this single administrative and procedural milestone came to a mere twenty pages (the comparable manual for the US Department of State, I'm told, numbers hundreds of pages). An extraordinary document.

All to prevent uncertainty.

CAMEO APPEARANCES

The cameo appearance is designed to foster the illusion of attendance.

A dear friend, whom I'll call Art and whom I deeply miss, probably spent half his time on the agency payroll moonlighting. He also spent an unbelievable amount of time away from the office. Luckily, the secretaries loved him; otherwise he might have gotten into real trouble.

To convey the illusion he was somewhere around the office, Art had perfected a technique he termed the *Cameo Appearance*, and God he was a master at it! He'd enter the office after one of his interminable absences, raise both hands in a victory sign, in the distinctive, celebrated manner of Messrs. Churchill and Nixon, and greet all who were present with "Cheers!"

In three minutes he'd be gone. One never knew whether he was down in Accounting haggling over a purchase order, drinking beer in the nearby bowling alley, or visiting a whorehouse—and knowing him, any of these activities seemed equally likely.

Then our boss would ask, "Where's Art?" and the secretaries or whoever was still around, would reply, "Jeez, he was just here two minutes ago . . ."

Other ploys that contribute to the illusion of attendance:

- leave a radio at your desk playing softly while you're absent.

- if it's cold outside, make sure your suit coat or overcoat hangs prominently in view. Nobody would believe you'd head home without your coat. I heard of one fellow who made a habit of leaving early without his suit jacket. (Caution: this gambit is recommended only if the janitorial staff can be trusted not to liberate stray garments.)

See also ABSENTEEISM and MOONLIGHTING.

CAUSES

...which revolve not only all the entrenched policies and procedures, but also a wide range of individual and collective behaviors that may have taken decades to evolve into their present form. And now, this pleasant (in some agencies, it might even be termed leisurely) routine is threatened by, of all things, a cause. Just imagine how the US Army Corps of Engineers regards the environmental movement.

Conversely, to a young agency, one in its early stages, a cause is invariably the driving motivation behind its founding, and adherence to that cause is a (it may well be *the*) prime motivation for its staff, right up to the agency head. Likeminded citizens make a wonderful public, a vocal, energetic interest group of outsiders.

Perhaps this dichotomy explains why established agencies often respond slowly, poorly, or not at all to major cause-driven attempts to change their mandate: there's nobody in senior staff who cares about the cause, so it gets short or no shrift from within.

This is as good a place as any to add that there is no dweeb like a cause-driven dweeb, be it one functioning as a professional citizen who assails the agency from without or as a committed idealist/true believer, even radical, from within. The absolute correctness of his cause imbues him with a strident moral authority that he wears with forthright conviction like Kevlar. This armor renders him insufferably arrogant and, thus, a royal pain in the ass to deal with, even to staff allies who espouse his cause.

Conversely, and mark this well, a disillusioned dweeb can evolve into a real problem child, a wounded tiger of a different stripe. Like falling out of love, disillusionment is among the most psychologically and emotionally damaging vicissitudes that life can throw at us, more so even than demotion. Its legacy: imprinting the psyche of the disillusionee in a most painful, corrosive way.

See also AGENCY EMPLOYEES, AGENCY LIFE-CYCLE, CITIZEN PARTICIPATION, PUBLICS, RADICALS, SPECIAL INTERESTS, and WOUNDED TIGERS.

CHICAGO ECONOMICS

...g ...~ ...~~. ~~..~~~~~ ..~~~~~~~. vvorse, this sordid institution teaches its students how, not what, to think. In this, Chicago-trained staff pose a double danger to an agency. I can't think of a more dangerous practice.

You're much better off hiring people from Harvard (and schools that emulate Harvard), where influence on government (and therefore, political power) is valued at least as highly as the knowledge uncovered there, and refrain from hiring Chicago-trained staff.

If I were President, my first executive order would forbid government funds to the University of Chicago—for any purpose—and I'd kill the tax-deductibility of donations to that institution.

I'd also shun Chicago-trained staffers. If I could, I'd burn 'em all at the stake!

See also HERETICS and INDOCTRINATION.

CITIZEN PARTICIPATION

A brilliant meld of psychology, law, marketing, and public relations; overall, an exceptionally powerful artifice of governance, especially under a putatively representative government: this could only describe *citizen participation*. Because of its extraordinary, multifaceted character and almost universal applicability, I rank citizen participation second only to intimidation in utility to an agency as a governing tool.

Citizen participation entails inviting (or enticing) interested citizens to express their views on the agency's prospective plans, projects and programs. Within this context, it can encompass a great deal. First and foremost, "interested citizens" means only citizens who favor agency programs. Almost equally important, citizen participation allows the head of the host agency and elected politicians to claim that the program they endorse or control has duly been put before the public, that "the people have spoken," and that it has received their seal of approval—but no more.

But citizen participation is more: for citizens opposed to a program, the process serves as an outlet for them to be heard, a safety valve to blow off steam—even though their views are unwanted and (since their opposition runs counter to staff desires) little is likely to come of their resistance. At least, nobody can claim that his objection went unheard, unnoted, or unrecorded.

Still, public opposition is unwanted. Not only because it can place a troublesome blot on the record, but because it poses additional work for the staff and publicly challenges the agency, it must be carefully dissected, then rebutted or otherwise derogated.* Beyond this, public input, real constructive input that is on target, though incongruent with program goals, is studiously ignored.

Often with good reason. Citizens whom I've heard testify generally fall into three groups:

---

* From the corridors of state government comes this excerpt from an internal memo: "... the citizen who continuously [*sic*] slows down the meeting with challenges, a Mr. ＿＿＿ was not in attendance ..."

1. "Professional Citizens," single-issue adherents, cause-driven dweebs, who invariably favor radical or impractical social goals (e.g., mandatory use of public transportation, licensing future parents, banning meat or fossil fuels. These dweebs would gladly spend 75 percent of the Gross Domestic Product on their pet issue, and they pursue their agenda with a fanaticism that makes the late John Brown of K

Membership in each group often is mutually exclusive. Often, the wishes and desires of each group hopelessly conflict. If the programs they support were fully implemented, the resulting cost to the public treasury would be excessive. Worse, the agency could be left without a mandate.

A caution: citizens who take time to express their views, no matter how stupid, ignorant, venal or contrary, should be treated with the utmost respect and courtesy, lest the agency incur negative points with the general public and become subject to complaints. To achieve maximum effectiveness, the participation process requires ostentatious faux courtesy and openness to all.

Resistance from the lunatic fringe is much easier to deal with than opposition that has been rationally and carefully thought out, because the rantings of loonies are easy (and for younger staffers, great fun) to debunk. Moreover, even if they are on target, recommendations that violate precedent are often impractical for the agency to carry out, because they would require changing or abandoning existing procedures. The likelihood of this is slim.

Worst case: when resistance is both well-reasoned and well-organized. Still, formal, organized opposition can be neutralized by packing the meeting with supporters and agency employees. If possible, stage the proceedings in a run-down section of town, so that "all citizens can be heard." An urban war-zone works best: usually, only a hard-core few are willing to run the gauntlet to show up at this forum. If you can, slap a time limit on testimony that promises to be unfavorable, and defer it till the end of the proceedings, when many attendees and, hopefully, reporters, will have departed.

Another time-tested tactic to minimize or, at least, water down unwanted public interference and yet produce a body of testimony that supports agency programs is to invite witnesses from other (preferably non-competitive) agencies that will benefit from the program, together with independent consultants ("expert witnesses") to endorse the benefits. Their testimony should be carefully reviewed beforehand. When necessary, it can be written by agency staff. Few, if any, observers will note (or care about) the conflict of interest here. These simple, easy-to-implement ploys guarantee that the record will contain a body of compelling arguments to proceed with any program at issue.

Lastly, for citizens whose views actually coincide with program objectives, every effort should be made to cultivate them and ensure their views become part of the public record. Sometimes, just as with the news media, sympathetic citizens can be primed with the "right" information before they testify. Citizens who stand to benefit directly from the program make dandy witnesses, and, as prospective beneficiaries, they promise to become vocally supportive members of the public the agency serves.

One federal cabinet-level department, which obviously agrees, recently developed a course for field office staff and local government representatives to incubate and cultivate grass roots support for its programs.

Eliciting positive citizen participation constitutes a full-time job at some agencies, and with good reason. Positive citizen response can only provide a powerful impetus for future programs; in fact, it could accurately be termed money (alternatively, political capital) in the bank. For this reason, it is critical that the process be controlled as carefully as possible. When this occurs, it provides a textbook illustration of Williams' Law (see page 432).

"PLUNK, DING-DING! PLUNK, DING, TINKLE-TINKLE!"

There you have it! This gem is excerpted from the testimony (no kidding: it really is) of a taxpaying citizen exercising his statutory right to speak out at a public hearing covering the annual capital spending plans of an urban transportation authority. What could his utterance possibly signify? Would you believe he was imitating the sounds that accompany the payment of a subway fare (coins PLUNKED down at the ticket window, a DING-DING bell that tells the rider that the turnstile is open and the TINKLE-TINKLE of his fare rolling down into a special, hold-up-proof safe)? Needless to say, this came from a professional citizen, a single-issue adherent—who else could unselfconsciously and naively utter anything like this, for the record and in a public forum? Without question, this testimony marked the high point in the proceedings.

As this suggests, not all public hearings are devoid of amusement. They can produce entertainment ranging from high camp to the sublime and the absurd.

Alas, the remainder of his testimony, and that rendered by other interested citizens, was not much more meaningful—and far less amusing. The real meat of the proceedings came from the testimony of (whom else?) outside consultants and the agencies which stood to benefit from our largesse.

See also COMPETITION, COMPLAINTS. CONSULTANTS CONTROL GAME

CLUING IN THE TROOPS

I've worked for managers who assign urgent new work to their people when a sudden crisis crops up. Such work eats up lots of time (and overtime) and energy, and distracts staff from their routine tasks. Later, after the crisis passes, and the office routine resumes, these managers never tell their staff what their overtime helped bring about. Maybe they are afraid to tell their people too much, maybe they just don't care, maybe it never occurs to them that the stiff who does the grunt work may actually be interested in what happened.

Whatever the reason, I can't think of a more effective way to kill staff zeal and motivation, especially among junior staff. This practice is guaranteed to force the best ones out the door. And hasten the metamorphosis of others into time-clock punchers and of a marginally productive department into an unproductive one—or mire an unproductive department more deeply.

Worse, keeping staff in the dark also kills something far more valuable: their loyalty. People need a cause to fight for. If they can't point to anything they've accomplished or claim membership on their boss's team, a blasé, disenfranchised staff has much less psychic incentive to rally around him when he comes under fire.

As a staff grunt, I can tell you it's nice to learn whether your labors bore fruit, and if not, why not. It's nice to be considered and treated as a member of the team. So, if you're a manager, unless you are so severely paranoid that you are congenitally incapable of sharing at all with your staff (some are), clue them in. Treat them as, or make them, members of your team.

Over the long run, this little courtesy will cost you little and can spare you untold stress and strain.

At an impromptu February department gathering over coffee and donuts, one staffer complained that nobody knew what was going on in the department; in fact, there hadn't been a full department staff meeting since November.

Much aggrieved, the department head, a Middle Eastern transplant, summoned all his formidable bargaining powers to defend this implied threat to his managerial acumen. "This is not true. We had a Christmas party in December, and so that was a staff meeting, and because of the snow in January (which had, in fact, cost the department ten staff workdays) we couldn't meet, and so you see that we've had a staff meeting every month!"

An awesome reply, bordering on non-sequitur. It is left to the reader to evaluate for himself its responsiveness to the staffer's plaint. Also left to the reader is to determine whether this department head can count on staff support in a pinch.

CODE WORDS . . .

. . . are used in place of everyday words that have taken on explicitly offensive or pejorative overtones (e.g. "person of color" has, through several replacement generations of code words, come to take the place of *colored person*) or are thought to convey potentially unfair or unfavorable connotations ("intellectually challenged" meaning *stupid*). In other words, code words are euphemisms or euphemistic; they allow academic and agency users to call a spade a spade in so many (more) words without seeming to be offensive.

This means that code words are the exclusive property of academics and agency staff who grapple with problems that require special verbal handling because nobody dares speak about them frankly or openly. Staffers who make a fetish of political correctness sprinkle their speech and lard their writing with code words. They jealously guard the use and knowledge of the most recent code word, because these denote who's on the inner circle or at the cutting edge in the field.

The more interesting euphemisms I've run across include: *issue* for problem, *concern* for fear, *leadership class* for (self-described) power seekers, *challenged* to describe physical or character deficiencies, and *deprived* or *deficient* to mean lacking in physical or economic resources. Thus, "penilely challenged" refers to an unfortunate cursed with a smaller-than-average male member, and "testosterone deficient" means the inability to get it up.

The downside of code words is that they need to be changed when with usage they acquire the same pejorative value or association as the offensive word or term they replaced. This only occurs when code words filter outside the agency into general public usage. Then, it becomes time to invent new code words, because the general public are neither knowledgeable enough to be entrusted with their use nor authorized to use them. The code word turnover rate is directly proportional to the emotive power of the subject or *issue* to which they refer.

While I am not aware of any studies on the subject, I suspect that the half-life of a code word can be measured by the time it takes to trickle down into the general public's awareness. When code words appear in movies and television sitcoms, and when kids in a school yard reduce a classmate to tears by deriding the unfortunate as *challenged*, you can be sure they're dated, and that a replacement term will soon be forthcoming.

See also ACADEMICS, CORRECTNESS, and THE PUBLIC.

COMMITMENTS, WRITTEN

A written commitment is, for all practical purposes, chiseled in granite: it's on record. The permanent record. So if you commit yourself or your resources in writing, you've put your obligation—and yourself—on record; and you will do everything in your power to honor your commitment.

In this respect, a written commitment differs markedly from one's parole, one's verbal commitment.

See also PAPER TRAILS and PROMISES.

COMPETENCE

Caution! For it to be meaningful, this assessment must be made first hand. Merely asking others, especially supervisors whose ideas of competence may differ from your own, could yield an inaccurate determination.

See also EXPEDITERS, NETWORKS, and PERFORMANCE REVIEW.

COMPETITION: TURF WARS

Outsiders tend to view government as a monolith and a monopoly—which, by definition, has no competitor. To a limited extent, they are correct. Government can and whenever possible does confer itself with a monopoly franchise (law enforcement, for instance), and has shown no hesitation in single-mindedly and forcefully using its enforcement powers to maintain that franchise and eliminate extra-government competition. Consider, for instance, the single-minded zeal with which vigilantism as an alternative means to combat crime is systematically prosecuted; citizen participation here is unwanted. All that shrill rhetoric about "a government of laws" and "trial by law" can just as easily be considered a rationale to banish competition from self-appointed, extra-governmental would-be crime-stoppers.

To be sure, the tranquil facade which the monolith presents to the public hardly suggests internal struggle. But the placid surface covers a seething competitive cauldron. Because competition is internal, few outward signs signal its intensity. But it's almost always present, at least as much as in the private sector; it's fierce; it's often vicious as the nastiest unfriendly corporate takeover—an excellent analogy, incidentally, except for one thing: sooner or later, all unfriendly takeovers are decided one way or the other, whereas within government, competitive strife usually continues on and on. The alleged struggles between the Departments of State and Defense are legendary, and one imagines that similar alleyway brawls take place daily among and between, variously, the Federal Bureau of Investigation, the Secret Service, the Bureau of Alcohol, Tobacco, and Firearms, and the Drug Enforcement Administration—or between any of these and the Department of Homeland Security, and between them and state and municipal police. These struggles would make the cold war seem tame in comparison.

But all for what? The competition is for turf—getting and keeping it—because turf is a proxy for power. Some may call it influence, others call it empire building, but what it comes down to is power, the motivational driver, the battery—or drug—that makes government tick.

Competition in government takes place at all levels—individual, departmental, agency. It takes place between the executive, legislative and judiciary branches: the desire to supplant another at certain tasks, to gain sign-off status on key—or

ALL—projects, for outright control over people, jobs, projects, programs, agencies, and more.

The closest private sector analog for turf is market share, but that term scarcely does descriptive justice to the competition that takes place within and between agencies. And as in the private sector, competitive behavior is oriented toward, and the largest rewards go to those who defer

This is as good a place as any to introduce the Principle of Silence: treat all turf war plans like military secrets, and I mean TOP SECRET. You never want your opponents or enemies to know what you are up to until you can confront them with a *fait accompli*.

Consider the following tale:

A computer vendor to a federal cabinet-level department received a telephone request from the department's Boston field office. "Please send us the specs for your Super-Dyno Deluxe Mega Processor." There followed an explanation that the Boston office planned to become the department's central service and processing center. This request was quickly filled. A few weeks later, the vendor received a call from the department's Dallas field office. "Send us the specs for a Super-Dyno Deluxe Mega Processor with a Hyper-Universal operating system with Ultra-Galactic Warp Drive and a Plasmoid Colonic Rectaculator." There followed an explanation that sounded eerily like the one tendered by the Boston office. This request, too, was honored.

A week or two later, the vendor called department headquarters in Washington, DC and spoke to his designated contact. "Hey Buddy," said the vendor, "I think you ought to know that I got a call from Aaron Aardvark in Boston, and he wants specs for a Super-Dyno Mega Processor."

"What? He can't do that! That's illegal, unlawful. Only our office is authorized to have a unit that big!"

"Well," continued the vendor, "then you probably will be interested to learn that Bubba Brown in Dallas asked us for the same thing, along with a Hyper-Universal operating system and all the bells and whistles."

"That son-of-a-bitch! He can't do that!" Then followed a couple of minutes of choice invective.

Clearly, the vendor had injected his presence into internal agency politics. Why would he do so? Was he not betraying, really screwing, the field office staffs in Boston and Dallas? Perhaps, but the vendor understood their motivation, voiced or otherwise, as well as or better than they did. Given the then-current tendency to federal downsizing, each field office was obviously trying to set itself up as *the* main service center for the entire department. So if the downsizing reaper came, the office that held the Super-Dyno Mega Processor would survive. By apprizing his front office contact of the survival plans of his rivals, the vendor gave him ample advance warning to ward off this threat and a priceless opportunity to defend his turf. The vendor, who was based in Washington, wished to deal with, and sell only to, the front office. While it went unspoken, it was implicitly expected that the new widget would be bought from him, not from a competitor—even if all other factors weren't equal (the vendor could write the justification memo, a small enough price to pay for having department business thrown his way).

The vendor knew the game, and clearly he could play it as well as the department's own staff, but then, in a broad sense, he was on the department's payroll, and he therefore would be expected to play the game in a way that would maximize his own rewards. Perhaps the field offices paid a severe price for their maladroit gamesmanship. Too bad . . .

Bottom line: silence is indeed golden. Keep your plans secret and trust no one, inside or outside alike.

See also AGENCY LIFE-CYCLE, CITIZEN PARTICIPATION, COMPETITION, INTIMIDATION, MUZZLE THE TECHIES, PERSONAL EMPIRE BUILDING, POLITICAL FAVORS, PROCEDURES, PUBLICS, REVENGE, THEORY OF THE AGENCY, TURF, VACUUM, and VALUATION OF TIME.

COMPLAINTS

...represents a little (occasionally, an enormous) green weenie pointed at your agency.

For this reason, complaints are to be avoided like the plague, and if they are received, great care should be taken and real effort made to diffuse (if not rectify) them.

Complaints from within (i.e., from staff) are preferable to complaints from outside. Because internal complaints are, by definition, not public, they more readily lend themselves to being covered up. This explains why a complaining letter from a citizen is apt to produce a far more satisfactory (and faster) response than an employee lodging a complaint. (It also suggests that if you as a staffer write a complaining letter as a citizen, you will be rewarded with a much faster, and more satisfying, response—if your agency identity remains secret.)

Most complaints take the form of someone who sought and didn't receive the services or other goodies your agencies dispenses, usually for good reason: the law, agency procedures or some other written *ukase* forbids him receiving them.

Track with care the source of, and reason for, external complaints. If their cause can be corrected (e.g., rudeness to the public), do so. As quickly as possible. Because you don't want too many green weenies pointing your way: accumulated weenies invariably come to the attention of your legislative oversight at the worst possible time.

Treat even the most abusive, obnoxious outside complainant as if he were a full-fledged member of your agency's financial oversight committee—in other words, with great respect, with the utmost (seeming) kindness and consideration. Likewise, treat every complaint, no matter how uninformed, stupid or trivial, as if it originated from your oversight committee. That way, nobody can (accurately) accuse your agency of arrogance or rudeness. Besides, you have no idea who a complainant's friends are—or to whom he may be related. And when you must say *no*, do so as courteously and (this is more important) as impersonally as possible.

A transit agency had a great way of handling complaints: along with the obligatory effusive letter of apology, every complainant received a token, good for a free ride. That simple expedient cheaply and swiftly diffused a great deal of ill-will.

The following complaint diffusion instructions were distributed to staff at a state agency. Because they are psychologically sophisticated, the instructions bear repeating:

"TALKING POINTS FOR INFORMATIONAL AND COMPLAINT CALLS

1. If the caller is upset, hear them [*sic*] out uninterrupted (even if they are misinformed).
2. Offer accurate information . . . more detailed information . . . if requested.
3. Offer additional help or information.
   — Would you like me to send you [printed information]?
   — Do you have other questions . . . I can help you with?

If the person is still upset, acknowledge it [*sic*] and say you hope you have helped in some way with information. You have written down the complaint and will personally let your management know the caller is not happy with the change.

Avoid passing the call to another agency or somebody else unless it is absolutely necessary for information purposes. Try to find the information yourself and give it to the caller—even if it means returning the call at a later time.

Be polite—but not patronizing—at all times."

This procedure is explicitly designed to diffuse public anger over a decrease in this agency's services. To an angry caller, the person hearing his complaint couldn't appear more empathetic, sympathetic or helpful. He was heard, his anger was (at least partially, one hopes) vented. How could he not feel better? More to the point, how could he remain angry with the agency?

Although the staffer who fields this call says he will "personally" notify his management, note that he doesn't say they will do anything to rectify things. Because they won't.

My department's policy on written complaints called for them to be rotated among professional staff, and mandated a reply go out the door no later than the day after it came in. One's turn to respond always seemed to crop up at the least opportune moment.

We also fielded telephone complaints, which came to our department from the agency switchboard operator and were doled out ...

... directed to an unpopular fellow in another department. Did she understand? Yes. Good! After he hung up, we all roared with laughter; then sat down to work.

A few blessedly complaint-free weeks later, the recipient of the chairman's spurious directive wandered into our department, scratching his head, musing, "Gee, I can't understand it. I've been getting all these complaints lately."

We shook our heads sympathetically.

See also BLAME-FREEDOM FROM, CUSTOMER SERVICE, THE PUBLIC, PUBLICS, and SAYING NO.

COMPROMISE . . .

. . . is basic to government. It allows an agency to act, enables programs to get started. It is the only way to ensure a workable agreement and therefore, garner the sign off, and the support, of all parties and interests. Absent this, no program can proceed.

It should be noted that while compromise enables things to get started, it always results in the initial concept being watered down to satisfy critics and opponents.

Whether to pursue a compromised project is a philosophical question that falls beyond the scope of this handbook. Once a program gets the go-ahead, however, into the pipeline with it.

Compromise almost always carries the day over optimization or conviction.

See also AGENCY BEHAVIOR, AGENCY EMPLOYEES, HIDDEN AGENDA, MUZZLE THE TECHIES, OPTIMIZING, THE PIPELINE, and SIGNOFFS.

COMPUTER THEORY

processing. There is no place for PCs in your agency. PCs, with the implicit privacy of their discs, are an open invitation to your people to pursue their own ends on agency time, which can include playing computer games, writing term papers, and even producing seditious material. As a matter of principle, you desire access to the work files and e-mail of everyone in your shop, and the only way to achieve this is through the use of a single, common mainframe.

This means your agency needs a mainframe. With one and a little judicious hacking by you or your Power Team, the work files of selected staff—of everyone—in the agency can be monitored. It may pay you to subject their files to random sweeps, just to find out what they contain. Your data processing manager, or a trusted assistant in that department, may be a useful, though silent, member of your Power Team.

One day an underground newspaper surfaced—almost literally: its news stand was the mens room urinal. The chairman's chauffeur showed it to his boss, who failed to see, and certainly didn't share, his driver's amusement over an unauthorized publication, especially one that so insolently lampooned him. So next day, the city cops visited the agency and checked every IBM typing ball in the house (clearly, this happened a few years ago). Naturally the flatfeet found nothing.

The unauthorized paper (it was well written and to non-members of the Power Team highly amusing), had anyone who bothered to examine its layout critically, featured two columns of text that were perfectly right-justified. Most agency secretaries could barely produce a simple three-line announcement without it appearing to have been typed by a chimpanzee. Two perfectly right-justified columns and no typos were far beyond their meager capabilities.

But not beyond the boys in data processing. They and they alone (this took place in the mid-70s, when word processing was in its infancy) possessed the expertise and smarts to produce professionally laid out copy.

Today, anybody can word-process, so the trick is to ensure data are stored in a way that allows them to be monitored at any time. Had this been the case when the underground newspaper came out, two or three data processing staffers could have abruptly found themselves out of work.

See also IN-BOXES, INTELLIGENCE, MOONLIGHTING, POWER TEAM, and THEORY Y.

CONFIDENCE, VOTE OF

2. *Sayonara!*

Antonymously misleading, a vote of confidence could more accurately be termed a vote of no-confidence. As allegedly employed by the Mafia, the technique includes greeting the votee with a kiss (they take the kiss aspect literally), followed by a great meal washed down with a bottle of fine wine before the votee is blown away—and then there are the most beautiful flowers at the funeral!

In government, the vote is far more mundane and prosaic—no food, wine or flowers. Barring a miracle, the unlucky recipient of the vote is on his way out. But in government the process boasts an extra fillip, too: a vote of confidence also contains two additional implied messages: don't look to me (the voter) for support anymore—for the record, I no longer know you and henceforth will not even acknowledge your existence, and perhaps more important, now you're on your own, pal.

Somehow the Mafia way seems much nicer—and considerably more humane.

See also PROMISES.

CONFIDENTIALITY:
CREATING, AND KEEPING, A SECRET

When an issue becomes hot or controversial, and especially when it becomes subject to hostile or potentially hostile public scrutiny, it pays the astute agency head to move relevant materials—files, etc.—swiftly and surely beyond the reach of anyone seeking Freedom-of-Information access to them.

There are two proven ways to accomplish this. One way to whisk sensitive material away from the public eye is to declare it *Secret* or *Confidential.* The defense, intelligence and law-enforcement communities are all masters of this technique (as well they should be). At the social welfare agencies, this ploy is tougher to carry out. Still, with a little creativity and the help of your lawyers, just about anything can be declared confidential and, therefore, placed out of bounds for a day or two, long enough to crank up the shredder or find a scapegoat or an excuse.

This ploy only works in shielding information from parties outside the agency. More often than not, information inside the agency, no matter how secret or closely guarded, will become known, either through leakage or guesswork, to the rank-and-file.

Also, clamping the secrecy lid on is a short-term ploy at best. Realistically, it can buy an embattled agency 24 to 48 hours, no more. After that, outside forces, in the form of courts and Freedom-of-Information writs, are likely to lift the secrecy veil. Then all bets are off.

The second method skirts confidentiality altogether. Sensitive, potentially damaging information, such as the findings of internal audits, are issued in DRAFT form. In this way, they cannot be classified as completed staff work. If any outsider asks to see them, he will be told, "Sorry, that work is still in progress," which means it isn't available to the public. Of course, it always will be, but the questioner never hears this. I know one county that uses this ploy most effectively.

At the root of both techniques is the public's "need to know." As with military intelligence, the less the public know, the better—except for information released by the press relations office to the media.

See also EXCUSES, LEGAL ADVICE, THE JUDICIARY, MANAGED NEWS, PAPER TRAILS, RUMOR MILL, SCAPEGOATS, and SHREDDER.

CONGRUENT COMMUNICATIONS

Why this protocol? Two reasons:

- If you receive a written communication—a memo or e-mail—even an innocuous one, from anybody, regardless of rank or title, answering it via the channel it came to you guarantees continuity and completes the record, which, if you perform your job correctly, is your ally because it covers your actions and insulates you from blame.

- If you receive a verbal message, reply verbally, not with a written record (you can still pen a memo to the file to protect yourself). To reply in writing could easily make the addressee wonder whether you are trying to set him up, and could be killer of mutual trust and thus of potentially productive working relationships.

See also BLAME-FREEDOM FROM and PAPER TRAILS.

CONSULTANTS

Consultants serve two roles: the first is that of a seemingly neutral advocate, with emphasis on *seemingly*. Their outsider's vantage, coupled with their (reputed) expertise, allows consultants to opine or recommend just about anything—including what you want them to. If you seek to initiate or implement some action or policy, infinitely greater weight is attached to opinion of an "outside expert" consultant than to the recommendations or opinions of your staff. You can then say, "Our noted expert, the consultant, recommends thus-and-so."

Since you control your consultant's paycheck, you control his opinion. It follows that you set up his contract so he reports to you. The public and your oversight alike seldom, if ever, worry about consulting fees: these have become universally accepted as part of an agency's cost of doing business. So pervasive is the use of consultants that Washington, DC has seen the growth and evolution of an entire industry known around the nation's capital as Beltway Bandits. (One presumes that this name stems as much from their desire to escape high DC taxes as from a desire to call themselves "outside experts." Then again, one cannot overlook what the term implies about their fees.) Smaller concentrations of "experts" tend to cluster around Harrisburg, Sacramento, Albany and similar watering holes.

A second reason to hire a consultant is to pay off a debt. The caveat is that care must be taken to make the service (the payoff) seem plausible to the public.

By way of illustration, some years ago the mayor of Chicago died. Naturally, his replacement wanted his own people in the city's key appointive offices. So he told his late predecessor's vice-mayor, "Look, I love you but I want *my banana* as vice-mayor. But I won't throw you out into the cold. I'll appoint you to a couple of boards which pay well and afford high public visibility, and I'll throw in a city consulting contract for $275,000."

And so the deal was done. The consulting contract turned out to be a study dealing with snow-removal. A summer intern cranked out twenty pages of paperwork on snow-plows or something, the resulting work product was labeled a snow-removal study, the intern's name was removed from, and the former vice-mayor's name was added to, the title page as author, and $275,000 duly changed hands. And everybody was happy.

But later Mother Nature entered the scene, throwing a wrench into this tidy, civilized transition of power by conjuring up the worst winter the city had experienced. Not one, but a whole series of blizzards

... surrounding the city's abysmal efforts to cope, there surfaced the story about the $275,000 snow study.

All hell broke loose. The media had a field day, and the story of the snow study was aired and re-aired, written and re-written, even as more frozen white fluff fell from the sky. The snow study may have been the straw that broke the electorate's patience. The replacement mayor was thrown out by angry voters.

The moral of this story is that it's OK to use a consulting contract to pay off a debt, only be damned sure to choose a subject not likely to blow up into controversy. It doesn't pay to make waves.

See also CONTROL, DALEY, DEPUTIES-SHUCKING, POLITICAL FAVORS, POWER TEAM, and THEORY OF THE AGENCY.

CONTACT AND LIAISON

If you have been designated the agency's official liaison or contact person with any other agency or other organization, allow your colleagues access to these outside counterparts only at the peril of losing your turf. Once other parties have been introduced to your opposite number, the door has been opened to triangulation; the boldest and most aggressive will not hesitate to approach your outside contact directly, without either the formality of going through you or the courtesy of informing you.

Once that happens, who needs you as liaison?

See also JOINT EFFORTS, SHARING, and TURF.

CONTROL

g g agency (or department) under control marks an important milestone in its maturation. And perhaps it explains the absolute fetish some agency heads make of control.

A good friend sums it up: "Never start anything you can't control."

See also AGENCY LIFE-CYCLE, BLAME-FREEDOM FROM, BUREAUCRACY, HIRING CRITERIA, and SCREENING PROSPECTIVES.

CONTROVERSY

Controversy is an inevitable accompaniment to the founding of an agency. Since it cannot be avoided, the only course of action is to secure the mandated turf and to hell with those who don't like it.

Otherwise, controversy is something to be assiduously avoided, because it means a squabble or argument, and these mean pro and (heaven protect us from) con, which can only mean blame.

Controversy usually arises out of an action, seldom out of inaction, which reinforces the axiom that inaction is preferable to action.* This applies both to external and internal sources of controversy.

If it is at all possible, the agency will move to eliminate the source of any controversy as quickly as possible. The more mature the agency, the more speedily one can count on remedial action being taken.

It's worth noting that controversy sells newspapers and grabs the attention of electronic media listeners and viewers. Which is all the more reason to dampen or prevent its occurrence in your agency.

---

*　The controversy arising from the ordeal of New Orleans following Hurricane Katrina stands as a conspicuous exception.

See also BLAME, THE MEDIA-SOME THOUGHTS, and SQUEEKY WHEELS.

COORDINATION

.... y to ensure that there are no secrets, to preclude one party making a stealthy power grab.

But a more important reason, I think, is to ensure that if something goes wrong, all parties to the process will stand firm and united against outsiders who might otherwise try to cast blame and criticism at any one of them. It's far preferable to have outsiders blame everyone than anyone; far better to blame the process, or the program, than those who run it.

See also BLAME, COMPROMISE, and SIGNOFFS.

COPIES AND ADDRESSEES

The single best official way to inform or notify is in writing. This means via letter for communications going outside the agency, and via memo for internal communications. A target recipient can be notified directly, as an addressee, indirectly, by copy, or confidentially, by blind copy.

It takes little imagination to see that blind copies can be great instruments for turf enlargement or defense, since the official addressee has no way of knowing that the information in the letter or memo is also being transmitted to other parties. Often the real addressee of a memo is the recipient of a copy—direct or blind.

See also BUREAUCRACY and DIRECTIVES.

CORRECT VERSUS BLAME

CORRECTNESS:
POLITICAL AND OTHERWISE

In thinking about political correctness (PC) in government agencies, one is admonished to consider the second word in the term and be governed by it. Period.

If you revel in being politically incorrect by uttering non-PC phrases, do so at your peril.

See also CODE WORDS and DALEY.

COST ACCOUNTANTS:

...populated world. How else can ...congenital, anal-retentive fervor with which he sorts a bunch of numbers, each into its special pigeonhole? This fervor doesn't stop with numbers, it covers all facets of office existence; accountants invariably insist that everyone in the office arrive precisely at 8:30 AM and leave precisely at 5:00 PM, with no more than one (1) hour for lunch. Most obnoxious of all, they may try to force other departments, regardless of the work they perform, to conform to this ideal. Their world simply has no place for a three-martini lunch, and in the mind of most accounting directors, the idea that half the time spent at one's desk is "lost time" (i.e., time not spent adding columns of figures) constitutes grounds for dismissal, even incarceration.

Accountants seldom, if ever, get to travel on business, which may explain why they take such vicious delight in knocking expense items out of others' requests for travel reimbursement.

Any time you submit travel, meal and lodging expenses, make sure that the numbers add across and down, and down and across, and that the totals equal. Otherwise, you focus unwelcome attention on yourself and subject your future expense reports to unwelcome scrutiny.

And if you feel your highfalutin status in the agency hierarchy entitles you to all-expense-paid-visits to topless bars, then be careful how you submit your reimbursement request. Share your travel secrets with no one. One trick: cabdrivers will often give you a blank receipt. Others will sell you receipts for a nominal sum.

Another way to minimize this potential problem is to ensure that each year, your accountants (at least, those who approve your expense vouchers) attend one or two out of town functions. Not in Philadelphia, either, but in fun places. It doesn't matter whether they learn anything on these junkets. What matters is whether they enjoy a few days on their employer's nickel away from the office.

And if anyone returns only to complain that the trip was a waste of valuable time, change his assignment and send someone else next time.

―――――――

But there's more.

A good accountant, I was told by a wise elder early in my career, is a priceless asset. By *good*, I mean the rare accountant who can find the alternative pigeonhole for funds when it becomes necessary to perform creative accounting. Who can bury or hide items and still withstand an outside audit—and keep you out of trouble. The ensuing years have proven time and again the wisdom of this truism. If you find a good accountant, one whose mind naturally and effortlessly seeks the alternative pigeonhole, attend well to his care and feeding, and make him an integral part of your Power Team, because you are many times blessed with his presence.

See also POWER TEAM.

COVERING UP, WHEN NOT TO

...material under the rug. No matter how painful this process may be, it's nothing compared to the torture that accompanies new, and embarrassing, public revelations after a Blue Ribbon investigative panel gets convened.

A second, riskier possibility: partial instead of full disclosure. Disclose only the facts that are obvious or that any cursory investigation will turn up. If there's more, keep mum, and hope no outsider or investigator finds out.

Best defense: a good PR guy who has systematically and thoroughly done his homework, which can dramatically improve the chances of controlling the damage.

If you set up someone in your shop to take your fall, do so only as a last resort, and know that this will almost certainly cost you the loyalty of your staff. Their correct reasoning: if he'd unfairly shaft good old George, he wouldn't hesitate to stick it to me. Often cover-ups do not hold inside the agency: what may be top secret outside the agency hallways is often common knowledge among staff—few secrets escape them.

See also CONFIDENTIALITY, DAMAGE CONTROL, PRESS RELATIONS, RUMOR MILL, and SCAPEGOATS.

CREDIT AND BLAME

A quick note concerning credit and blame:

Of the two, IT IS INFINITELY PREFERABLE TO AVOID BLAME THAN RECEIVE CREDIT.

See also BLAME.

CREDIT STRATEGIES:

g———, ·· ···· ····· ·· ··· ·······························s rational economic man. Because of this, a great deal of jockeying and gamesmanship takes place at all levels—at the agency, the department and the individual, to secure credit.

To catalogue all the ploys and strategies used to garner credit lies beyond the scope of this manual; instead, two general guidelines are offered.

The first and most obvious: if you or your department or agency accomplish something genuinely laudable (as opposed to, say, some image-enhancing gig cooked up by the Press Relations Officer), take credit for it so that everyone above you and outside your agency perceives you (or your shop) as deserving all the laurels. *Do so promptly*. (Parenthetically, men seem to understand—and react to—this concept more swiftly and proficiently than women.) This helps ensure that nobody else can snare the laurels you—or your staff: it helps to remember them—truly deserve. Conversely, if credit goes unclaimed, claim it for your agency. Even if it means jumping the claim of someone (or agency) more modest. Above all else, remember that to fail to claim credit that's rightfully yours is to invite claim-jumping and thereby forfeit any claim at all.

Claiming credit with observers above or outside an agency is an oft encountered and entirely understandable behavior for its head. Simply put, many senior staffers succumb to a tendency to poach, to grab for themselves credit for the best, most creative and impressive work of their subordinates. In doing so, they risk lowering their standing in the eyes of knowing superiors and outsiders—why's he doing that stuff instead of running his department/agency? Worse, their subordinates invariably will find out about when boss appropriates what they rightfully regard as theirs, and this can cost him valuable loyalty points: after all, a manager who steals credit when it's not legitimately his to claim is a manager who, perforce, stabs his staff in the back.

A preferred ploy, if you're secure enough to share: claim that your managerial perspicacity created the climate within your agency that enabled all that good work to get done—which may be true, and will be far more credible to superiors and outsiders. Given the stage in your department's or agency's life-cycle, it may well represent an incredible feat. In any event, the determination of how much credit to claim is like purchasing liquor by the drink in hitherto dry jurisdictions—local option, strictly up to the individual manager.

The second law regarding credit is much more subtle and, thus, often overlooked by many unsubtle managers. It involves awarding it, spreading it around. To assign credit is to recognize and praise laudable work or behavior. Assigning credit should always be done publicly, more that others may know what efforts bring favor from on high than to engender good feelings in the person recognized. Subordinates appreciate it when their best efforts are duly—and equitably—recognized.

Two important restrictions hold: the effort which receives praise must be uniformly perceived as truly praiseworthy, not as some half-assed job by a favored courtier. This creates the impression of fairness and, all other things being equal, is more likely to secure the loyalty of a staff behind their manager. Some managers, themselves, either don't care about or realize this, or perhaps they think that credit is merely one more perk, one more goody, to hog. In this they are wrong: when credit is truly deserved, there's always enough to spread around.

The other restriction is subtler: praise the work, not the worker, "Bob did a great job," not "Bob is great." That way, if he screws up later, Bob's ego is less likely to be bound up in criticism.

See also AGENCY EMPLOYEES, AGENCY LIFE-CYCLE, BLAME, CREDIT, COMPETITION, GENDER DIFFERENCES, IMAGE, LEADERSHIP, LOYALTY, PRESS RELATIONS, TURF, and VACUUM.

CUSTOMER SERVICE

Here's why. First of all, providing, or attempting with great fanfare to provide quality service could unreasonably raise the expectations of a public who for decades have been assiduously conditioned to be treated with contemptuous indifference: in other words, like dirt. To alter this perception could cause major, long-term problems with an up-to-now somnolent public. Second, the tax-paying "customer" pays anyway, whether or not he requires, requests, demands—or even receives— government goodies, services and handouts.* We're talking users, not customers.

Moreover, with few exceptions (the Postal Service comes quickly to mind; there may be others), the agency that provides the service holds a monopoly on it. A customer-taxpayer is not free to punish poor service by withholding his tip, much less by taking his business elsewhere. No direct link exists between service quality and reward or punishment.

To be sure, there exists one easy, time-tested way to improve the quality of government service: allow government employees who offer prompt, courteous service to accept (and keep) tips. Or simply offer a two-tiered service, standard (no tip) and expedited (tips, please). Better yet, to encourage customers to select the upgraded service, why not make the tip tax-deductible? Cynics may point out, though, that this practice already exists, tolerated if not officially sanctioned.

As can be seen, customer service is a soggy reverie whose time is yet to come. In the meantime, let the customers wait their turn, thank you.

---

* By my lights, the all-time topper: On April 15th, Pay-Up Day for the taxpaying public by the Internal Revenue Service, a TV news story on the IRS refers to taxpayers as *customers*.

Perhaps, though, this is merely an awesome piece of *IPSE DIXIT*, though this the reader will have to judge for himself.

Your typical agency can, and more often than you'd imagine, does offer customer service rivaling the better efforts of four-star establishments. This is bestowed only on the publics who count; those which exercise disproportionate influence on the providing agency. Neither the general public nor the mandate public is among these. It is rumored, for example, that the State Department thoughtfully dispatches to the offices and homes of cabinet members and Congress a courteous, friendly staff professional to assist them and their families with passport applications. (One wonders whether these applications take the standard three to six weeks to be processed. One thing for sure: these applicants never have to stand in line for three hours, only to be told that their passport picture is too large.)

To cite another case, a well-connected staffer in my agency needed to renew her driver's license. She mentioned to her political patron her concern over passing the written test. Hey, *no problemo!* A quick phone call from the patron brought her to a window at the license bureau that opened especially for her, sparing her the inconvenience of waiting in line. A most helpful DMV clerk completed her written test for her, though she actually had to sign the papers herself, and then processed her application on the spot. Talk about service! She didn't even have to study for the test. Think how well she might have done if she'd studied!

These examples, I think, provide a pretty fair indication that most agencies are fully capable of providing private-sector-quality customer service, service that would be the envy of any customer-driven corporation—as well as clues to who rate it. This is service in the best sense, taking care of the customers who have it in their power to take care of you if you don't. Just as in the private-sector, there's a clear economic incentive to go the extra mile. Guidance in this matter can be gleaned from the listing of the agency's publics elsewhere in this manual: use that list as guide and you'll never get in trouble.

As for members of the general public who expect, but do not receive, customer service, let them pay tips. If they balk at that, let them get elected.

See also BRIBES, FIND A PATRON, INTIMIDATION, *IPSE DIXIT*, THE MEDIA-SOME THOUGHTS, THE PUBLIC, PUBLICS, and TAXES.

CUTBACKS:

.... ploys to defuse or kill them outright.
Some examples:

- Many municipalities, when their expenditure of funds is threatened by ignorant, mean-spirited, reform-minded citizen-vigilantes, immediately announce major cuts to the police and firefighting payrolls. This assures attention from a captive media, and is guaranteed to produce howls of protest from all corners of the community. After listening to these howls, it's a tough city councilman who is still willing to support the cuts. And your payrollers (patronage placements) are safe, too, which is what you really wanted in the first place.
- Public Broadcasting Service (PBS), when congressional budget cutters turned on the network as a waste of money, responded with inspiration. It immediately announced that cutbacks would mean the suspension of its flagship show, *Sesame Street*, which, in a stroke of marketing genius, it had previously positioned alongside traditional American motherhood-and-apple-pie values. Few politicians would dream of cutting *Sesame Street*. After a brief but intense firestorm of protest (supported enthusiastically by the TV media, for whom the threat to PBS may have felt too close for comfort), the threatened funding cuts to PBS died stillborn.
- A flagship state institution, the University of Maryland, reacted to prospective cuts from the Maryland legislature with all the brilliance that one would expect from a major center of higher learning. Calmly, the university's president announced the impending dismissal of faculty who taught courses required for undergraduates to earn their degrees. Were this action to be carried out, the resulting teacher shortage would force thousands of undergraduates, who came from all over the state and comprised by far the largest component of the university's student body,

to spend an extra year, at great expense (college doesn't come cheap, even in Maryland), to finish up school.

The results of this strategy were predictable. Voter registration among undergraduates reached an all-time high, and thus empowered, students went home to lobby for the restoration of the announced funding cuts with the youthful conviction, energy and enthusiasm that only an undergraduate can muster. Needless to say, educational budget cuts, if the state legislature ever enacted any, came at the expense of other institutions.

(What prompted the newly recruited army of undergraduate customer-voters to lobby intensively for full funding instead of demanding cuts to the university's Paper Mache Department, which emerged unscathed, provides a telling comment on the university president's understanding of the malleability—and gullibility—of youth. Moreover, no faculty member felt troubled by this shameless exploitation of their youthful customers—most undergraduates were under 21—but then, all is fair in love and war, and make no mistake, battling budget cuts is war!)

From these examples, two points become clear. First, in targeting services to be pruned, your focus should be the most highly valued (by outsiders, not by your Power Team) and visible services your agency provides. Ensure all announced cuts are truly draconian. When you can directly mobilize the recipient public by scaring or intimidating them, by all means do so. Senior citizens who are mentally deteriorated have been bussed to protests over real or imagined Medicare cuts; elementary school students have been instructed to write (often abusive) letters to school boards to support the teachers' union during contract disputes.

Second, enlist the media in your crusade. Invariably, they will take your side, and their sympathetic reportage is critical to the success of your campaign to retain your rightful funds. If you're lucky enough to have drawn a minority reporter to cover your story, emphasize the damage of the cutbacks to minority citizens, particularly infants, children, women, the poor, and the elderly. Whether it's true or not—they won't check. This guarantees you their strongest, most sympathetic coverage.

The foregoing, I think, should put to rest any criticism that government workers are lazy and stupid. As the foregoing examples clearly suggest, government workers can act aggressively, decisively and with the greatest inspiration, creativity and resourcefulness, even with genius, a term I do not employ loosely.

See also ACADEMICS, GENDER DIFFERENCES, INDOCTRINATION, INTIMIDATION, MARKETING, THE MEDIA-SOME THOUGHTS, PATRONAGE, POWER TEAM, and UNIONS.

THE CUTOUT

yourself, or designate another to take the task.
This tactic is practiced most effectively when your target is out of the office and isn't around to object, complain to his patron, or otherwise protest your action. Long vacations are ideal and protracted trips out of town work well—especially when you dispatch the traveler. When the victim can no longer claim the work, he has effectively lost it.

See also PURGING and TURF.

DALEY, RICHARD J.:
PATRON SAINT OF PUBLIC LONGEVITY

If you accept the proposition that the essence of genius resides in simplicity, then the late Richard J. Daley, Mayor of Chicago (1952 to 1976), surely qualifies.* Into two devastatingly short, simple sentences, *Da Mayor* distills encyclopedias of political wisdom:

> "Don't make no waves. Don't back no losers."

Together, these timeless gems constitute Mayor Daley's formula for political success. The power and elegance of these simple rules is extraordinary. I personally rank them among the classics of human creativity, a landmark in civilized human achievement on the order of Einstein's $E=mc^2$, in that both expressions set the paradigm for an entire field. Every major failure in the public sector, be it personal or organizational, political or diplomatic, inevitably violates one of these precepts.

Don't make no waves. Don't back no losers. In management jargon, these two rules form the unwritten (until now) constraint set for your agency, for your actions. All of them.

The second rule is self-explanatory. If a person, program or idea is a winner, support it, push it for all you're worth; if it's a loser, shun it like the plague. The rule is universal. It cuts across military, diplomatic, legal, civic, economic and social issues alike. If you cannot tell whether a person, program or idea is a winner or loser, then handle it like a porcupine (with great care); by no means support it blindly.

The first rule deserves discussion:

---

*   Although Mayor Daley was merely an elected official, that in no way detracts from the genius and wisdom of this giant's observation.

"You get in trouble for what you do, not for what you don't do," observed a colleague. In the sense that he meant it, he is absolutely right. In an agency, personal initiative means making waves, and organizational norms of conduct go out of their way to prevent deviation from previous behavioral patterns and punish—often severely—those who deviate: sins of commission incur a far greater measure of opprobrium and censure than sins of omission.

...the rules as I have—they're not difficult—and let them be your guiding mantra.

HIGH PROFILE EXAMPLES OF PEOPLE IN HIGH PLACES WHO VIOLATED THE DALEY LAWS ... AND SUFFERED THE CONSEQUENCES

Jimmy Carter	Voted out of office in part because he appeared to waffle over American hostages in the US Embassy in Teheran. Root cause: he supported the Shah of Iran and, thus, backed a king-sized loser.
Richard Nixon	Resigned the presidency because of role in conspiracy to cover up Watergate break-in. In doing so, backed conspirators (losers).
John Tower	Denied Senate confirmation as US Secretary of Defense because his earlier actions when he was a Senator alienated colleagues. Made waves.
James Watt	Fired as US Secretary of the Interior for promoting anti-environmental friends and programs. Backed multiple losers.

A soldier who was decorated for valor under fire in Viet Nam provides a unique, colorful illustration of the perils of wave making. The unlikely venue (combat) only enriches the illustrative, pedagogical value and power of his narrative, and highlights the universal wisdom of Mayor Daley:

"... I exhaled strongly as I walked toward the man's office. Here we go. I knocked twice.

"Come in."

I stepped into the room, noting the first sergeant standing against the far wall. Must be some administrative business, I figured. Well, let me have it. "Sir, Captain Carhart reports to Colonel White as ordered."

[Colonel White] returned my salute silently, and then reached for a manila folder lying on a corner of his desk. "Captain Carhart, here is your Two-Oh-One personnel file, and the Officer's Efficiency Report that I have just completed for you. There's a flight to My Tho in half an hour. You're to be on it with all your possessions. Tomorrow you will make your way to Can Tho, where you're being transferred. The first sergeant will escort you back to your quarters to pick up your gear. Then he'll make sure you're on that flight. Army regulations require that I be available to answer any questions you may have about your OER, so take a quick look at it and see if there's anything you want to ask me about."

I was stunned ... the total score I received was 78 [out of a maximum 140; a score lower that 135 effectively put its recipient on probation and severely jeopardized any chances for future promotion. More than merely a poor evaluation, a score of 78 can be regarded as no less than a career-ending blackball.] I looked up at Colonel White. "Am I being relieved, sir?"

"Yes, I suppose you could say that. Any more questions?"

"No, sir."

"All right, you'd better get a move on to catch that plane. If you miss it, I'll really be upset ... Now move out!"

... I walked out to the hallway in a daze ... When we got to [my quarters] I gathered my few possessions ... [and] ... hefted my duffle bag back to the kitchen.

The first sergeant stepped forward and took it from me. "Let me get that for you, sir." He disappeared out the door, leaving me helpless with Dick and Jess and Norm. We walked back into the bedroom as I related my experience with Colonel White ... Jesse and Norm were shaken and didn't really know what to say, but Dick was outraged. "Shit, sir, I knew something like this was gonna happen. You didn't get relieved because of that medal; this is all because of Phoenix!"

"What?"

"Hell, yes, sir. This province has always been safe for the [Viet Cong], and the Ruff Puffs [provincial South Vietnamese guard units] don't do shit, we all know that. Colonel White has had a sweet deal; no killin', no dyin', a "pacified" province and a good OER for him! Shit, he's on everybody's "good guy" list, and *all he cares about is making general. He doesn't give a fuck about fightin' the war. In fact, he wishes it'd go away; it's only trouble for him* [emphasis added]. And then you come along, and in the last month, you've been out on three Phoenix [aggressive, clandestine seek-out-and-destroy] operations ..."

"Four," I corrected him. "I went out again while you were in Hawaii."

"Okay, four, and of course Colonel White knows that, too, and what's happened? Those two visitin' VC big shots got knocked off in the middle of the night, and a bunch of bodyguards, too, and now all the rules of the fucking game have changed on White, and he's runnin scared."

"C'mon, Dick, you know I wasn't the ...

g ... ... [emphasis added]. And he was probably getting pressure from our allies to get rid of you, too. Don't forget how all our Ruff Puff operations have been compromised, and the VC sure don't want you around! So some piddley shit thing happens, provides him an excuse to get rid of you, and he kicks you out of the province, and now he won't have to worry about his sweet deal and his nice letter from the province chief he advises. No, sir, you got relieved because you were trying to fight the fuckin' war, that's all!" (Carhart. *The Offering*, New York, Morrow, 1987)

This account speaks volumes. Even combat in a war zone is neither immune to, nor exempt from, Daley's First Law. The narrator, variously, and in no particular order, violates (unwittingly, it must be added in fairness to him—many really don't know the criteria for advancement, and clearly the author's military indoctrination emphasized all the wrong things) numerous rules and protocols cited elsewhere, but especially, "Don't make no waves." A military theater director in a combat zone has far greater discretion and latitude for eliminating a troublesome presence than his civilian counterpart, and Colonel White took full advantage of a deck stacked absolutely in his favor.

Because they were unexpected, the wounds from this episode probably were much longer lived and far more painful than those the author received at the hands of the Viet Cong. Agency staff who work outside combat zones should mark this well.

See also BEHAVIORAL GAP, BLAME STRATEGIES, BRIBES, COOPERATION, CRITERIA FOR ADVANCEMANT, ELECTED OFFICIALS, FACE, IMAGE, JOINT EFFORTS, THE MEDIA-SOME THOUGHTS, PERFORMANCE REVIEW CRITERIA, PICKING FIGHTS, PURGING, RULES AND PROCEDURES, SCAPEGOATS, SHOWING UP THE BOSS, SIGNOFFS, and VOLUNTEERING.

DAMAGE CONTROL

The term for damage control in Washington DC is "Spin Doctoring" (what positive spin can a "doctor"—a media specialist—impart to an otherwise unfavorable news story?). Spin doctoring is self-limiting to communications with the news media: a man accused of sexually molesting pre-adolescents "has been recognized for his intense involvement with children".

Spin doctoring comes under the heading of defensive media relations. As such, it is a piece of damage control, an important piece, to be sure, but only a piece.

In the broadest sense, damage control means insulating the agency and its senior staff from blame and from the assaults and aggression of rivals. It not only encompasses defensive, but offensive media relations. It encompasses assembling the Power Team, internal policies and procedures, barriers to public access, purging extra documents—shredding and burning, if necessary—the whole nine yards.

The agency head who plans to stick around would do well to review the status of his agency's current damage control procedures.

See also BLAME-FREEDOM FROM, CONFIDENTIALITY, ERECTING BARRIERS, and POWER TEAM.

DECISIONS, LOCUS OF

.... consequences. Later, as the agency progresses through its life-cycle, decision making becomes concentrated (along with the action) at progressively higher levels. And fewer decisions get made.

At the final life-cycle stages, with decision making now lodged at the top of the agency, paralysis sets in, and even the most basic decisions go unmade.

See also AGENCY LIFE-CYCLE and HIERARCHY.

DECISIONS: MAKING AND AVOIDING

Decisions can be difficult, stressful things to make. Worse, a decision maker may one day be held responsible for what he decides. This explains why some managers, even entire agencies, go out of their way to avoid making them. So they postpone till tomorrow what they could decide today—or figure a way to pass the buck.

Decisions aren't all alike. Some are easy to make, some aren't; some are fraught with great consequence, both in financial and human terms, others are trivial. But the issue is not whether a decision should be ducked, sloughed off, deferred or otherwise avoided, because sometimes it is necessary, or at least expedient, to do this. No, the real issue is what kind of decision is avoided.

I sometimes wonder whether managers who have become exceedingly adept at decision avoidance become, in the process, so reflexively scared of deciding anything that they've even become gun-shy of simple, day to day decisions. An acquaintance tells me that following a holiday, her office found itself grossly understaffed. She told her boss help was needed, and asked if he could avail himself of some by picking up the telephone to ask for additional people for a day or two.

Her boss couldn't do this.

If a manager or department head can't determine whether the office Christmas party should be held over a long lunch on a weekday or during the weekend, if he appoints a committee to determine coffee-break policy, and refuses to sign any form that isn't officially sanctioned by the Records & Information Management Department, that speaks louder about him (and, implicitly, his boss and his boss's boss) than a thousand state-of-the-union addresses. Ditto if he can't tell the difference between these and decisions involving billion-dollar expenditures.

Speaking of decision avoidance calls to mind a recent little epic, related by a friend in an office run by a decision-challenged manager:

The aforementioned manager was promoted into his former boss's job. Who should fill his old slot? Two "reliable" subordinates who had his ear and enjoyed his trust seemed qualified. So which one gets the job?

The solution seemed positively Solomonic, blazing new trails in the science of public management. In fact, Solomon himself would have marveled at its sheer brilliance as a mechanism for decision avoidance—although the implications involving accountability might have left him a little nervous: until a "permanent" manager could be chosen, the two subordinates were named "acting department co-managers."

No doubt they planned it this way all along.

My colleague Goeff, a first-level supervisor, was the perfect subordinate for Mutt, his insecure, paranoid, hanger-on boss. A shrink would examine Goeff with wonder: he exhibited no ego. Nor to anyone's knowledge, did he ever manifest the slightest sense of self, at least, not around the office. Goeff was congenitally incapable of making even the most menial decision, deferring instead to his boss—who just loved it.

You could argue with Goeff over something truly critical, like punctuation. After the argument, Goeff would say, "I'll ask Mutt," and adroitly passing the buck upward, put it to his boss, "Mutt, should we punctuate this sentence with a dash or a colon?" and then, when Mutt replied, Goeff would turn back to you and say, with a straight face, "Mutt says use a colon."

A totally repressed sense of self. The perfect subordinate.

See also BUCKPASSING.

DEPUTIES, SHUCKING

"You are getting old, and we are worried about your health. Have you though about appointing a vice president?" asked a reporter.

"It's precisely to the fact that I've never had a vice president that I owe my longevity," purportedly replied former Philippine President Ferdinand Marcos.

This exchange brings us to the subject of deputies. Many senior staff and agency managers agree with Marcos. If you agree, too, and if you inherit, or your organization chart calls someone your Number Two, your deputy and you do not wish him to act in this capacity, proven methods have been devised to denigrate his position and, if necessary, demean its incumbent.

- One sure-fire tactic: ignore the organization chart, and go around him, directly to "his" subordinates. If you do this in front of him, you demean him in their eyes. You also destroy his power base.

- Another can't miss tactic: make him responsible for a project, and then give the work to someone else. Route all correspondence, paperwork, and other information and material that relate to his project to the other but not him. Periodically, require him to give a detailed status report on his project.

Together, these two, easy-to-use ploys are guaranteed to keep your unwanted deputy off guard and on the defensive, even drive him bugs. One thing for sure: if he's perpetually on the defensive, he'll find it exceedingly difficult to undertake an offense against you, to plot against you or scheme for your job.

See also PURGING and TRIANGULATION.

DEVIL'S ADVOCATE VERSUS HERETIC

...ing ...ith not being on the team, and perceive the questioners as heretics.

Do not be confused: if it seems moderately difficult to sell a new idea or a new program internally, I can guarantee you that it will be many times more difficult to sell it outside the agency to people whose pay and promotion you do not control. And if your staff can think up reasonable objections on short notice, then just imagine what external rivals and opponents, with all the time in the world at their disposal, can come up with. To survive real world trials in the legislative and public battle ground, your idea needs all the annealing your staff can give it.

To stifle the hard questions now almost guarantees your idea will fall flat on its face, will cost you *face*, or worse, place you in the position of backing a loser. Condemning your staff for supposed (versus actual) heresy carries an additional penalty, one much more costly than any short-term losses you stand to incur from backing a loser: it will unfailingly isolate you and cost you their loyalty.

From the halls of state government, Great Moments in Idea Trials:

Recently, a friend was denounced as a non-team playing heretic because, at an inter-agency meeting, where her boss presented a wonderful new initiative, my friend's body language—her BODY LANGUAGE—agreed with a critic.

Now my friend had said nothing at this presentation. Nor did she express her views in writing (maybe she should have). Ironically, she supported the new program; her only concern was how it could be most effectively presented to the public, and her concern was shared and forcefully articulated by an elected official in attendance. In the eyes of the presenter, her disagreeable body language branded her a dissenter, a heretic, not a team member. (Significantly, the presenter had nothing to say about the response of the elected critic—perhaps because he felt powerless to do anything about it.)

Fortunately, when my friend expressed her concern to her boss after the meeting, who had called her in to explain her apparent heresy, she was able to convince him that she was still a true believer—or at least still a team member.

I describe this event not so much to amuse as to highlight how constructive criticism in many quarters is welcomed and to urge you to consider carefully how you might react in similar circumstances.

See also AGENCY LIFE-CYCLE, FACE, HERETICS, LOYALTY, PRESS RELATIONS, and YES-MEN.

DIRECTIVES, WRITTEN

~~~~~~~, you are expected to respond via the same channel you receive it.

Written directives are enormously useful instruments. They can set up someone to take a fall. They can curtail the activities of someone whose presence is no longer desired. If he violates his written directives, *ZAP!! Got him!* Grounds for disciplinary action.

And sometimes written directives merely seek to link the addressee with a project which has turned, or is about to turn, sour.

See also CONGRUENT COMMUNICATIONS, PURGING, and SCAPEGOAT.

DOING SOMETHING:
GUERILLA EFFORTS

_____

Occasionally, an achievement-oriented government employee gets tired of being hemmed in by all those overbearing, all-encompassing, time consuming, energy sapping rules and procedures, or frustrated from spending all his time helping his boss or agency avoid blame. Sick of it all, he takes it into his head to just do something, to actually accomplish something . . . anything.*

This is the individual counterpart of stealth. And the analog holds here, too. As with the stealthy agency, the trick is not to have your guerilla effort discovered, or at least, have it go undiscovered until it is completed.

So just do it. But proceed with caution. Remember, in your boss's eyes, you're now acting independently and thus without authorization, without the requisite internal consensus and signoffs. You are out of control. Keep the profile of your effort lower than the belly of a snake. Tell nobody. Above all, keep your boss and the agency hierarchy out of your work, or they'll interfere and mess it up, gut it or kill it—and maybe you in the process. Bootlegging provides a good operating model. Maybe the agency's competent network can be quietly tapped.

If your effort reaches fruition, be prepared to forego any credit or to share it with your boss or members of the Power Team.

_____

*   This urge should never be confused with offensive behavior (i.e., grabbing turf). Offensive behavior is seldom the handmaiden of real accomplishment, so it is unlikely to contribute to this urge to achieve.

See also BLAME-FREEDOM FROM, BUREAUCRACY, CONTROL, CREDIT-TAKING, DALEY, EXPEDITERS, MOONLIGHTING, NETWORKS, POWER TEAM, SIGNOFFS, and STEALTH.

DOWNSIZING: STAFF BUYOUTS

Why? Simple: most often, staff who opt for early retirement are the competent ones.

The implications of this with respect to the inevitable life-cycle change which will accompany the buyouts should not be overlooked.

---

*   In exchange for a lump-sum, a staffer takes early retirement.

See also AGENCY LIFE-CYCLE and GRESHAM'S LAW.

DRUGS AT THE OFFICE

Widespread drug use at the office signifies an agency well advanced in its life-cycle.* The more open the substance abuse, the more mature the agency. Like sex in the office, drugs are an escape, a sign of low morale.

Over lunch, our August Chairman enjoyed having a tall, cool one. One entire fifth of his favorite sour-mash, that is. And lo! After lunch, he was as ugly and abusive and irrational as he was a model of charming, rational decorum before noon. His Jekyll and Hyde persona quickly became known to the staff; in fact, in some dark corridors he was clept, neither lightly nor inaccurately, "Half-Day Harmon."

One fine afternoon, a consultant brought a twenty-page document for him to review and sign. Upon being presented with the paperwork, Chairman Hyde began to rant and rave. He castigated the presenter to the point of abusiveness, called the work sloppy and sub-par, decreed it be redone and that the revision had better be brought to him early tomorrow morning. First thing next day, a charming Chairman Jekyll graciously received the revision, quickly reviewed it, and signed it without hesitation. "This is perfect. Why didn't you have it done this way yesterday?" he asked, reasonably.

The consultant hadn't changed a comma.

This points up a lesson: if you must deal with someone who drinks, snorts or shoots up at noon to make his day pass more quickly, best to catch him before lunch. Otherwise, don bullet-proof clothing before you visit.

The first (and only) time this same chairman addressed his entire assembled staff, he made a serious tactical blunder: he scheduled the event immediately

---

* By drug use, I include alcohol along with coke, pot, meth, and other controlled substances. However, I exclude tobacco products.

after lunch, thereby guaranteeing that what should have been a pleasant, low-key, "Hi, I'm Harmon Smith, your new chairman, and I expect we'll all accomplish great things together" affair instead became an abusive, adversarial thirty-minute harangue to clerical staff and division heads alike on coming late to meetings with their Appointed Leader—some had straggled in late, no doubt engaged in something more important, perhaps...

EDUCATION

Education is one of the few things, if not the only thing, the government cannot take away.* Consider: government can, and increasingly does, strip citizens of their dignity, of their worldly possessions, even (for those who fail to pay child-support) their children, but it can never take away what one has learned.

From this, it follows that education, defined here as accumulated learning, skills and experience, is a store of non-transferable wealth, and it pays you to take advantage of every opportunity to add to your fund of knowledge.

If classes are available, and reimbursement is offered by your agency, by all means look into and pursue them.

---

*   Not to be confused with indoctrination. No exemptions apply to government employees.

See also GOVERNMENT AS GOD and INDOCTRINATION.

ELECTED OFFICIALS: THE STAFF VIEW*

the proverbial Harvard men, you can always tell them, but you can't always tell them much (come to think of it, many probably attended Harvard). Worst of all, if prevailing political winds dictate that they do so, they can—and will—turn on your agency, its budgets, its programs, and you, at the drop of a hat. Controlling elected officials is next to impossible: the best any agency can reasonably hope to achieve with them is some measure of influence.

Treat elected officials with extreme care. Once their staff, who are usually organized along functional lines, have been socialized to respond to the agency's cues, they inevitably become far more knowledgeable on agency programs and legislation than their boss. This can be good, because, if their boss is smart, he knows he cannot follow every issue, so he will rely on his staff for guidance on how to vote—and on how to respond to agency business.

If an elected official proves to be impossible to work with, just bear with him. Chances are the agency will be around long after he has been cast out of office.

---

* This view, it must be noted, comes from below the officers who have been appointed to head the agency. Those at the upper rungs do themselves a disservice, however, to ignore it.

See also *IN EXTREMIS*, KEEP 'EM WAITING, LEGISLATIVE STAFF AIDES, MANDATE, MUZZLE THE TECHIES, PROMISES, and PUBLICS.

EMERGENCIES

Emergencies constitute the one stimulus capable of suspending the defensive games and turf wars, and getting everyone to work together. Never mind that inquests, hearings, Blue Ribbon panels, Task Forces, and the like will likely be convened in the aftermath to study the matter, but just after the disaster, all hands, including men whom one would ordinarily never leave alone together in a room with a loaded weapon, will work in concert for long hours, days, even weeks, until the crisis is resolved or subsides.

The motivational power of an emergency is not to be believed. It is far stronger than, say, a presidential exhortation. If ever an agency were fated to move mountains, then an emergency might provide the impetus. Partly, I think, the non-routine nature of the event poses an unusual challenge to all concerned, and partly, sheer adrenalin kicks in. This holds especially when the emergency threatens agency employees.

Oh yes, the emergency must involve the welfare of the agency, not that of its mandated public.

See also MANDATE and PUBLICS.

EMPLOYEE UNIONS

- senior staff has gone out of its way to alienate workers over a lengthy period.

These conditions apply to your agency. The workforce never wake up one morning and collectively decide, on the spur of the moment, "Hey, let's form a union today." On the contrary, employees are driven into organizing by the insensitivity, stupidity and weakness of management, and the worst of these is all of these. All things being equal, no employee wants union dues skimmed off the top from his monthly paycheck, and most professional employees would just as soon dispense with the periodic union meetings, elections and other trappings of symbolism and solidarity that characterize the Great American Labor Movement (GALM).

If you actively seek union protection, my advice is, "If you're gonna be a bear, be a grizzly." When you organize, find the meanest, toughest, no-bullshit representation available. Twenty years ago, I'd have opted for the Teamsters; today, I'm not sure which brotherhood best fills that role.

If you are in the "Management" of an agency being unionized or threatened with unionization, the action taken by the rank and file means you have blown it—particularly if the positions to be unionized are patronage slots; once a union becomes ensconced, control over these plums may pass from the party in power to the union. You can be sure that the power brokers at city hall or the state house will be highly displeased that their ability to reward and punish has been compromised, and you can probably expect changes in the agency's executive suite.

Oh yes, interfere with union elections only at your peril, because doing so violates federal labor law, and can bring the US Department of Labor down on your head—and one hardly needs to be reminded of its bias in these matters.

In one sense, a union is like a government agency: it is formed to protect a special interest. Once it has become established, it will be almost impossible to dislodge.

One fine day, every professional and clerical employee at my agency received a letter from the aforementioned Teamsters, detailing a list of particulars against "management" and asking whether you really wouldn't rather have a union to prevent and protect you from these abuses. If you wanted such protection from the Teamsters, continued the letter, indicate *Yes* on the enclosed form and return it. The abuses enumerated in the letter were factually correct.

Reaction was swift. Word swiftly went out (no doubt after a hasty phone call to the agency lawyers) that no manager even discuss the Teamster's letter. Senior staff were scared enough that none did. The Teamsters were voted down, perhaps because the guy who signed the letter sounded like John Gotti's grand-nephew, and perhaps because the payroll was top-heavy with political placements who owed their job to patronage, not to GALM, and with professionals who felt membership in any union, especially the Teamsters, beneath them.

A few weeks after the receipt of the Teamsters' letter, the replacement of our chairman was rumored, and a few months later, he was gone.

See also AGENCY LIFE-CYCLE, GOVERNMENT MONOPOLIES, LEGAL ADVICE, PATRONAGE, RUMOR MILL, and URSINE THOUGHTS.

ENFORCEMENT: CREATIVELY USING

goods on anyone in the agency who A) is out to shiv you and B) whom you are out to shiv. Given his mandate, it is much more difficult, if not impossible, to turn him loose on rivals outside the agency. His is not the last word—it is not he who informs the victim that he is fired, for example; that job properly falls to your Hatchet Man. But absent the Inspector General's investigative spade work, there may be no last word.

The investigative powers of the Inspector General's office are tailor-made to keep you in power.* With ready and complete access to all records in the agency—and he doesn't have to tell anyone why he wants to review them—the Inspector General can without challenge gather damaging evidence on anyone you wish to remove—and there's nothing the victim can do to prevent this digging. Better yet, if the victim tries to impede or otherwise interfere with the process, he can be reprimanded for obstructing an investigation.

Perhaps the best combination of investigative skills is a creative accountant filling this slot (assuming you can find one), or pairing him with someone with an investigative background—an ex-cop or an investigative reporter.

It goes without saying that the Inspector General is an important member of your Power Team.

---

* J. Edgar Hoover understood and, more important, practiced this better than anyone else I know of. As Inspector General Plenipotentiary of the nation's capital, all the resources of the FBI were at his personal disposal (an amazing accomplishment), and all of official Washington was his to investigate. Hoover made the most of his opportunity.

See also HATCHET MAN, HOOVER, PERSONAL EMPIRE BUILDING, and POWER TEAM.

ENGLISH: THE HOMETOWN ADVANTAGE

If you speak and write good English, here is one way to keep out or at least at bay many (beware: not all) who grew up speaking another language.

You may be able to use your native language as a weapon. Often, a strong command of English, a tongue rich in nuance and filled with homonyms, is not just lacking, but sorely lacking, in those who grew up speaking some other tongue (caution: I assume that your knowledge of English is excellent, otherwise forget this. Ditto if you are an engineer or otherwise technically trained: most techies choose their vocation, I believe, because they are congenitally incapable of using the Queen's English competently.)

If you can use twenty-five cent words where five-centers should do nicely, you may be able to mislead or keep a colleague with a poor command of English from understanding a critical point in a memorandum that you don't want him to understand. If differences between inter—and intra-, super—and supra—are indistinguishable to a colleague, then you may be in luck. Try these out for starters by purposely misusing them for your audience. The beauty of this: if they don't understand the difference, there's nothing they can do about it.

Increasingly, this ploy may work well with others who did grow up speaking English, as command of the language has been emphasized less and less over the intervening (or is it intravening?) decades since I finished high school. Come to think about it, it may work equally well on techies (I recall one department head saying of her technically trained assistant, "Some people simply have to be muzzled outside the office.")

Some may decry this ploy as unfair. And in a sense it is, because you force someone to communicate in a foreign (for him) idiom. But that's the point; if he cannot use English well, and if you enjoy a markedly better command of the language in which government—and most other—business is conducted in this country, then his deficiency in his adopted tongue precludes his advance. So be it. At some level in the agency hierarchy, there exists a dividing line between those who must communicate in our native tongue clearly and effectively with senior managers and elected officials outside the agency, and those who jabber in strange tongues around the coffeepot.

Knowledge, lest we forget, is power.

Corollary: If you know your English leaves much to be desired, then look up big words in memoranda and letters f...

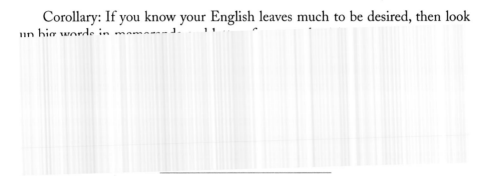

The subject of staffers whose first language is not English brings to mind an amusing though cautionary tale, rich in lessons. Smedley (not his real name), a foreign-born systems manager at our agency whose mother tongue was completely unrelated to English, became captivated and intrigued—perhaps a bit puzzled—by the bewildering alphabet soup of technical names, terms, and acronyms that he had encountered, so he determined to compile a dictionary of relevant terms and acronyms. All on his own initiative—a red-flag if ever there was one. Into Smedley's dictionary went a bewildering assortment of federal, state, and local agency acronyms, legislation, and downright interesting terms that intrigued a mind not yet familiar with idiomatic English.

This effort, I reemphasize, was undertaken at Smedley's initiative. It ignored the fact that any professional not long associated with the agency would have been grossly incompetent if this amateurish effort at dictionary compilation proved even remotely informative. Maybe the fact that Igor, Smedley's boss, was himself foreign-born and shared Smedley's lack of general American office acculturation explains why Smedley's dictionary progressed as far as it did.

Anyway, prior to releasing Smedley's magnum opus, Igor circulated it in draft form for comments at a weekly meeting of department heads. One attendee, seemingly no fan of *émigré* would-be Diderot*-systems techies, or most likely just bored and seeking a little amusement, kept his copy and presented it to the beat reporter from the city's largest daily, along with an explanation of what it

---

* One of the brightest intellectual lights of the Enlightenment, Denis Diderot produced the first dictionary.

represented. Next day's *Times* carried a sarcastic article, its headline naming the agency's chairman, and asking if this were how his staff spent its time . . . which, of course, it did.

Saddest of all, after the paper hit the newsstands, Smedley entered the office with a broad, innocent smile on his face. He was greeted by a co-worker who was more attuned to American office culture. "Smedley, did you see the newspaper article about your dictionary?"

"Yes. Izz wonderful, izz not?"

"No, Smedley, the article makes fun of it." There followed an explanation.

As the enormity of his gaffe sank in, and his loss of face became increasingly apparent, Smedley could only reply, "Ohhh, ohhh, I do not feel well. I must go home."

Mercifully, we need not dwell on the lessons that this vignette provides.

See also AGENCY LIFE-CYCLE, DOING SOMETHING, EDUCATION, FACE, LEAKING NEWS, MUZZLE THE TECHIES, SCREENING PROSPECTIVES, SIGNOFFS, and VOLUNTEERING.

ENTHUSIASM

of the contact will naturally blunt any criticism that may otherwise fall on the agency for institutional foot-dragging.

And if the agency backs the project enthusiastically, the project manager's added enthusiasm will give it that little indefinable extra, the creativity and oomph that push it into the pipeline, overcome objections and maneuver around internal obstacles.

In this way, waves are avoided, or at least, their frequency and amplitude are minimized, and potential blame is side-stepped.

See also BLAME-FREEDOM FROM, COMPLAINTS, DALEY, and PIPELINE.

ETHICS

Ethics in government—what do you think of them?

This question, posed to friends in federal and state agencies, provokes gales of cynical laughter.

See also BEHAVIORAL GAP, GOVERNMENT-A BRIEF ESSAY, and UNDERSTANDING THE GAME.

EXCUSES

Some slippery customers can contrive excuses for everything, almost as if they have a list to draw from—and maybe they do. Such people would much rather avoid blame if their assignment goes awry than garner praise for a job well done. Their mind set, when they are presented with an assignment, is "Am I being set up to take a fall? How can I dodge blame?" and not "What must I do to complete this assignment?"*

I don't trust them, maybe because they play the game too well. Expect never to nail them if things sour: the paper trail they'll have laid will always be two to three steps ahead of you. The astute manager assigns their work so as to eliminate all excuses for not having it performed to specifications and completed on time.

---

* To be fair, their suspicions may be well founded: it all depends on the supervisor who hands out work.

See also BLAME-FREEDOM FROM.

EXPEDITERS

If your Power Team provides the foundation for your full term in office, then expediters comprise the structural skeleton on which the rest of the agency hang, especially if the agency is in the later stages of its life-cycle.

Expediters produce. Quick results. A product that outside publics will deem credible and saleable. Expediters are the movers, the shakers, the staff pros who know the system backwards and forwards, including and especially the leverage points, the buttons to push to get things done. They identify relevant decision makers and cut through procedural bumpf, foot-dragging and red-tape. Despite institutional tendencies toward inertia, expediters get things done in a hurry—or at least, ahead of schedule and under budget. Projects they manage move through the procedural pipeline at near muzzle velocity.

All without winking at regulations and procedures; without getting anybody indicted or investigated by a Blue Ribbon Panel two years later. And despite the non-cooperation of lazy, hostile, indifferent or incompetent colleagues whose effort and participation are nonetheless critical to the project's timely completion.

Because expediters are often scarcer than hens' teeth, they are exceedingly valuable to have around. As a rational onlooker, you might quickly conclude that it behooves managers, department and division heads to identify and devote great energy to the care and feeding of such people in their organization BECAUSE IT IS THEY WHO WILL ACCOMPLISH WHAT LITTLE WORK THEIR DEPARTMENT OR DIVISION IS LIKELY TO PRODUCE. Since expediters, like diamonds and mink coats, are always in demand somewhere, a frustrated expediter can be expected to leave if he is not rewarded.

(My research discloses that useful work, when it does get accomplished in mature organizations—outfits staffed through and through with obstructionists, non-performers and incompetents—gets done by an informal network of a few competent people who actually produce the results. Perhaps, on reflection, you know examples of this. When one of the competent people leaves, the organization sinks to a new low, and nobody understands why.)

Two corollaries: Never, never, never let an expediter go, not without a fight; and, if you don't have one, then go and find one. One last word: if, as a manager or agency head, you desire to find an expediter, don't expect the Personnel Department to identify the producers. They will bring in losers, not winners. So save yourself the aggravation, and look elsewhere.

But it often doesn't work this way. M

.... and he will respond by giving his expediter subordinate unfavorable performance reviews.

If you are a card-carrying expediter, and if meaningful work needs to be done, relax. There's no need to volunteer. If the work is critical, sooner or later, your services will be explicitly sought out. Someone will come to you; he'll have to, if he wants the job done right. Two out of three times, the work will be assigned specifically to you over the protests of your immediate boss and, quite likely, his boss, both of whom are threatened by the recognition that is attached to your competence, and resentful that they have been directed, in no uncertain terms, not to interfere with you.

The relationship between one federal bureau head and an expediter five levels beneath his on the organization chart works this way: when he needs her work yesterday, he cannot afford to wait the three days to two weeks that it would take to buck instructions to her, so he calls her directly. He wants to deal with her alone, not with a host of meddling intermediaries and not with her today, and someone else next time. He makes himself personally available if additional guidance or clarification is required, and ensures the expediting staffer knows and takes advantage of his accessibility. This is mandatory if their relationship is to be productive. Managers at intervening levels know better than to meddle here, they have been socialized (ordered) to stay the hell out of the way. To keep them out of the way, the bureau head runs interference for her so that nobody who gets by-passed can punish her for his circumvention. Equally mandatory to ensure a productive relationship, this precaution precludes any incompetent, threatened, or obstructionist underling from inserting himself or his court favorite into the proceedings, or from punishing the expediter. In this case, the bureau head even directed that one intermediary to initiate the paper work to promote her.

If you occupy an intervening position and find yourself by-passed, fear not; if you refrain from interfering, no harm will befall you; in fact, some one may even copy you on the completed correspondence. That's probably the best you can hope for.

See also AGENCY BEHAVIOR, AGENCY LIFE-CYCLE, COMPETENCE, DALEY, TRIANGULATION, and VOLUNTEERING.

FACE

one stands to lose.

By this measure, elected and senior appointed officials, who hold the highest positions in government, clearly have the most face to lose. And they can be predicted to go to the greatest lengths to save it.

Why? Because in public service *loss of face is the governmental equivalent of castration*. Embarrassment and shame, the fears that underlie loss of face, are among the most powerful human emotions, and their motivational force is extraordinary.

As with sex, loss of face must be experienced first-hand to be fully appreciated.

There exists a species of stroker which, I believe, tends to appear more in government than elsewhere and owes his position to massaging the ego, building the face, of his boss. Weak department and agency heads are particularly susceptible to ego-massage; some surround themselves exclusively with ego masseurs and masseuses.

To cause one's superior to lose face, whether studied or by accident, can affect him profoundly, to say nothing of how he subsequently perceives his defacer. This makes doing so either a psychological ploy of great impact, if it is done deliberately, or an incredible gaffe, if it is inadvertent.

Conversely, to enable a superior to save face is an act of greatest kindness, which can result in incalculable good will toward the face-saver. Best of all is when face saving takes place with seeming unconsciousness of the event by the saver.

See also ASSISTANTS, CREDIT, IMAGE, POWER AS A CORRUPTING INFLUENCE, SHOWING UP THE BOSS, and YES-MEN.

FORMER EMPLOYEES:
OUR ALUMNI ASSOCIATION

Former employees, agency alumni, align themselves conveniently into two mutually exclusive groups: those out to shiv you and your agency, and those whom management or staff would skewer in return. Of the two, the ones who view you with revenge uppermost in mind should concern you most. I have seen alumni with blood in their eye devote an inordinate on-the-job (publicly funded, for those who remain in the public sector) time and energy to sticking it to their old agency or former boss, sometimes with success.

When employees depart (and join the agency's alumni association), it is to your advantage that all, or as many as possible, feel positive toward their former employer (and especially toward you). Once an employee (appointed or staff, doesn't matter) has landed in greener pastures, he has, for all practical purposes, escaped the greatest leverage you and your agency can exert over him: the power to terminate his employment. After he's off your payroll, your influence over him drops to nil. And the last thing you need is a vengeful tiger with blood in his eye, who still retains information pipelines deep into your agency, over whom you're your control has dwindled down to zilch, landing in a position from which he can stick it to you and your agency. Such a vendetta, carried out from a vantage that confers its prosecutor with influence, can cause their former agency no end of grief—and once they start stabbing, there seldom is a damn thing you can do to stop them. Among these efforts, the most effective you never find out about. And don't think retirees are exempt, either: someone who may have had no stomach for games while on the payroll but nonetheless harbored a strong grudge may succumb to the urge to settle old scores after being liberated and receiving his first pension check.

Counter-intuitively, the same applies in reverse to senior staff who've moved on, especially those who have much to lose, especially if their tenure at their old agency was fractious. Those who were liked (which means leaving in good graces, and respected and popular among staff) are free to get on with life, professionally and personally. Those who weren't would do well to look over their shoulder because they may become subject to slings and arrows from former colleagues the launching of which they are powerless to prevent and which can cause their career enormous harm.

To sum up, agency alumni earn their relatively high standing among an agency's publics for good reason. Hopefully, this has been demonstrated to the satisfaction of the reader.

.... latter, which in time would prove unfortunate.

When his appointing regime fell from power, he returned to the private sector to take the reins of a company in the industry his former agency dealt with (no surprise). Shortly after he arrived, company finances took a turn for the worse, and it declared bankruptcy. It was forced to operate in receivership while trying to turn itself around.

Congress drafted legislation to help companies such as his, and the company applied for an infusion of federal cash, which, by curious coincidence and pursuant to the recent legislation, was dispensed by the very agency its CEO had recently headed. Grant requests were duly filed, but no federal cash was forthcoming. The company continued to file for help, but its requests kept getting deferred, studied. In time, a trusted employee was dispatched to Washington to find out why no action had been taken.

By day, he and the agency staff pored over the company's funding application, and one evening he took a staffer out to dinner. After a few drinks, the staffer told my friend (off the record) that the problem wasn't the company's grant request; that was in order. No, the grant wasn't the problem: the sticking point was that the company would never receive a nickel of federal aid as long as the prick who previously headed the agency was company CEO. Period. And it never did receive a nickel, either. Absent federal financial aid, the company eventually was liquidated, its assets auctioned off sold by the bankruptcy court.

See also LOCK THE DOOR, PUBLICS, PURGING, REVENGE, THEORY OF THE FIRM, and WOUNDED TIGERS.

GENDER DIFFERENCES: RANDOM THOUGHTS

When you cut the baloney about differences between the genders, it is worth noting that most men and women process information (i.e., think) and communicate differently. Men are logical and linear; women are metaphoric and use imagery. Each sex sends and decodes different meta-messages differently. Rare is the lady who alone can participate fully and equally in a meeting of the boys, and rarer still the man who can hold his own among a klatch (or clutch) of women. This means that when you impart a message to a member of the opposite sex that you wish to be received and decoded, you may face a real challenge. Rather than belabor this point, I'll cite a reference: by far the best book I've found on inter-gender office communication is Deborah Tannen's *Talking From 9 to 5* (Morrow, New York, 1994).

This having been said, women possess several competitive advantages which, I suspect, go underutilized (and under compensated) in office politics, and one can make a strong *prima facie* case for having women represented proportionately with men in one's network—women are masters at unearthing information—and one or two women as full-fledged members of your Power Team.

Many men, for example, will frequently share with a woman confidences that another man could extract from them only with thumbscrews. A little patient rapport building and a willingness to listen can elicit a cornucopia of valuable information from a man. Add to that a smile, a bat of the eyelashes, a wiggle of the fanny, a soft touch, eye contact—and many men turn to Jell-O. If that doesn't work, tears do—few men know how to take it when a woman bursts into tears.

But it doesn't stop there: men may say things in the presence of—not to, but in the presence of—a woman that they would never say if another man were within fifty feet. Seemingly, such men can't differentiate between a woman and a piece of office furniture. This phenomenon is much more apt to occur in the presence of males rooted in Mediterranean, Middle Eastern or Asian cultures, who, even after a generation or two of family acculturation, still presume that a women's place is to produce and raise babies, keep house and perform the most menial, boring, repetitive office work (incidentally, psychological studies of women in factories suggest much truth in the latter).

Many women managers exhibit the "Gold Star Syndrome." Remember, back in the fourth grade, when the girls would receive a gold star for keeping their desks clean and tattling on those (usually the boys) who misbehaved? Women who retain this mind set make an absolute fetish of the truly important things around the office, like unplugging the coffeepot at the end of the day, turning out the lights at night, rebuking staff for being five minutes late to a meeting—that sort of thing. They'll pull someone deeply enmeshed in an important assignment off to attend a three-day-long, out-of-town seminar on Defensive Driving or AIDS Awareness or Sexual Harassment (note the proper use of caps—they would) because the departmental quota must be filled. Gold Star syndromers who pursue emptying the wastebasket with the fiercest anal-retentive fervor are often completely oblivious when their department lags six months behind schedule on a major effort, because they cannot distinguish between the truly important (the project) and the seemingly important (the wastebasket). By these signs you may recognize this subspecies and understand the basis on which your performance will be evaluated and you, rewarded.

Someone (probably a women) pointed out that women are disproportionately over represented in the "caring" fields (i.e., welfare agencies). Assuming this true, one is inclined to question whether it stems from "Gold Star" attentiveness during indoctrination or whether "caring" is inherent in women, a behavioral trait embedded deep in their genes, a function of all that progesterone. I suppose this question is only an extension of the tedious nature/nurture debate, which, like determining whether the chicken precedes the egg, is unanswerable. Still, it points up an interesting side phenomenon: seemingly, women starting out in the agency are willing to work harder and longer without compensating pay, or even recognition, than their male counterparts—long after a man has eased off and conferred a raise on himself, a women is still caring away, burning the late evening oil. Whether for this reason, or because as a lady friend suggests, women feel impelled to work harder to compensate for not being a man, such industry will only tempt her (usually male) manager to take advantage of her industry by piling on the work, which leads the other men in the office to grumble about curve-busters and quietly invoke sanctions designed to curb or otherwise punish female industriousness. Women would no doubt term this practice cynical and exploitative, and they may have a point; still, when one leads with one's chin, one leaves herself wide open . . .

Women make up over half the population (51 percent), and unlike men, they tend to be more right-brained (metaphoric and emotional—caring) than left-brained (logical, rational). From this, and assuming that the same proportion of women as men cast votes at election time, it follows that it will handsomely pay agencies in the "caring fields" to pitch their message emotionally—to women voters. The marketing implications of this demographic nugget can scarcely be overemphasized.

The Women's Movement tries to have it both ways. It encouraged women to wear dresses that reveal four fifths of their boobs and come two inches below their twat, thereby encouraging (well, at least not discouraging) glances and comments from admiring or interested (or, occasionally, horrified) males, and then sue the admirer for sexual harassment. This makes me wonder whether women's clothes aren't designed by attorneys who specialize in sexual harassment litigation. Be forewarned: look (discretely), but don't touch, and if you must say something pleasant, best to do so away from witnesses (come to think of it, how would it be construed if, instead of rendering a compliment, one observed, "that looks horrible!"?).

This brings to mind an amusing tale. Martha, a young, bright and talented, good looking professional colleague, one day showed up at work wearing a casual fishnet top that revealed a great deal (Martha boasted a lot to reveal) and openly invited admiring stares. Seizing a quiet moment, I called Martha into my office, wishing I'd known and dated someone who could wear this outfit so effectively when I was in high school, and told her, "Your outfit looks terrific. And every business has its own uniform. The one you are wearing is perfectly suited to advertising, where I've seen women walking around in outfits with their boobs hanging out. But this is a public agency, not an ad agency. So you might want to think twice before you wear that top to work here. In the meantime, I reserve the right to enjoy the view." I leave her in a gale of laughter.

country.

Despite all one hears about the elimination of gender (or sexual preference, take your pick) in promotion, women still face a (decreasingly) uphill fight to reach the upper tiers of public management: the executive suite remains mostly a man's world. Many male managers persist (whether consciously or otherwise, I cannot say) in assigning to competent, highly educated women, tasks that are clerical in nature ("Get me this file," "Copy this document,") and far beneath their capabilities. A feminist acquaintance in state government puts it more bluntly: men engage in a game of keep away to prevent her and other women from gaining access to the juiciest, most challenging and highly visible projects, and thus, to the executive offices on Carpet Corridor. Only to her, it isn't a game.

Assuming her assertion correct, I ascribe it partly to the fact that women generally do not crave power as nakedly, shamelessly, and remorselessly as men, and partly to the fact that an agency is nothing if not a magnet for power seekers. (Alternatively, women do crave power, the power to curtail masculine excesses; in other words, the power to emasculate.)* Recall that the wolf pack only has alpha males; some females enjoy higher status than others, but there are no alpha females. Men are drawn far more strongly to the executive suite than their female counterparts—and, I believe, are socialized to do so far more strongly than women. Maybe if someone invented a "power pill" for women, their representation in senior slots would improve. Alas, I fear it would contain large, or at least non-random, concentrations of testosterone.

---

*   Hilary Clinton stands out as a conspicuous exception.

GIVE YOURSELF A RAISE

increase. Naturally my friend was aggrieved. In comparing his accomplishments with his peer, he personally sucked $20 million out of the feds when their policy explicitly forbade it, while his back-stabbing co-worker couldn't write a simple sentence and left his accounts in shambles. He felt the system (to say nothing of his boss) had screwed him. Big-time.*

In his bile, my friend decided to reward himself for work well done. He simply did less work. His workday grew no shorter, so he received the same salary for less output. His pay for actual hours worked increased, so he had effectively given himself a pay raise.

In one sense he was lucky: his department was so poorly managed that the drop in his output went undetected for months.

During this time, he was not idle. Far from it. He wrote papers for graduate school, brought his resume up to date, wrote a masterpiece on industrial organization for an industry he hoped to work in someday (he shared this with me)—all on "company time".

I mention this because I have observed any number of employees, scattered throughout various agencies, who have done as my friend did. And if you work in an agency where your best efforts go unrewarded, chances are that consciously or unconsciously, you are doing, or will do, the same.

---

* My friend was equally at fault because he failed to recognize the criteria by which his performance was being evaluated.

See also MOONLIGHTING and PERFORMANCE REVIEW.

GOVERNMENT—A BRIEF ESSAY

Definition: Government: The constant struggle by those in government service [elected, appointed or merely hired—it doesn't matter which] to a) attain maximum control over people's lives, and b) maximize the number of lives they control.

Some related thoughts:

- From this definition, it follows that to govern is to control.

- This control (or power—the two terms are used interchangeably here) cannot be exercised without the acquiescence (forced, tacit or freely granted) of the governed. Whether they willingly cede this control, or whether government forces it on them is a chicken-and-egg question, and is thus an irrelevant distraction. I personally believe that power, meaning the desire to control—both its acquisition and retention—is endemic in all social hierarchies, and since *Homo sapiens* is nothing if not social, that power is a drive embedded deeply in our genes.

- Given that it takes constant struggle to acquire power, it follows that once power has been acquired, or ceded, *those who possess it will go to the most extreme lengths to retain it.* This may explain why power is never willingly relinquished: in fact, to reverse its acquisition, to overthrow it, entails nothing short of revolution—be that at the level of the civilization, the nation-state, the agency, the department, and the individual.

- Qualifiers: Our definition has nothing to do with whether the people to be controlled are citizens or not. Nor has it anything to do with wealth production, consumption or distribution. The quality and quantity of services provided, moreover, are almost comically irrelevant. Lastly, this definition has nothing to do with either ethics or morality: "good" and "bad" are as irrelevant as the quantity and quality of services.

- Marx might smirk knowingly at the word "struggle" in our definition.* And for many practitioners, Marxians included, this struggle is practically—if not morally—akin to war, whether declared (*jihad*) or undeclared (cold). On occasion, it spills over into armed combat, though more often it is fought with less bloody memos and procedures.

---

* On second thought, maybe he wouldn't. Marx's driving obsession with uplifting the downtrodden masses scarcely qualifies him as a laugh-a-minute.

See also AUTHORITY, *IN EXTREMIS*, PROCESS-FOCUS ON, THE PUBLIC, and THEORY OF THE AGENCY.

GOVERNMENT AS GOD

The goodies that government giveth, government can taketh away.

It must be remembered that this law applies to government employees, too.

See also GOVERNMENT AS RELIGION.

GOVERNMENT AS RELIGION

⊔⊔⊔⊔ a heaven (material security), and its heaven compares favorably with the Christian version because you don't have to die to get there because it's here on earth. Its followers fervently look to and petition (pray to) Government to protect them and provide for their welfare. Just as Judaism and Christianity boast a long succession of prophets (Abraham, Isaiah, Moses, Jesus, and St. Paul), true believers in government also point to their prophets (Plato, Locke, Rousseau, Jefferson, Lincoln, Marx, Lenin, Franklin Roosevelt, Gandhi, and King).

Government worshipers also have their own utopian vision, all-embracing answers, community of believers, traditions, schisms, heretics, and even churches—Republican and Democrat. Like medieval Christianity, Government increasingly seeks to provide an integrated, all-inclusive view of reality, an interconnected whole which embodies the organization of all significant knowledge, a frame of reference within which all possible questions of importance are or can be answered.*

In common with other institutions, religions need money. Certainly no religion amounts to much of a presence without funds. In recent decades, Government's ability to tax has come to supersede by a wide measure the ability of its religious rivals to enforce tithing discipline. Ironically, this has made them dependent on government financial support, since government (with mounting reluctance) subsidizes its rivals by permitting their worshipers to deduct "religious" contributions from their income taxes. By eliminating this subsidy (which I for one favor—like any other rational human, I dislike competition; certainly, I resent my employer subsidizing it), Government's adherents could severely crimp the flow of funds to rival sects and thereby consolidate its position as the leading provider of welfare and security, and so cement its claim to being the leading religious order in the land.

---

* Not author's original words. The descriptive format was excerpted from a journal. Applying it to government, however, is strictly the work of the author.

When, not if, but when this occurs, Government worshipers will have at long last succeeded in separating church from state, truly as the drafters of the Constitution envisioned. And when that day comes, Western Civilization will have attained a victory so subtle yet so massive, that Mary Queen of Scots' systematic persecution of Protestants pales in comparison to it. Indeed, to find an event of comparable significance in Western Civilization, one must look all the way back to the fourth century when Emperor Constantine decreed Christianity the official religion of the Roman Empire.

Some, probably most clerics, may disagree, perhaps violently, with this characterization of Government. Yet assuming it accurate, it puzzles me that churchmen who depend on charitable contributions for their livelihood and whose most important ministerial work—helping the poor, ministering to the sick, social counseling, educating the populace, and promulgating to their congregation a common system of moral and ethical values and behavior—are being or already have been taken over by Government. Maybe they just don't see the competitive threat to their true ministry, much less to their livelihood and the institution to which they have dedicated a life of service. Or maybe it's because contributions to the Church that pay their salary are tax-deductible.

It's not that their services will be no longer provided; it's just that their providers will be publicly employed.

"For love of God and Country" is now a meaningless expression.

During the last fifty years, Government has come to represent "country" in the minds of the electorate and government workers alike. This means that the expression could be rewritten to read,

"For love of God and Government" (1)

However, during the same time span, Government has replaced God as the creature to whom citizens both pray for material blessings, and to whom they look increasingly for spiritual guidance. Thus, expression (1) could be reworded,

"For love of God and God" (2)

which is nonsensical, and therefore, meaningless.

Sadly, even though it may not be accurate, "for love of Government" provides a poor substitute for the original expression: it does little to stir the passions and get the blood running, so it may be best to keep the original phrase, flawed though it may be, until some true believer comes up with a suitable, politically correct replacement.

See also COMPETITION, CONTROL, CORRECTNESS, INTIMIDATION, MARKETING, TAXES, and THEORY OF THE AGENCY.

GOVERNMENT MONOPOLIES

Picture this: a long line of people waiting resignedly at the passport office or the post office or to apply for benefits at the unemployment office or to register a car with the Department of Motor Vehicles. At the service window, a bored, indifferent, overweight clerk processes paperwork with studied, mechanical unhurriedness, and you know that he wouldn't speed up even if the place caught fire. Without warning, he closes his window and puts up a crude, hand-lettered sign: ON LUNCH BREAK.

Happened to you? Happened to me, too. All the standees share something in common (besides irked impatience): the agency with which they are dealing holds a monopoly on supplying whatever good or service they seek. Closing down the service line without notice is a classic action of a monopolist. Customer service is an alien concept . . . or a sick joke.

This should come as no surprise to any of us. After all, government can, and frequently does, confer monopoly rights on numerous institutions, especially its own agencies. And no fooling, the power rush that accrues to the guy who without warning knocks off for lunch, leaving a line of people frustrated and without recourse, probably counts as one of the two high points of his day (the second: when he heads home at quitting time).

But monopoly can be a two-edged sword, and even if an agency boasts a monopoly, it pays its senior staff to understand whether the monopoly is real (like, say, that enjoyed by the Department of Defense—hey, what other government agency could realistically operate the "Defense Triad?" HHS or HUD?), or merely apparent (like that of the U.S. Postal Service. Extensive competition from overnight express companies and a growing tendency to internet bill payment and personal correspondence threatens to turn the Postal Service into a subsidized delivery system for junk mailers).

The Post Office offers an interesting—and sobering—case study of a monopoly broken. Its peak (measured by the quality of the service it provides) came between 1920 and the early 1950s, when intercity mail was actually sorted (on trains) en route to its destination, and the public enjoyed two deliveries per day. Service has gone downhill, and competition has heightened ever since (in the early 1970s, its work force unionized, and coincidently or not, Federal Express, now FedEx, came into existence). Today, even government agencies use private delivery services when something has to arrive tomorrow for sure.

In not recognizing, even as its service continued to decline, that technological innovation had long ago ended its monopoly, the postal service may have cost itself its very existence, because it is woefully unprepared to engage in market-based

See also AGENCY LIFE-CYCLE, COMPETITION, CUSTOMER SERVICE, and OVERWEIGHT STAFF.

GRESHAM'S LAW OF PUBLIC MANAGEMENT

Just as bad money drives good money out of circulation, so does bad (weak, incompetent) management drive out good (strong, competent) management.* This phenomena can have external and internal causes. Internally, competent senior staff desire to work for an organization where the material they require from other departments comes to them on time, or gets done properly. Or they become tired of dealing with professional obfuscators and dawdlers who dedicate their zeal and energy—along with that of their staff—to a zero-output strategy. When these occur, the competent senior staff leaves the agency—and leaves the incompetents in charge.

Externally, the appointed or elected board members desire a man running their agency who will do their bidding, regardless of whether it jibes with the agency's mandate—or even makes sense. When this occurs, you can be sure that the last thing a weak agency head will do is surround himself with strong, competent subordinates.

Once they're ensconced, the weak senior staffers stick together. Although they may compete vigorously against one another, if a competent replacement comes along, they can, and invariably will, forge an implicit alliance among themselves to rid the agency (and themselves) of the newcomer and the threat he poses. Even if they cannot stomach one another, the arrival of a competent peer can be counted on to unite them as few other stimuli can. And if they can't get rid of him, they can at least drag him down to their level, much as rate busters are assailed in a union shop.

The insinuation of incompetents in key senior staff slots can take awhile, perhaps years, or it can occur at the outset. It all depends depending on the quality of the agency head and the importance attached to the agency's mandate. But ultimately, it happens to all agencies.

---

*   Economists term this phenomenon "Gresham's Law."

See also AGENCY LIFE-CYCLE, BLAME-FREEDOM FROM, and EMERGENCIES.

HANDLING THREATS OF INFLUENCE

...........t, and he threatens to go running to a powerful big-wig friend and patron, someone presumably in his pocket, who will move heaven and earth to have you fired, demoted or transferred to Skagway if YOU don't sign on the dotted line.* INSTANTLY. But if you sign, you risk, at minimum, a reprimand for bending or violating established procedures, and at worst, being indicted for sanctioning a possibly illegal or unlawful scheme. What do you tell the bully?

My suggestion: Courteously but firmly inform the bully that his request cannot be authorized unless it conforms to departmental rules, regulations, and guidelines to regular procedures. If he threatens to call his patron, fine, that's his privilege. And if the patron values this bully (or his money) enough to call your boss, or your boss's boss, or otherwise bring pressure, or even get legislation passed to grant him the privilege or favor he sought, that's fine, too. That's his privilege. But under no circumstances sign the authorization for him there and then.

If your boss or your boss's boss directs you to sign on the spot, it is your place to remind him, and mark this language closely, that established written guidelines/regulations/law-of-the-land preclude authorization without the appropriate internal review and approval (you know the procedural jargon best). This wording makes the procedures, and most important, not you, the sticking point. If you are still directed to sign, reply, "I will be pleased to sign when I receive written instructions and authorization to do so." This phrasing avoids the personal pronoun *you*, which many subconsciously internalize as a threat, yet by passing the buck up the line, it takes the twin monkeys of accountability-and-blame and non-cooperation off your back and transfers them squarely where they belong—on your boss's or his boss's. If after this your superiors are dumb or desperate enough

---

* By "special treatment," I mean seeking to be accommodated in a non-routine, non-regulation or extra-legal manner.

to put the directive in writing, that's fine—that's their problem. If the bully gets someone else, someone more pliant, to sign the paperwork, that's fine, too; it's now the other guy's ass, not yours, that may get fired, demoted or consigned to Skagway if irregularities in this matter ever get questioned.

If the authorization is signed thus—committing agency resources in an irregular manner and without the usual due process—take the original and substitute a photocopy in departmental files or agency archives. *You* keep the original in your "Life Insurance" folder, off the premises, and preferably in a safe deposit box. You could use this to advantage later—against the bully or your boss, or against whoever finally signed.

But signing the form on the spot just to get a bully off your back is not reason enough to risk a blot or worse on your record, much less put yourself *in extremis.*

See also BUCKPASSING, INSURANCE, INTIMIDATION, and SAYING NO.

HATCHET MAN

ui cold water on the not (usually radical) ideas that you don't want implemented (face it: you don't want the record to show that they were even considered). As Lord High Executioner, he personally fires malefactors and, most important, in your place, sticks it to your enemies and rivals.*

Several qualities are required in a first-rate Hatchet Man.

- He has a hide of toughest leather, and (unlike you) he harbors no congenital need to be loved. He must be tough enough—and willing—to take the heat for unpopular moves, policies and decisions. I can unequivocally guarantee you that he will be respected and detested—and feared. If he walks the halls unfeared, then he's the wrong man for the job.
- He must have your complete trust. The closer the working relationship, the more effective it—and he—will be.
- His title must convey sufficient seniority to guarantee him credibility in dealings outside the agency.
- Most important, he must be absolutely devoted to you.

Your Hatchet Man functions as your lightning rod. He becomes the focal point for internal (and external, if you can swing it) ire and ill-will that otherwise

---

* When the axe does fall—when bad tidings must be delivered or some draconian action must be taken—guess who swings it? And while the Hatchet Man delivers the bad news or fires someone or announces a staff pay cut, you make it a point to be vacationing in Maui, visiting the field office in Yuma or Sioux Falls or attending a seminar on better government in Miami—in other words, someplace far removed from the office.

would be directed at you. This may save your hide, because he may attract mortal blows and sanctions that would otherwise be aimed at you. And his carefully cultivated tough guy persona allows you and him to play good cop/bad cop with the staff, your Santa Claus to his Grinch—or perhaps Attila the Hun. You want to be the guy who delivers good news, because you want your troops to think good, or at least non-bad, thoughts about you.

Because he will be the natural focus of ill-will and internal disloyalty, he will need and must have your unquestioning support. If you are unwilling or unable to supply this (in other words, if you will not or cannot take care of him), then it is ludicrous to even consider having a Hatchet Man. At worst, because he will know where your skeletons are hidden, you needlessly make a powerful enemy of one whom you should otherwise count among your staunchest, most loyal supporters.

"Chairman Mel seems like such a great guy. Agreeable, easy to talk to. I just can't understand how he can suffer a close-minded, uncooperative Neanderthal like Lecter to be his right-hand," opined a staffer. Guess which one was the Hatchet Man?

See also LOYALTY, POWER TEAM, RADICAL THOUGHT, SAYING NO, SAYING YES, and URSINE THOUGHTS.

HERETICS, PURGING

makes the agency "bad." Some even exhibit open hostility to the agency's enabling legislation. They espouse ideas like free-markets, freedom from government regulation, that sort of thing.

When you encounter such a devil worshiper or idolater on the payroll, there's only one way to treat him: brand him a heretic and then purge him and his beliefs. As expeditiously as you can. His level in the organization is irrelevant: you don't want him; you don't want anyone who openly opposes your team (and, thus, you): people like him spill the beans to Rush Limbaugh.

Highly instructive are the speed with which heretics are dealt and the severity with which they are punished. These sanctions suggest a pathological underlying fear of them and their beliefs.

To illustrate the fervor with which entrenched bureaucracies deal with heretics, one need only consider the bloody end to which Leon Trotsky came and the death sentence under which Salman Rushdie lives. A more mundane

---

*   Heretics must be distinguished from Time Clock Punchers who may exhibit indifference, scorn, or active hostility toward the public the agency serves, but still pay token homage to the inherent value of the agency's authorized mission. Heretics, on the other hand, are Committed Idealists who oppose its mission.

†   A specialized branch of government, political thought control, heretofore thought unique to totalitarian governments, bears the sole responsibility for determining what thoughts are politically acceptable. What remains a specialized division of labor in absolutist governments (solely the turf of political officers and commissars) is the task of all committed employees in the more liberal form of government encountered here.

example appeared a few years ago in the alumni newsletter of a leading university (University of North Carolina-Chapel Hill) incubator of graduate-level urban planners, policy analysts and public administrators:

> "[a 1965 graduate reports] . . . the [incumbent administration] are doing their best to eliminate the Federal domestic sector, [and] this includes a special effort to eliminate urban planners who they believe over-regulate private development and otherwise do nothing of value. In an ironic twist, HUD Assistant Secretary Savas, a point man for these . . . policies, wrote [his latest book] *Privatizing the Public Sector* using HUD research staff; for this illegal act, *he may be privatized . . .'* [emphasis added]" (University of North Carolina at Chapel Hill, Department of City and Regional Planning, 35th Annual Alumni Newsletter/1983, page 20)

Assistant Secretary Savas was "privatized," soon after this squib appeared. Given the heretical nature of his book and the fact that he had little incentive to call outsiders' attention either to his alleged moonlighting or appropriating agency assets (employees' time) for his personal use, one concludes that incumbent HUD employees (and school alumni) not only cheered, but also actively participated in, his departure. One also concludes that when he departed, few tears were shed by his self-appointed privatizers. The end of Savas's tenure at HUD was not quite so dramatic (and certainly not so violent) as Leon Trotsky's, but by having him removed under a cloud, the guardians of the faith still may have dealt his career, and thus his future livelihood, a crippling blow.

Had Assistant Secretary Savas's book been entitled something like *HUD's Positive Influence In The Allocation Of Housing To Underclass Strata*, it is likely that little or nothing would have been said (or done) to remove him from the payroll.

Thus do agencies deal with heretics.

See also GOVERNMENT AS RELIGION, INDOCTRINATION, MOONLIGHTING, PRIVATIZATION, and PURGING.

HIDDEN AGENDA:

... . This ritual most often produces little or no long-term effect on the rest of the agency. So pervasive are the rules and regulations, so intimidating and immobilizing the prospect of dealing with outsiders, especially the media and the Prime Public, that they can reduce an insecure or untalented appointee to little more than a kept man, incapable of independent action or initiative.

While appointed senior staff, competent or otherwise, may come and go, the permanent (career) agency staff, the technical employees, remain. And with them, their agenda.

The staff know best. And the permanence and continuity they enjoy, irrespective of who's in charge, confers them with a measure of staying and absolute power that few appointed heads enjoy (one conspicuous exception: J. Edgar Hoover). This, in turn, gives rise to behavioral norms within the agency that exist despite the appointed or elected officials who nominally run the place. In fact, I would further argue that these norms lie beyond the control (and often beneath the awareness) of the Power Team, which by definition has its ear to the ground.

These norms take the form of an unwritten agenda that is pursued apart from, or even despite, the efforts or wishes of elected and appointed officials. Unwritten into statutory program plans and probably recognized by few insiders, this agenda nevertheless becomes woven as deeply into the agency's mission as its statutory duties, becoming part of its ethos. Its presence explains why certain programs and issues seem to take on a life of their own. But so subtle is this agenda that the Power Team may not even be conscious of it: to them, it may exist only subliminally, like advertising messages.

This explains why the staff agenda is often pursued with stealth, and why it accounts for the preferred treatment of certain publics quite apart from how they may be treated by the Power Team.

The roots of this behavior are lodged deep in an agency's institutional consciousness. By dint of their academic training and long experience with an issue or problem, the staff know (or believe they know) best, or at least, better than the Power Team, and certainly better than outside meddlers like the legislative oversight committee and the media, how to deal with a problem: no "temporary" (i.e., appointed) agency head, and surely no legislator, knows an issue or better than the permanent staff. To long-time staff professionals, the elected and appointed officials are often as ignorant as the general public, maybe more so.

Virtually nobody in the general public knows of this phenomenon, and few elected officials are aware of it, either. Of these who are aware, I suspect that just a small number understand, much less appreciate, either its influence or its pervasiveness within an agency. Indeed, I believe that many agency heads pass their full term from being sworn-in to being cast out totally unaware that it exists, which makes them easy to deal with, i.e., they can be virtually ignored. Better yet if they fall into that blissfully ignorant subset of bosses who isolate themselves from agency goings-on.

Recognizing the existence of this off-the-record agenda, it may pay the inexperienced staffer not to disrupt any programs undertaken pursuant thereto.

The hidden agenda is best kept that way.

Quoting again from the University of North Carolina-Chapel Hill alumni newsletter, another alum reported:

> "We recently updated the Comprehensive Plan for the County and now are revising the Zoning Ordinance. A major target is to clean up the Agricultural Zone (A-1) which covers 64,000 acres or over 2/3 of the County's land area. This *notorious zone* [emphasis added] allows everything. Apparently a deal was cooked up in 1975 to get a [zoning] plan adopted then. Zoning was allowed around [town] if the rural area was left with *no zoning controls. It's time to change this* . . . [emphasis added]" (University of North Carolina at Chapel Hill, *Idem*)

This alumnus, one senses, has taken it upon himself to set things right. His brief synopsis suggests whatever zoning initiative he plans to invoke will take place despite, not because of, the efforts (or, more likely, the non-efforts) of elected officials or those appointed to run his agency. When he calls the zone "notorious" and declares, "It's time to change this," he clearly speaks for himself and perhaps a few like-minded staffers, probably not for the townspeople, not for the residents of the rural areas, and certainly not for the elected or the appointed officials whose 1975 deal he would quietly overturn.

In other words, it's his agenda, not theirs. While, so far as his fellow alumni are concerned, there's nothing "hidden" about it, I suspect that this may not be so with the officials and good citizens of the town and further, that his purposes would remain best served if it were kept that way.

It's also worth noting that the focus of his efforts is "control"; he solely intends to bring additional

HIERARCHY: THE CASTE SYSTEM

The hierarchical pyramid—what an extraordinary accomplishment! The Romans invented it, and it has endured more than two millennia for a simple, elegant reason: no one has come up with a better way to organize authority and responsibility. To be sure, there have been minor adjustments and changes (one doubts, for example, that the Romans ever distinguished between line managers and staff pukes), but a superior system for structuring an organization has yet to be invented.

One inescapable aspect of the pyramid is the resultant layering of authority, which, as an agency matures, results in an increasingly rigid caste system. The Brahmins who run the agency perch majestically at the top, and the Untouchables (the janitorial staff, the copy room gang) toil on the bottom. By definition, there are many more Untouchables than Brahmins, and employees at these two extremes never, and should never, deal directly with each other.

And seldom do they deal with, or talk to, anyone in the middle, either. This is a manifestation of the Two-Level Rule, an unwritten protocol that forbids conducting business with anyone more than two levels above or below you. The Two-Level Rule extends even and especially to finding scapegoats. Why? Because there's no credibility if you hang the janitor—unless he truly was guilty or unless you run the janitorial staff.

The hierarchical pyramid forms an integral part of the bureaucracy, as much a part as all those rules and procedures.

Departures from this model usually signify a weak manager or a sick organization. To be sure, there are exceptions. At agencies that perform major, intensive, non-standard work (cutting edge research and development in the sciences, the space program, and the wartime military, where the hierarchical pyramid may be disrupted, all come to mind), technical knowledge and performance may temporarily supersede rank.

Among the departures I've encountered are the Sow-and-Piglet Model (everybody reporting to a single boss, invariably a reluctant delegator), and the Totem Pole (Number 4 reports to Number 3, who reports to Number 2

170

who reports to Number 1, with nobody else reporting to Numbers 1 to 3, an arrangement almost sure to guarantee constant conflict between 1 and 2, 2 and 3, 4 and 3, because each is responsible for the same task). Then, there's the Moving Sun, or Temporary Center of the Universe Model—one employee having specialized knowledge or technical competence calls the shots until the need for his expertise is finished

See also AGENCY LIFE-CYCLE, RULES AND PROCEDURES, SCAPEGOATS, SHARING TURF, and WHO'S IN CHARGE.

HIRING CRITERIA

My main criterion in bringing in someone new is, assuming that the professional knowledge and experience he brings to the table meet the nominal requirements for the position, will he play ball with me? For me? Can I control him? Will he, if it proves necessary, fetch, beg, roll over, even play dead?

If he will not, then I don't care how great he is: I don't need him; I don't want him. I don't want individualists: I want people who (preferably) are happiest playing a team role and a subordinate role at that.

It's that simple.

See also CONTROL and SCREENING PROSPECTIVES.

HIRING INDEPENDENTLY

Here's why: the implicit threat of job loss effectively keeps most employees on a tight rein. For most people, the enormity of this threat cannot be overemphasized. If they are fired, they can kiss goodbye all their accrued benefits, they can be blackballed from government work in their immediate locale, and after they have worked long in government, many companies won't even talk to them, much less hire them.

Because people of independent means can afford to ignore this threat, they are immune to it. A friend coarsely, but accurately, terms independent wealth *fuck-you money*. Employees fortunate enough to be endowed with fuck-you sized checking accounts can walk anytime. And by being able to leave without incurring financial pain removes a—perhaps the—key hold you have over them. And this, no rational boss will accept, unless he has absolutely no choice.

So if the resume of a young Rockefeller or a Kennedy, or a comparable dilettante comes across your desk, buck it, if you can, along to the next guy and save yourself much heartburn.

See also CONTROL, HIRING CRITERIA, INTIMIDATION, LEADERSHIP, and PURGING UNWANTED EMPLOYEES.

HOOVER, J. EDGAR:
A BUREAUCRAT'S BUREAUCRAT

J. Edgar Hoover, the late director (for Life) of the Federal Bureau of Investigation, was, quite simply, a bureaucrat's bureaucrat.

Hoover built and carefully cultivated a far-flung network of informants all around Washington, DC, both in and outside the government, that kept him up to date on all of the dirt on anybody who mattered in the nation's capital. Who was sleeping with whom, who was a closet homosexual, who was receiving kickbacks or bribes, and so forth.

The beauty of this network is that it was maintained by the Bureau and paid for through federal authorizations. While the information gathered went into files at the Bureau, it was for Hoover's personal use. Hoover's intelligence network and his extensive files together constituted the most extensive—and effective—power base ever seen in Washington. In fact, they may well have been be the most effective such weapon ever created in the history of government in the free world.

No president ever took Hoover on. Not even Lyndon Johnson, who is still renowned for playing Oval Office hardball, dared oppose him. Nor would Congress cross him. While most federal employees retire when they reach age sixty five, J. Edgar hung in as director until shortly before he died at the age of eighty—just as he wanted it.

Few use the power of their office so effectively.

I often think that one of the best moves a player in the Washington game could make would be to start up, perhaps as a silent partner, his own escort/massage service, a la Sydney Biddle Barrows, New York's celebrated "Mayflower Madam," or Heidi Fleiss, who arranged sex for sale to the stars of Hollywood. In short order, the list of clients would almost certainly be more than enough to keep the entrepreneur forever on the federal payroll.

See also INSURANCE POLICY, INTELLIGENCE, and NETWORKS.

IF YOU ARE BLAMED . . .

nand them your scalp: make 'em earn it by proving you guilty.

Remember, the burden of proof lies with them.

So cover up and stonewall.

Marshall your defenses.

Above all, never, never apologize: remorse or contrition will be taken as a sign of prior knowledge, and therefore, culpability.*

---

* Exception: unless, of course, you are convicted.

See also COVERING UP and DAMAGE CONTROL.

IGNORANCE

At times, ignorance is bliss. It may pay you not to know the whys and wherefores surrounding a hot, controversial, non-standard or illegal issue. You just want to be able to truthfully testify, if you are later summoned before a Blue Ribbon Panel, "I didn't know that."

On the other side of the coin, eager beavers who seek to know too much too fast are seldom to be trusted. In this case, their ignorance is your bliss. The wise staffer will be content to remain in the dark until amplifying information is volunteered.

See also INTELLIGENCE, POLITICAL FAVORS, SOLE-SOURCE PURCHASES, and TASK FORCES.

IMAGE

- It behooves you to learn, when you start out in a new job or get a new boss, whether you will be rewarded for solid performance or for making him *look good*. That way, you can adjust your efforts to maximize your reward. If he wants to look good, fine; only make sure it's his signature on the paper work when finger-pointing time rolls around.
- A man's physical appearance and grooming reveal a great deal about his core values. To me, one whose suits are impeccably cut and cleaned, who always sports a perfect haircut (not a hair too long or out of place) is an image hound who owes his position to appearance rather than achievement. I personally harbor a deep-seated aversion to any man who compensates for baldness with hair implants or combs his remaining hair over the bald crown of his head to "cover up" an apparent visual deficiency.
- Navy ship inspections sometimes fall into this category. I have seen inspecting officers mark down a machinery compartment for a spot of grease on the overhead while overlooking rust in the bilges or ignoring the condition of fire-fighting gear and damage control fittings. Image guys. The best inspector I ever met: a tough, grizzled, salty, no-bullshit captain who really knew his stuff. While inspecting a machinery space, he'd overlook grease, but he'd order the sailor presenting the compartment to start up a pump or check a fire extinguisher horn for cigarette butts.

  The irony: this captain's ship not only worked, even and including machinery out of sight down deep in the bowels of the ship, but because it consistently delivered, its image far outshone all other ships of its type. This captain was a rare manager who did not mistake image for performance.

In sum, know (and perhaps beware) the manager who would have you believe that his scat issues forth from a Chanel No. 5 bottle.

IN EXTREMIS

When an agency comes under siege, expect the senior staff to prolong their term in office as long as possible, to do all in their power, be it fair or foul, to forestall their removal, regardless of the consequences to all others—including friends, the agency, the government, even the country. *Nobody* willingly relinquishes power.

The behavior of the Nixon White House in the aftermath of Watergate and the Clinton White House after the Lewinsky Affair, when the twin specters of criminal prosecution and presidential impeachment hung heavy over the most highly placed and powerful men in the world, is most instructive: the continuous stonewalling and covering up, the paranoid defensiveness, the unrelenting search for scapegoats and leakers of damaging information, the charges and counter-charges, the lies—regardless of their corrosive effect on the general public's perception of its government, the attack on another country (Serbia) to deflect the media spotlight, all are classic. Ditto for the Japanese and German high commands late in World War II: when it had become obvious that losing everything—the war, their office, their power—was all but a foregone conclusion, they stubbornly held out, even as their cities were incinerated and untold thousands of innocent, or at least non-combatant, civilians were killed. But to the leaders it must have been worth it: they remained in power until the bitter end.

Likewise, if the leaders of your agency come under fire, expect them to behave the same way—except they probably lack the authority to attack Serbia.

If, God forbid, your agency is besieged, and you do not belong to the Power Team, then understand the need to protect yourself. As their predicament becomes more and more precarious, expect the senior staff to become increasingly irrational. They'll be searching for scapegoats, someone, anyone, to take the fall in their place, with all the desperation and fervor that one saw among the last few to escape Saigon. When things get really hairy, anyone will do, culpable or not: the Two-Step rule is suspended indefinitely. In fact, all rules, all norms of trust and civility, are suspended. So buckle up your flack jacket, pull on your crash helmet and crawl into your foxhole until the storm blows itself out.

See also COVERING UP, GOVERNMENT-A BRIEF ESSAY, NEWSLEAKS, and SCAPEGOATS.

IN-BOXES: TWO THOUGHTS

It goes without saying that you may wish to safeguard your in-box from their prying eyes.

An unobtrusive way to accomplish this: stop in the mailroom—it's easy to find out when the mail clerk starts his appointed rounds—and while you're there, offer to pick up your department's mail. On the way back, you can gather your mail and screen anyone else's in relative privacy.

Many in-boxes become a purgatory, a place where projects and assignments die a quiet, moldy death. In your constant quest to avoid blame, you want to push the papers on. If paperwork is fated to die a quiet death, best it happen in someone else's in-box.

See also BLAME-FREEDOM FROM, INTELLIGENCE, and PAPERWORK-ROUTINE.

INCOMPETENT PLACEMENTS—
DEALING WITH

From time to time, your agency or your office will become home to a political placement whose incompetence is so massive and absolute that he not only embarrasses, but even threatens, the whole organization.

What action can you take to neutralize some bozo who, just because he owes his job to the Speaker of the House, thinks, talks, and acts as if his shit doesn't stink?

Call the Speaker's office, get his administrative assistant or someone who has the Great Man's ear, and ask whether it's true that Desidarius Doofus, who just signed an order authorizing the draining of the Everglades, owes his position to the Speaker. More often than not, a patron will not wish to float a turd in someone else's punch, because doing so make waves—and casts aspersions on the Speaker. If this is so, then perhaps the patron or, if the placement holds a position of comparatively minor importance, his duly authorized representative, can call Doofus and tell him to cool it.

Sometimes, this may not be possible, so other measures are called for.

One possibility is to reorganize duties around the office so that Doofus cannot legitimately inject his unwelcome presence into sensitive business. I refer to this as the "Useless Gambit," since the reassigned person is useless for anything more than collecting his paycheck. Or, send him to the Omega Department. There exist, I'm convinced, scattered throughout government, entire departments, maybe even whole agencies, filled with placements from whom nobody expects—much less wants—any output: the employees are only there to collect a paycheck.

See also AGENCY, ISMS, and PATRONAGE.

INCOMPETENTS AT HIGH LEVELS:

that turkey gone, we can really accomplish something now."

Nine times out of ten, their optimism is short-lived and sadly misplaced. Chances are, the replacement will make the departed turkey look great.

Why?

If your agency is far enough down its prime public's or appointing administration's priority list, nobody with the clout to appoint a successor will care whether he's competent—only that he obeys orders, pays his party dues, stays out of trouble and doesn't louse things up too much worse than they are. Perhaps this explains why HUD hasn't accomplished anything noteworthy in over 18 years spanning two Republican and two Democratic administrations.

When a stiff is replaced, more often than not, the job will go to some hard-luck or otherwise challenged incompetent who is well connected and rates a favor. Coming in at mid-term almost guarantees that he will be a third-stringer: the varsity were appointed at the first go-around (what does this say for appointees of an administration that has been in office for two or more consecutive terms?).

I am reminded of a replacement department head who took the place of a bright, engaging non-performer who over-promised and under-delivered once too often.

- On his first day at the office, the new man greeted a passably good-looking female employee with, "I'd like to roll in the hay with you, but I'd don't want to become emotionally involved."
- His staff soon discovered him to be alcoholic. A couple of beers before breakfast would put him in the appropriate working frame of mind.
- To curry political favor, he interfered with the established, agreed upon budget for a minority party contractor, thereby undercutting the commitment of, and embarrassing the higher-ups in, his own party.

181

One day, an accident tragically and prematurely claimed the life of his political patron. The replacement's tenure on the payroll did survive, by forty-eight hours, the announcement of his patron's death. However, his firing preceded his patron's funeral.

INDEPENDENCE, FISCAL

sun rising in the East. Together, these conditions guarantee your agency its virtual independence from the legislature.

This happy state occurs only when voter loyalties to the agency are so strong and pervasive that a legislator opposes your authorization stream only at peril of not being returned to office. To best appreciate this fiscal idyll, one must have toiled in an agency whose funding stream has been threatened.

Fortunately, time-tested ways to ensure its continuance, or at least neutralize any misguided efforts that seek to counter it, are catalogued elsewhere in this handbook. With luck, attaining this pleasant state won't entail a revolution, or even open warfare (exception: defense agencies). In fact, attaining fiscal independence is a central *raison d'etre* of this manual, and underscores our thesis that, collectively, agencies constitute our fifth—and previously undiscovered—branch of government.*

---

* As shown elsewhere herein, its isolation (or insulation) via the legislature from the voting public, its ability to sway the legislature (and less often the executive branch) and the media—the second and fourth branches of government—and the right and tendency of its employees to vote at elections to retain agency programs, all effectively confer separate "branch status" on the agency.

See also CUTBACKS, MARKETING, and PUBLICS.

INDOCTRINATION

By indoctrination, I mean inculcating in the general public the idea that government alone (our agency) can solve their problems, that they must look up to and support government in all its endeavors, that government is "good."

The (sometimes) implicit meta message is that all institutions which compete with government are, perforce, "bad." In this way, the credibility and influence of competing institutions is slowly eroded, a bit at a time, until they fall by the wayside. Except for the free market, I can think of no competing institution which is explicitly denigrated much, but then, there's no need to. There's little enough competition from them, and what competition exists, is decreasing with the passing of older generations.

The church provides an instructive example: once upon a time, not so long ago, the church educated children and ran so many colleges and universities that church-affiliated institutions dominated higher education (even today, the only first-rate private research universities that come to mind which claim no prior religious affiliation are Cornell, Johns Hopkins, and Stanford).* Today, the role of churches in education (the Catholic Church is a notable exception) has diminished to insignificance. The other great private research universities—Harvard, Yale, Princeton, Chicago, Columbia, Duke, Emory, Northwestern, and NYU: the list goes on and on—make a fetish of being non-sectarian. All were church-affiliated early in their existence. No college which remains church-affiliated ranks with any of the schools noted above.

The primary institution for indoctrinating the young is the schools. From earliest childhood, children learn the credo set forth below.† Indoctrination reaches

---

* Education is but one field where the churches have abdicated their social responsibilities to government. Welfare—the entire field—was once almost the exclusive province of the church; it ministered to the sick, ran hospitals, and helped the indigent. In welfare as in education, the role of the church has similarly diminished.

† Government is good. Government will provide for you—feed you, clothe you, shelter you, educate you. Government will solve your pressing social problems. Government will protect you and guarantee you a living. Government is good—and you can depend on it.

184

maximum intensity when a kid reaches college. Once they reach adulthood, the media assume this burden as the primary agency for public indoctrination.

It is not by accident that maverick educators bemoan the lack of critical thinking skills taught in schools and even (and especially) most colleges and universities. It is probably best that the young are not taught to think

MEDIA-ACHIEVING CONTROL, and THE MEDIA-SOME THOUGHTS.

INERTIA: PARABLE AND LAW

When some firebrand or radical comes into your agency seeking to change the world, give him wide berth. The laws of physics tell us that most systems tend toward inertia, and these same postulates can be applied to government, in spades. If the agency undergoes a paradigm change before (or in spite of) its time, it can usually expect to undergo a speedy "ectomy" soon afterward, and with it, its proponents.

Change, real change, occurs slowly. We're talking evolution, not revolution. Consider the following parable:

Given the human toll in misery and in inner city violence, given the vast powerful multinational criminal cartels and rogue nations, financed mostly by American dollars, that produce and distribute their product, given the drain of billions of dollars for *enforcement* (whatever that accomplishes), for all these and other excellent reasons, suppose, just suppose that somebody proposed that the sale of controlled substances—addictive drugs—be legalized.

If this policy were implemented, then, with a huge consumer market (current users) guaranteed, reputable companies possessing efficient (and legal) distribution networks would soon dominate the market—and supplant the drug cartels controlled by foreigners. The power and influence of the huge Asian, Middle Eastern, and Latin American crime cartels and rogue governments would swiftly fall. Competition and the removal of the risk premium a seller now tacks into the price of his product would lower the price of a high, so the constant need to feed an addiction would be less likely to bleed cash from low-income families with users. With the lure of easy big money gone, young hoodlums would lose the single largest economic incentive to kill each other (at present, no other illicit activity boasts anywhere near the market size or payoff as selling drugs), to addict or recruit relatively innocent ten-year-olds and induct them into a criminal life. Felonies attributable to raising cash for a quick fix would decline. Perhaps with no, or less, stigma for using, the naturally rebellious inclination of kids to try addictive drugs might subside. If it became mandatory (or even optional) that buyers present identification at the point of sale, perhaps they could be approached for treatment and detoxification. The general public (i.e., non-users) would benefit too: less crime, safer streets, and fewer tax dollars for enforcement, interdiction, and the resultant huge bureaucracies these efforts spawn.

Sounds good, doesn't it? The trouble is, it is good. Too good. The number of interests vested in maintaining today's less than ideal *status quo* would amaze you. I suspect that by far the loudest protest would come from the drug treatment

substances as addictive as heroin, meth, pot or cocaine (as if a rational non-user will walk up to a counter to buy a couple of lines of coke). Clergy would decry the amorality of the idea. The law enforcement community, aided by the Department of Defense, the CIA and especially the Drug Enforcement Administration, would come up with a jillion creative reasons to question and challenge this policy (after all, if this came to pass, think of the reduction in off-the-books income just for cops—to say nothing of others—who moonlight on the payrolls of drug dealers! Dear reader, you and I could comfortably retire many times over on that sum). Drug-producing nations which enjoy friendly diplomatic relations could be expected to bring diplomatic pressure to bear on us, and to retaliate for decriminalizing their produce would ostentatiously increase their propensity to "buy Asian." Last but not least, the crime syndicates themselves, which have mountains of disposable cash and an excellent economic incentive to spend a great deal of it to safeguard their franchise, could be expected to spare no expense to fight such a policy: they could easily buy the services of politicians and journalists who would then duly brand this policy vicious, ignorant, misguided, discriminating against minorities, and so on.

Finally, in the face of mounting opposition to this increasingly hotter potato, the incumbent administration would suspend the initiative pending exhaustive investigation by a hastily constituted "Presidential Blue Ribbon Task Force on Drug Legalization." Bet that after a few hearings no report would be forthcoming.

From this, it follows that if one proposed this policy or came up with an alternative which promised to eliminate drug-related crime for $1,000 per state, the last place to expect support would be the US Drug Enforcement Administration: the policy would remove their mandate, put them out of business. In response, DEA could be expected to do all in its power to frustrate, block, obfuscate, delay, derail and otherwise resist the implementation. Count on the media to give more than equal time and sympathetic coverage to the opponents. Similarly, if one discovered a way to house the homeless or eliminate illiteracy or air pollution, the last place one could expect (much less receive) support from would be HUD, the US Department of Education and EPA, respectively.

This gives rise to the Williams law of Continuing Social Ills (alternately, the law of reversed effect): any agency which has been constituted to address a pressing social problem can be counted on to cultivate, but never solve, the problem.*This explains why we never "win" any social war: [†] they are fated to remain on-going. In this one case, agencies have discovered that to win is to lose; here, in fact, it pays to back a loser.

The *status quo*. God bless it . . .

---

*   Whether the legislators who enact the mandate that creates an agency envisioned it would solve the problem or milk it forever—or whether they simply don't care— remains unknown. This question, however, suggests an excellent topic for research.

[†]   So far, the military seems to have kept combat (i.e., shooting wars) outside the range of social wars, but recent evidence (e.g., Desert Shield) suggests this may be changing.

See also BRIBES, KILLING THINGS, THE MEDIA-SOME THOUGHTS, MOONLIGHTING, and TASK FORCES.

INOCULATION

It can be seen that inoculation is a defensive weapon; it can be used to defend and retain sales and market share, not expand them. It is a form of indoctrination for existing customers.

Incumbent politicians use this technique. All the time.

The use of inoculation in an agency is the same. If you suspect *a priori* a line of attack by a rival, it is possible to inoculate your agency's relevant publics from his claims beforehand, thereby defusing them before he attacks. *But you must get your licks in first. Otherwise, you've lost the battle, and maybe the war, before you've fired your first shot.*

If it is used intelligently and with appropriate timing, inoculation can be a defensive weapon (against blame and turf incursions alike) of devastating power.

See also BLAME, COMPETITION, INDOCTRINATION, PUBLICS, and TURF.

INSULATION

A phenomenon which can be fully appreciated only after it has been encountered, insulation is encountered at all levels in the agency, not, as one might imagine, merely at the highest levels. Its root cause: insecurity and fear, specifically, the fear of reality. This fear causes an employee or manager to shrink away, to insulate himself, from unwelcome contact with anything that smacks of the real world—other people, outsiders and his staff alike—and decision making.

Together with revenge, fear ranks among—if it isn't the—most powerful motivators, as the actions of an insulatee will reveal. The more fearful the victim, the more strenuously he will use all available agency resources to provide himself refuge.

An insecure, fear-driven agency head will surround himself with yes-men and layers of assistants to insulate himself from the public and his staff alike—from anyone who could possibly question, challenge or probe his decisions and actions, who might force him to decide an issue or answer a question, or otherwise expose him to the harsh, cold light of reality.

Likewise, an insecure, fear-driven staffer will insulate himself from contact with the public at large and with his boss and peers to the maximum extent possible. Lots of seemingly legitimate avenues are open to, and beg, this behavior. Staff development lectures or courses—if they remove him from office and he is paid for the time spent taking the course—work well. He may also suffer the most Monday/Friday flu. Other proven techniques for avoiding contact: time outside the office for coffee and smoke breaks, and lengthy bathroom visits. The technological revolution in telephony has become a wonderful ally, too, offering refuge from callers in the form of voice mail, call forwarding, and phone menus that feed studiedly and inexorably into a Kafka-esque dead-end loop.

Knowing and recognizing the symptoms are but the first steps in dealing with self-insulators. This is much more difficult than it sounds, because many, especially managers, have painstakingly erected formidable defenses against direct access via any channel, and as a general rule, the higher the personage, the less accessible he is. One doesn't just walk into his office—no open doors here. Instead, one must negotiate an obstacle course of suspicious, uncaring, unsympathetic assistants and secretaries, which to many isn't worth the effort. Which is exactly what he wants.

Still, it may be possible to reach his underlings. For example, if you work in the same agency, you can intimidate them by showing up at their office and dealing with them in person. Or you can join the "team" and become another assistant

INSURANCE POLICY

From time to time, there rolls down the work assignment road a nonstandard, sensitive, confidential project that nobody wants to take credit for; in fact, everyone runs for cover to avoid not just the credit, but the very fact that they even worked on it. If knowledge of it or how it was handled became public, life could become extremely unpleasant for many people, including your boss, his boss and perhaps his boss, and so on up the line. Somehow, you become privy to the paperwork, complete with your boss's, or his boss's, initials authorizing the work.

When that happens, when fate gives you the original (a copy is next best), complete with signoffs, place a photocopy in the appropriate files, and keep the original. It's best to store it in a safe deposit box, not at home. *Never* keep it in the office.

This is your insurance policy. Any insurance agent will tell you, with justification, that the more insurance you carry the better off you are. Mention the policy only if you are placed *in extremis* (i.e., if you are threatened with termination or someone tries to make you the scapegoat). If your boss is smart, he'll know you're insured, so he won't mess with you.

Controversial contracts, CYA memos (yours and others) that bear evidence of someone else's knowledge or written OK, the authorization or signoffs of department or agency heads on sensitive correspondence, these and similar evidence that clears you and/or proves the prior knowledge of higher ups all make excellent stuffing for you insurance file.

The head of a major big-city agency had a problem. Arrested in the men's room of a downtown bus station while performing an act that most would judge sexually perverted (certainly his action violated statutes that render it illegal in public venues), he was taken downtown by the cops for questioning and booking.

One quick phone call got our man off the hook. He told someone with the clout to squash the record of his arrest or else there could be a problem: the beat reporters knew of his arrest; he knew enough and more important, had years of documented evidence, which could cause all sorts of problems at City Hall—he knew closet skeletons that nobody else was even aware of; he could interrupt the flow of desperately needed federal dollars for key social services his agency provided in the city and adjoining county; his arrest, if it became public, would provide a sordid, unwanted and unneeded embarrassment for City Hall finally, he had a mere eighteen month

...tion, or at least without messing things up more than he ordinarily would have, until he retired. He also behaved himself (to the best of my admittedly limited knowledge, he was never again pulled in for doing anything licentious while he was still employed). After he retired, he lived happily on his fat city pension.

And all because of his insurance portfolio.

See also BLAME, CREDIT, DECISIONS-MAKING AND AVOIDING, HANDLING THREATS, *IN EXTREMIS*, SCAPEGOATS, and SIGNOFFS.

INTELLIGENCE

Intelligence means information. Specifically, information that is not common knowledge, that may not even be public. It tells where the hidden mines lie; nobody wants to blunder into a minefield. Beyond that, intelligence is knowledge, and knowledge is power, and the less common the knowledge, the more power it confers on those privy to it. How it is used is another matter.

Government agencies spend an inordinate amount of time (and money) gathering intelligence, variously, on other countries and governments, on terrorists, criminals, and more. Politicians gather as much intelligence—read dirt—on their opponents as possible before elections, as much as (sometimes more than) they can afford when their race is close.

At the level of the agency and the staffer, intelligence is equally valuable. J. Edgar Hoover built more than a career; he created an empire, all on intelligence he gathered. It can be most helpful to know the plans and intentions of rivals, how they might attack your turf, to learn of the legislators on your agency's oversight committee—their vulnerabilities and where they can be attacked, swayed or manipulated—and a whole lot more.

There are two aspects to intelligence: gathering information, and figuring out what it means. Intelligence comes from many sources: from someone else's in-box, through the rumor mill, from the media, who tend to be extremely well plugged in to goings-on, from one's information network, and from a host of other sources. For the agency head, the Power Team is an ideal source of information on happenings in and outside the agency; in fact, one of its chief purposes is to gather information.

But raw information alone is only a part of the puzzle. Once gathered, information must be sorted, pondered and analyzed. Few enjoy the resources that Hoover could tap; still, the scope of available information and analysis can be surprisingly formidable.

Most evenings after work, a small group from my department convened in the bowling alley to sort out what happened that day. Others occasionally joined us for a beer, no doubt thinking we had merely gathered for a tall cool one at the end of a hard day, and we did little to dissuade them. The regular attendees came from different backgrounds, and besides friendship (and an unwritten mutual aid alliance), they brought their respective strengths to the effort; in this case, investigative reporting, political and police connections (we could, and occasionally

---

* If access to the police seems farfetched, then consider this: I read that a Washington, DC prostitute (through a reliable, trusted client, one presumes) ran potential new clients through the FBI's computer net to ensure she wouldn't find herself confronting an axe-murdering maniac—or the vice squad. One presumes that among her profession she was far from alone in taking this precaution.

If hookers can gain access to this resource, any agency staffer worth his salt could, too—or find a call girl who can!

See also COMPETITION, IN-BOXES, NETWORKS, PERSONAL EMPIRE BUILDING, POWER TEAM, PRESS RELATIONS, PUBLICS, RUMOR MILL, and TURF.

INTIMIDATION

Intimidation, the threat of government sanction, has quietly outgrown its use as a simple compliance tool by regulatory and enforcement agencies to enforce their procedures and rulings and their monopoly franchise into one of the preeminent techniques of governance in the United States. More the pity that the subtle elegance and power of this technique are fully appreciated only by a select (and privileged) few. Indeed, the mere threat of protracted (and extremely costly) litigation, involving THE FULL WEIGHT OF THE LAW—or OF THE GOVERNMENT, which amounts to the same thing—leading to potential fines, sanctions, even criminal prosecution, is an ordeal few wish to face, much less endure. To be sure, one can resist, but the advantage rests overwhelmingly with the intimidating agency; it can bring unlimited resources, including funds and, especially, staff time, to bear against a resistant opponent. In sum, a weapon of enormous persuasive power over individuals, corporations, industries, even entire states and other government agencies and other governments.

To be effective, a threatened sanction must occasionally be carried out, lest the parties whom the agency is supposed to regulate or coerce completely ignore it. A good analog, one observer noted, is the frontier sheriff who every now and then publicly pistol whips some cowpoke, not necessarily a guilty cowpoke, proactively, gratuitously, graphically and severely enough to demonstrate the fate awaiting potential troublemakers—and to show lawful citizens that he's not sitting down on the job.

The impetus for a sanction occurs for one of two reasons: when an agency decides to show via deed instead of word that it really means business, or when a bunch of eager Young Turks, aggressive true believers all, take it upon themselves to punish, curb, make an example of or otherwise secure the attention of a supposed transgressor. When both conditions hold, the results can be awesome: the attempt by the Anti-Trust Division of the US Department of Justice to break up IBM furnishes an instructive example. Consuming twelve years and untold millions in legal expenses, all to no otherwise publicly discernable end—IBM remained intact—the effort provided years of employment for hundreds of lawyers. Certainly the proceeding guaranteed the Anti-Trust Division the undivided attention of IBM's management and, presumably, that of companies enjoying similar preeminence in their industry—and of the entire legal profession. At this, the IBM breakup attempt succeeded brilliantly.

Intimidation is used much more by the federal regulatory and enforcement agencies (FDA, EPA and, especially, the IRS) but little, if at all, by the welfare agencies, the handout and subsidy bureaus. On occasion, the threat implied by

vulnerable employees can be bullied into performing questionable (unauthorized, illegal, immoral or unethical) acts.

Having said this, the tactic works best as a short-term interpersonal motivator because intimidation can be a double-edged sword. The downside: it can be a real wave-maker. Over the longer term, an intimidator risks making enemies and becoming a target for revenge from those who were unable to reply in kind, but did not forget the loss of face implied there from. Hence, I believe that unless you feel the congenital need to step on each staffer's head, intimidation is best suited to dealing with external publics.

Guys who get off on intimidation are special. Even more so are those who invoke sanctions (reportedly, the Clintons are masters of this technique). Perhaps the women's movement offers a biochemical explanation for this phenomenon: excessive testosterone. Whatever the reason for their actions, intimidators are the people who make government special. Know and understand this species well.

The following blurb was excerpted from the *Washington Post* of May 2, 1995. It is worth noting that because it appeared as an opposing editorial, it subtly highlights that paper's welcome pro-agency bias:

> "... the [US] attorney general has ordered the Justice Department to file ethics complaints with the state bar authorities against non-government lawyers who dare complain of ethical lapses by government lawyers. One ... defense lawyer who forsook ... [his] ... state bar grievance committee to file a confidential complaint with ... [the US Department of Justice's Office of Professional Responsibility, which one supposes, exists to preserve the appearance of curbing or somehow policing ethical lapses of Justice

Department lawyers] . . . alleging misconduct by a federal prosecutor found himself slapped with a lawsuit for libel.

"Federal government lawyers already enjoy "sovereign immunity," a . . . concept based on the notion that "the King can do no wrong." What this means . . . is that federal prosecutors who abuse their . . . privileges don't even have to pay fines imposed by judges as a penalty for breaking the rules of litigation. The . . . Senate bill would legitimize an elite corps of government lawyers who are exempt from judicial control. The most zealous would simply be out of control . . ."

This passage is rich with material from all corners of this handbook, but above all else, it fairly exudes intimidation. "If you mess with us, we'll ruin you," is the explicit message sent to opposing lawyers who would deign to protest unethical behavior by their Justice Department counterparts. To me it enumerates both the quintessence and the ideal of intimidation. How can you lose if you are given *carte blanche* to act without "judicial control," and, most important of all, with protection from all actions that are unethical or unlawful guaranteed by Congress?

If I were fresh out of law school, these working conditions would sure make me consider applying for a job in this shop. And they give rise to related questions involving other agencies, namely, "What's so special about Justice? How can we secure similar rights and protections for our own staff?"

For the insecure supervisor who needs to keep his staff perpetually on the defensive, there are proven, easy-to-use verbal gambits to guarantee that their consumption of Maalox and other stress relievers remain frequent enough to threaten their health—or drive them away. Samples:

- "As you know . . ." whether he 'knows' or, most likely, does not, is a wonderful introduction to an assignment and can be counted on to place a staffer immediately on the defensive. If he admits he doesn't know, he reveals ignorance (which most are loathe to admit); and if he corrects his boss on this item, he disagrees with him at the outset, which is a poor way to start a conversation or assignment. Works most effectively in front of others.
- "We had agreed [although we really haven't] that . . ." places your staffer in the unenviable position of having to disagree with his boss at the outset. Another powerful psychological arm-twister. Especially fun to pull this nifty little ploy on yes-men and watch them squirm.

- "As I told you [even though I never did] . . ." Most intimidating of all: not only must a subordinate disagree with his boss, but by disagreeing he implies that his boss is a liar.
- Also, preceding any declaration with the word "you" is guaranteed to send a momentary flash of terror through a previously cowed subordinate, even

to gravely inform him to *stick close to the phone because Mr. Bashmeister is calling from Seattle and wishes to speak to you next* . . . This ploy, whether studied or not, produced an enormous quantity of stomach acid for so small an organization.

See also AGENCY EMPLOYEES, AUTHORITY, BRIBES, COMPETITION, CONTROL, DALEY, ETHICS, FACE, GENDER DIFFERENCES, GOVERNMENT MONOPOLIES, HIRING INDEPENDENTLY WEALTHY EMPLOYEES, JUDICIARY, LEGAL EAGLES, POWER AS A CORRUPTING INFLUENCE, PROMISES, PUBLICS, REVENGE, URSINE THOUGHTS, YES-MEN, and WHISTLE BLOWING.

IPSE DIXIT*

The power of this technique, especially when it is carried off well, can be extraordinary. It works like this:

Someone—an elected or appointed official, an agency head—excitedly informs the public (via the media) that a hot new program has been implemented, that reinvigoration and beneficial changes are occurring, that even now the public is realizing significant benefits. Classic big-time examples of this technique include the multiple on-going social "wars"—on poverty, drugs, crime, etc. Even the New Deal. Judging variously from their duration (some for decades), from the sums expended on them and most of all, from the increasing numbers of government employees working in them, and from the increasing numbers afflicted by the social ills that the programs are said to address, the wars can only be termed, by these measures, extraordinarily successful (maybe the way to ensure steady growth in future authorizations is to declare war more often).

Former Vice President Al Gore's widely ballyhooed *Reinventing Government* effort bore all the classic hallmarks of *ipse dixit*.

Recall that for most agencies and all politicians, the appearance of reality far exceeds in importance reality itself. Moreover, if a message is repeated often enough, everyone—the media, elected officials, even the public—actually begins to believe the program is working—and thus, in the program.

For it to work best, this technique should be applied to an issue that is not currently hot. If, say, Iran had bombed Pearl Harbor yesterday, few would attach much credence to "I personally met with the Iranian foreign minister, and I can report that meaningful progress has been made . . ." This technique also demands the full, unquestioning complicity of the media. Having a first-rate press relations officer helps, too.

---

*   Latin for "I said so."

Several commonly used *dixits* bear note:

- *Progress* is among those most frequently invoked.
- *Problem:* a perceived opportunity to expand turf.
- *This Will Create Jobs!* is another. This almost always means shiftin~

- *Investing* means spending money. Thus Social Wars become *investments* in social *progress.*
- *I am a leader* or *We are taking the lead* means we have found someone or some procedure to follow.
- *Greed* or *Greedy.* The ideal (irrefutable) characterization of one's enemies and rivals. Since, by convention, only a minuscule (and probably troubled) percentage of the world populace prefer having $1 to $2, be assured all human beings are greedy; thus, this claim can never be convincingly counter-argued.* Besides, the media and the general public lap this up, too. The perfect stigmatization.

---

* Economists term this phenomenon *rationality.*

See also CODE WORDS, IMAGE, LEADERSHIP, MANAGED NEWS, MARKETING, THE MEDIA-SOME THOUGHTS, SAFETY NETS, SPECIAL INTERESTS, and THEORY OF THE AGENCY.

ISMS—RACISM, SEXISM, ETC.

When you throw away the rhetoric, this means choice in hiring and promotion—surrounding yourself with your, versus someone else's, bananas—and is not to be confused with political appointments.

You can ignore *isms* on a micro level, meaning you can surround yourself with whomever you want, but ignore them at the macro level (on a department—or agency-wide basis) at your peril.

This implies that the higher your position in the hierarchy, the more choice you enjoy in hiring and promotion, and the greater the creativity that may be needed to give the illusion of pay, perks, power and prestige to those favored by quota but not by you. Countervailing hiring and promotion may be necessary to balance your choices.

Excellent tactics have been devised to meet this threat.

One: if you need to fill the agency's Martian quota, make sure to hire or promote a Martian whose paper qualifications seem impeccable, but whom you know will prove, at best, barely marginal. This guarantees that the chosen Martian will move heaven and earth to retain his lofty position, and thus prevent other, more talented and competent Martians, whose presence you don't want (in chosen slots anyway) from displacing him (or confronting you). This also gives you license to drag your feet in hiring and promoting additional Martians ("Hey, we appointed one in good faith, and see what a turkey he is—we don't want to promote any more of them"). Best of all, it leaves any truly capable and ambitious Martian on the payroll with but a single recourse: leave.

Two: designate (unofficially, of course) one department as the agency's EOC dumping ground. Planning and Human Resources Departments often serve this purpose admirably. When this occurs, you can be sure that the department head ranks last among his peers (often he serves as the designated verbal tackling dummy at senior staff meetings), and whatever function his department ostensibly serves, bet that it will have little if any bearing in the overall mission of the agency. Certainly nobody expects anything meaningful from it. As such, it serves as the quintessential, diametrical opposite of the Alpha Department, so I'll term it the "Omega Department." At one agency, we called it "The Department of Useless."

Still another: make sure the job

English. Th

CAL, ENGLISH,

MENTS, POWER TEAM and SCAPEGOATS.

"ISSUES"

Agency-speak for real problems and constraints. The concerns of your critics, rivals and enemies.

See also CODE WORDS and *IPSE DIXIT*.

JOB POSTINGS

...posting advertising is a formality that perpetuates the charade that from coast to coast we've sought out all interested and qualified candidates, and here's the lucky winner.

The more highly rated the opening, the more likely the posting process is nothing but window dressing.

See also PERSONNEL OFFICER and SCREENING PROSPECTIVES.

JOINT EFFORTS—FORGET 'EM

One of the most commonly held images in the eyes of the public, oft put forward by academics and the media, is that of multiple agencies, marching together arm in arm, joining together to solve all the problems that afflict society.

This is bunk. As anyone who observed the post-Hurricane Katrina cleanup in Louisiana can attest.

In any interagency effort, unless the tasks and scope of responsibility are clearly spelled out at the beginning (and often even despite that), the two or more parties will end up jockeying for turf or pointing accusing fingers at each other for work that fell between the cracks. Think for a minute about the problems faced by the Department of Homeland Security, which must coordinate efforts of the FBI, CIA, and Department of Defense, among others. I posit that the stage in each agency's life-cycle ultimately determines which outcome ensues.

One experienced boss, a grizzled veteran of inter-agency turf wars, had a great way to combat this. After we'd met with staff from another agency, he'd pen a letter outlining which party was to do what. His technique was less than subtle—his letter would contain a section entitled "You Do/We Do," and there would follow under each column all the tasks assigned each participant.

He was smart and experienced enough never to show joint responsibility for any single task: each discrete task was assigned to one, and only one, actor. That way, the respective agencies didn't waste time jockeying or jerking each other around.

See also COORDINATION, INDOCTRINATION, and MEETINGS.

And the basis for their appointment or being slated on the party ticket lies in their connections, or perhaps as a payoff. In any event, they can be counted on to support the system that seated them on the bench—and to uphold our agency and its mandate because it owes its existence to the same process that rewarded them with their seat. Also, the agency's Power Team invariably belongs to the same political party.

Federal judges are altogether different.* Appointed by the president for life, some are chosen for the same reasons as other judges, but others are selected for the bench for a doctrinaire adherence to some ideal, and less for their political reliability. And because Republicans have held more than equal sway in the White House over the last thirty years, adherents to a wide range of ideals may be encountered in the federal judiciary. Consequently, seated federal judges are in the aggregate far less likely to play straight patronage politics (and support our agency) than their state, county and municipal counterparts.† For this reason, federal judges constitute a collection of unpredictable, unreliable, and therefore dangerous goofs (with the Supreme Court comprising the most dangerously talented goofballs on the government payroll). It becomes a real crapshoot as to

---

* Federal Administrative Law Judges are excluded from this generalization. Their focus is narrow, usually on process, and because they are paid by the agency whose rules they enforce, they can be expected to uphold the rights and primacy of the agency they work for over those of any and all other parties.

† An important and enormous exception involves a federal appellate court overturning California's Proposition 187. Its overturning by a federal appellate court marked a landmark triumph for the primacy of all agencies over the will of the voting public. In magnitude, it promises to do for agencies in general what *Marberry V. Madison* did for the entire judiciary—guarantee their independence.

whether federal judges can be counted on to uphold agency interests in a legal dispute—even if a federal agency is a party to the dispute.

So if you have a legal battle to join, your best bet for winning it is to fight it outside the federal courts. And if your agency is a federal agency, you probably have no legal venue outside federal court, so you'd best secure the highest powered legal counsel you can lay your hands on.

See also GOVERNMENT—A BRIEF ESSAY, HIDDEN AGENDA, LEGAL ADVICE, PROCESS, and REGULATORY AUTHORITIES.

KEEP 'EM WAITING: RESPONDING TO

before he receives a response to his query. Respond by all means with the utmost courtesy (this is your Prime Public, after all), but in your own good time. "Make 'em suffer," says a friend who pens a response to her fair share of these. Besides, what does an inquiring congressman really think he is—the voice of the people or something?

Seriously, there's good reason to socialize an impatient congressman to wait for his reply. For one, it shows him his real place in the world and conditions him to lower his expectations when it comes to being waited on: an agency has better things to do than waste precious staff time answering his chicken-shit query. Moreover, the complaint almost certainly was originated by some third level aide, not by the legislator himself. And most responses are run-of-the-mill and formulaic: usually, a constituent without clout has demanded service which the agency, for one reason or another, invariably statutory, cannot perform, and after the agency has declined his demand, he runs to his congressman, hoping for vindication and retribution (not always in that order).* In short, niggling everyday stuff. After it receives the agency's reply, every congressional office has its own canned response to aggrieved, and unsatisfied, constituents.

Most important, this practice buys the agency the extra time it may need to respond to the occasional difficult (i.e., substantive) complaint.

---

* The very fact that a complaint is transmitted through this channel means that the complainant is clout-less. Had he possessed real influence, his congressman or, more likely, his senator would have called the agency head directly. That this has not happened reduces the entire process to a *pro-forma* charade, in which the final answer will almost always be, "No! Our governing laws preclude bending the rules for you . . ."

See also PRIME PUBLIC, PUBLICS, and SAYING NO.

KILLING THINGS: SOME THOUGHTS

From time to time there will crop up dumb or radical ideas, or ideas you find uncongenial and wish would go away. If you have reservations or concerns about an issue but for political reasons you do not wish to, or cannot, publicly voice them, do not despair. There are time-tested ways to kill it outright or alter it so radically that its proponent can hardly recognize the remnants and will be reluctant to support it.

- One good way to kill a project—especially if it is a hot potato—is to hand it to the Planning Department. Planners are the least concerned of any governmental department with the here-and-now. With a little luck, the hot project or idea may be placed on hold forever. I know one planning department in state government whose hierarchy actively seek to accomplish nothing because they may one day be held accountable for their output. This department has elevated this strategy to an art form: I marvel at their efforts from afar. They'll study a problem to death. Or come up with a variant of the initial project that is so irrelevant or weird or perverted (and I use these terms deliberately) that even its proponents will be pleased to see it die. But most often, they simply do nothing, and wait to see whether anyone bothers to follow up: numerous projects have died a moldering death in the departmental in-basket.
- Another way to dispatch an unwelcome project: send it to a Blue Ribbon Committee or Task Force for review. By the time the finished project comes out of their homogenizer, you can be sure that it will bear little resemblance to the working idea that initially went in there. Sometimes merely convening a Blue Ribbon Panel gives the appearance of progress while nothing actually happens. In this way, Blue Ribbon Panels serve the same purpose externally as convening a meeting does internally.
- A variation of this gambit is to send an initiative first to an intra-agency panel for internal review; later, after it emerges, send it on to an inter-agency task force or review committee for additional study. The more reviewers who enjoy license to express concern, and the more diverse the departmental or organizational interests they represent, the more

you can be certain that little of substance will be accomplished, and the greater the chance that the idea will be watered down or otherwise altered, or, better yet, that nothing will happen. A once-over by a joint agency review panel will usually result in the sponsor wishing he'd never brought his idea up. If it's deemed a sure loser, you, or better yet, your

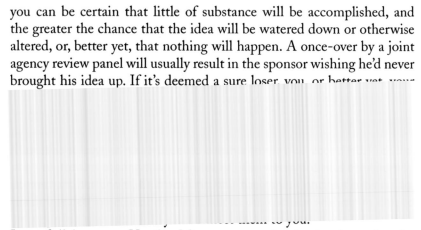

- Last of all, have your Hatchet Man unceremoniously give the project the thumbs-down.

In addition to killing ideas that could mean a great deal more work, these are great ways to prevent eager beavers, crusaders, one-term political appointees, and people you just flat don't like from bringing their ideas and pet projects to fruition, much less getting credit for them.

See also BLAME-FREEDOM FROM, HATCHET MAN, MEETINGS, POLITICAL FAVORS, PROGRESS, SAYING NO, SIGNOFFS, and TASK FORCES.

KNOWING THE RULES

Every agency boasts at least one dweeb who knows, down to the last comma, the rules and regulations that govern agency programs and services. Invariably, the mindset of these dweebs is to limit what the agency (and, therefore, you) can legally do. To them, those rules and regulations are everything—the be-all and end-all for their existence. Maybe it's their way of carving out turf for themselves, conferring themselves power, in a sphere where nobody really wants to tread—or poach.

I knew one such fellow. He could, and frequently did, cite chapter and verse (he had actually written some of the scripture he proudly invoked) as to why his boss couldn't take this or that desired action.

While his knowledge had undeniable value (it kept his boss out of trouble when he proposed action that ran blatantly afoul of the regs), and undoubtedly conferred him with job security, he would have been twice as valuable if his mindset had instead been, *here are the rules—and here's how we can finesse 'em.*

See also BUREAUCRACY.

LEADERSHIP

And that's why leadership, real leadership, is rarely, if ever, found in government. In my thirteen years of public sector life (which include a two-year military hitch) I've encountered only one real leader in a senior position (more about him in a moment), and my observations suggest that he is a real anomaly.

Now, most public managers (and all elected officials) will reflexively call themselves leaders, but this self-serving self-description confuses leadership with title or rank. Alas, these would-be Pied Pipers lead in the manner derisively propounded by the late Professor Peter, ". . . they lead only in the sense that a carved wooden figurehead leads a ship." (Peter and Hull. *The Peter Principle*, New York, Morrow, 1969).

So as leadership role models, they are worthless. If you really want to learn how to lead, expect nothing from the staff who run your agency: most likely, they are walking, talking examples of how not to. Had they been assigned a rifle platoon to command in Viet Nam, many, perhaps most of them would have been fragged (shot in the back by their own troops) within two weeks. Nor will you find anything in the personnel manuals, employee handbooks or job description boilerplate on how to lead. These are only written to encourage you to follow.

No, there's little to be gleaned by watching or asking or reading, except in a negative sense. But if you still want to know how a real leader actually functions, or whether one even can function in public life, then read on.

Leo (his real name) was a leader. The real thing. His title, General Manager, really had little to do with his job description, which was to run agency operations and keep his flighty chairman firmly rooted on solid ground.

As one might guess from the apparent conflict between his title and job description, Leo wasn't perfect. Far from it. Although he had a wealth of practical

---

213

experience, and was highly thought of nationally in his field, Leo wasn't well educated (I'm not sure he even went to college), and by his own admission, the people he chose as his trusted lieutenants weren't all that hot ("I just can't pick 'em," he remarked with rueful candor late one Friday afternoon); physically he seemed too old and frail to perform his job—he'd fall asleep at meetings, and one used to wonder whether he'd even wake up from these siestas; and undoubtedly other warts and zits marred his performance. Yet that menagerie which was our board of directors treated his word as gospel, and his troopers worshiped the ground he shuffled over.

Why? Well, Leo had backbone, real backbone, a scarce enough commodity in public life, increasingly so as one ascends the organizational ladder in any agency. And everyone respected him for this. Among his stoutest vertebrae:

- Honesty. Leo (with a single curious exception, which I'll explain shortly) never conned anyone. *Anyone.* Not his board, not his chairman, not his counterparts at other agencies, not his troops, not his friends, not even his enemies, not anyone. And everyone knew this. While lesser department heads, when the truth became an unpleasant tale to bear, tiptoed and tap-danced around it as though it were a landmine, Leo approached it head-on; he never backed down. When he was forced to deliver unpleasant news to the chairman or the board, Leo would unhesitatingly do so. He'd preface his message, quietly but forcefully, with, "These are the facts," implying that nothing we can do will change them so let's deal with them now so that we can get on with business.

- Ran Interference. Leo went out of his way to insure that every obstacle to the smooth performance of his people's work was removed. No buck passing here—Leo took care of any obstacles himself. And if he had a bone to pick with someone, Leo approached him head-on and forthrightly, never from the back or with a knife.

- Set a Personal Example. Leo would never ask his staff to do anything he wouldn't do himself. No downward buck passing here, either. And so he set the standard for his department.

- Accountability and Loyalty. Leo shouldered ALL blame, and backed his staff to the hilt. He used to say, especially and emphatically to the chairman and to the board, "My people never make mistakes. *I make all the mistakes.*" Ironically, this is where he conned the world, and the world knew it was being conned, and conned fairly often, because sometimes Leo's lieutenants were, to put it politely, prone to err.

- Corrected Instead of Blamed. When he could, Leo would correct his people instead of blaming them.

- Reprimanded in Private. No doubt, when one of his troopers really messed up, Leo dressed him down behind closed doors. But the front he presented to the world was that of a harmonious team: it never included blaming, dressing down, berating, demeaning or otherwise bashing his staff in public—in or away from their presence

...(too bad none of his lieutenants absorbed this lesson; but then, being a leader doesn't necessarily entail being a good teacher).

So here is a man who tells the truth, sets a positive example, corrects instead of blames, backs his people, and goes out of his way to ensure they can do their best and receive all due credit for their effort. For this Leo earned the unbridled respect—not love, respect—of all. Leo's people would have killed for him. So would I, were I lucky enough to have had him for my boss. If Leo had asked his troops to swim Lake Superior in January, to a man they'd have jumped in and given the task their best effort, even with little chance they'd get far. Perhaps they'd do so knowing that if anyone could part the waters for them, Leo would.

Now Leo did have one advantage over most of us: he enjoyed independent means and didn't need his salary, so if anyone ever tried to pressure him to do something he didn't want to do, he could walk. And everyone knew he would.

But even though he was blessed with fuck-you money, step back and ask yourself, how many people in authority, elected, appointed or just staffers, junior or senior, have I encountered who 1) won't bullshit me under any circumstances, and 2) would never blame me in public? I suspect your answer is the same as mine: damned few.

Jeez, think what Leo could have accomplished if he were smarter in choosing subordinates!

Corroborating our assertion that true leadership in government agencies is neither valued nor desired is this gem from the corridors of state government:

"INTEROFFICE MEMORANDUM

From: Human Resources
To: Distribution
Subj: Leadership Training
The following leadership classes are being offered . . . :

Class # 1: **MAKING THE DIFFERENCE**

DESCRIPTION: This class makes participants aware of their ability and duty to make a positive impact at [our agency]. It reviews the role communication skills play in living [the agency's] Purpose, Mission, and Values and fosters recognition of job, interpersonal and action skills as keys to effective performance. It develops the skills of how to meet people's (*sic*) personal and practical needs. ***This . . . is a prerequisite to all other leadership courses*** [emphasis added].

Class # 2: **OVERCOMING RESISTANCE TO CHANGE**

DESCRIPTION: Builds awareness of the need to manage change in the workplace. This course demonstrates how to anticipate and handle employee concerns about change and how to deal with resistance. Course activities lead participants through discussions with employees about implementing change."

Note how closely the definition of leadership implied by this memo ("communications skills" and persuading—manipulating, really—resistant employees to change their *modus operandi*) corresponds with our definition—*motivation*. Can you imagine Leo manipulating his people? Alas, I suspect this memo speaks for many, perhaps most, personnel folk.

Here follows an illustrative tale of leadership. Alas, it is a negative example . . .

One drizzly, overcast winter afternoon at the agency, while we toiled to solve the problems of the world, work was interrupted by the fire alarm. Of course our first inclination was to treat the insistent clanging bell as a malfunction (in a city infamous for corruption in the building inspector's office, who ever took the trouble to test the fire alarm?), but then came word that this was a real fire. *Everyone evacuate! Leave the building. Use the stairs, not the elevator. Stay calm.* And sure enough, the acrid smell of smoke became stronger and more pervasive.

When a real fire breaks out, who *should* be the last to leave, and then only after making sure everyone had left the office? To my quaint way of thinking, the managers, the department and division heads, bear the responsibility for the well-being of their employees. So who were among the first to reach the street? You guessed it! The department and division heads.

building as agency fire marshals. It would have been interesting to start another fire just to see how they'd react.

I wonder what Leo would have thought of all this . . .

See also BUCKPASSING, CORRECT VERSUS BLAME, IMAGE, *IPSE DIXIT*, LOYALTY, POWER AS A CORRUPTING INFLUENCE, and SETTING THE TONE.

LEGAL ADVICE

Outside the judiciary, I suspect, the best legal talent on government payrolls clusters in two areas: the US Department of Justice, which represents the federal (and, in a sense, all) government's legal interests in court; and among public prosecutors at all levels, whose ranks include tough, smart, ambitious Young Turks who intend their success in this arena to provide them a sure ticket to bigger and better things.

For my money, the remaining legal talent in government isn't worth a continental damn. You can be sure the staff lawyers at your average agency didn't finish in the top ten percent of their law school class at Yale or Columbia, didn't clerk for a Supreme Court Justice or any other justice; in fact, you can scarcely trust them to correctly draft the boilerplate on run-of-the-mill contracts, much less add anything substantive to documents that require routine legal review or comment. And that's about all they're good for.

Still, at some point, every agency (or agency head) will need top quality legal counsel, in the worst way and immediately.

So where do you find it?

My advice: have a senior partner at a top law firm in your city or state capital on retainer. Consider him an integral member of your Power Team. His professional demeanor and unassailable character should command eminent respect in leading business and professional circles, and from both sides of the aisle at the legislature. He has 24-karat contacts at City Hall, in the State House, or on Capitol Hill—in other words, he is far better connected than you. He will hear long before you rumblings that can adversely affect your agency. The quintessential fixer, he can smoothly and quietly solve potential problems with a single phone call or with a few words at a cocktail party or on the golf course. Best of all, he will put the interests of his agency client (and you) uppermost and always keep them in mind—remember, he has an economic stake in the survival of his client agency.

What's even better: two firms on retainer, each with strong ties to its own side of the aisle.

Expensive? In dollar terms, perhaps, but for its value, the best investment you could ever make. To me, securing top-flight legal counsel is as important as finding a competent, reliable secretary. Maybe, if you are forceful and persuasive, you can arrange for outside counsel on retainer as part of a payoff package, since the lawyers are likely to be plugged in better than you

LEGAL EAGLES

Never one to mince words, Leo observed one day that "in Washington, every other son of a bitch you bump into is a lawyer . . ." Leo's heartfelt feelings about legal eagles are shared by many, and not just by those in government, either. Yet it's true that relative to staffers with other advanced professional and technical training—engineering, economics, accounting, planning—lawyers are disproportionately represented in the upper levels of the agency hierarchy and push the buttons and pull (some would say *yank*) the levers of power with far greater frequency than people trained in any other profession. Based on its obvious influence, "the law" is truly the alpha profession in government.

Why is this so? An important part of the answer involves language and linguistics. Law has a language all its own, and legal reasoning is a thought process unto itself. Together, these require special training, and that gives us lawyers.

Legislation means making laws, and making laws means money and raw power. Money and power: those two magic words attract lawyers like clover attracts honey bees. Statutes can be crafted loosely or tightly; loopholes are deliberately thrown open or closed. To do these jobs right, or to best advantage, requires legal training and so ensures the administration and legislature, and their respective staff, will be top-heavy with lawyers.

Then, too, lobbyists, to function effectively, must be able to create the loopholes they push—must know how to word the statutes, and find their way around all legislation which promises to decrease or increase their clients' quality of life. It helps that they speak the same language—and attended the same law schools—as the legislators and their staff (ironically, there are no truly top-tier law schools in the nation's capital). Knowing the language also means knowing what not to say—lawyers seldom get in trouble (make waves) for their outspokenness.

Further, large numbers of cause-driven zealots and dweebs have opted to receive legal training so that, socially, they can *make a difference*. Thus legally empowered, many become extremely effective advocates for their cause. Ditto for consumer advocates and labor unions.

Of the three branches of government, the judiciary exclusively involves the courts, and legal training is mandatory for anyone who counts for anything in this milieu. To interact on equal footing means that the other branches *must* have their own lawyers to deal with or through the judiciary. The law provides the only common language.

Outside the enforcement and regulatory agencies, those which use intimidation as their chief weapon have discovered that it takes a lawyer to bring the full weight of the law most effectively and heavily on a violator. Or to threaten

But the influence of lawyers in the agency doesn't stop here; it goes much deeper. Lawyers are masters at determining why some action can't be undertaken. So for an agency head who doesn't wish to pursue an action, access to legal counsel is mandatory. Conversely, if he wishes to undertake something but (ostensibly) can't because the rules or the law hamstring him, a lawyer can supply justification which will result in him getting neither fired nor indicted.

Finally, lawyers tend to cluster together. Knowing that they're on to a good thing, they restrict entry to their profession via the bar exam, more, I think, to keep their numbers down (and fees up) than to ensure the professional competence that passing the bar exam supposedly confers. Like any religious or ethnic minority or other guild, they tend not to just cluster, but to network, to promote and reinforce each other—lawyers against the world. And because lawyers are disproportionately represented in the highest, most powerful levels throughout government—the judiciary, the legislature, lobbyists, the enforcement agencies—nothing short of a revolution is likely to change this happy state of affairs.

Put it together and you have an inordinate demand for the services of lawyers in the nation's capital—and in state capitals, county seats and city halls to boot. And know why lawyers predominate in government over the other professions. Like the opposite sex, you can't live with them, and you can't live without them. Maybe that's why even staff lawyers of indifferent quality often carry themselves with the smug cockiness of alpha department staff.

And maybe why Leo felt as he did about lawyers.

But Leo wasn't a lawyer.

See also ALPHA DEPARTMENT, BLAME, HIERARCHY, INTIMIDATION, JUDICIARY, KNOWING THE RULES, LEGAL ADVICE, LOBBYISTS, and MUZZLE THE TECHIES.

LEGISLATIVE STAFF AIDES

Especially in Washington, but also in Springfield, Harrisburg, and Annapolis, there are just too many issues for our elected senators and congressmen to keep up with. So these distinguished gentlemen, not wishing to appear more ignorant than they really are, rely on their aides, not only to determine the merits and demerits of issues, but even to tell them how to vote.

As a practical consequence of this, if one is examined, either informally or even in a hearing, the questioner may be a kid just out of college, voicing concerns, popping zits and posing questions that could involve the transfer of billions of dollars.

To take a zit-popper lightly is the mark of an amateur, since it is the popper who serves in absentia as his boss's antennae. The smart staffer treats all aides, adults and poppers alike, as full-fledged members of the agency's Prime Public.

See also PUBLICS.

LOBBYISTS

Fixing pays well, which explains why the woods around Washington, DC, state capitals, and city halls are full of them. Most lobbyists exercise their persuasive powers with (and distribute largesse among) the legislators, so your dealings with them are likely to be nil. But if one comes to you, as agency head, and asks for a favor, treat him with kid gloves ("don't make no waves"), in fact, treat him as you would any member of the public—but not as if you are a monopolist. And if he makes unusual requests or demands, such as bending or breaking the rules for him or his client, weigh carefully the consequences of bucking him. Remember that his ability to cause harm is directly related to the friends he boasts in the legislature and the size of the favor he wants. If a lobbyist threatens, remember that to bring you to heel he must call in fire support from some politician in office, and in the process, lose a few chips. Still, you do have a few bargaining cards. The fact that he has come to you directly implies he doesn't want his friends in the legislature to know it. If you choose not to play ball with him, and he threatens to go to his friends, tell him that that's his prerogative, and if they direct you or the agency to help him, you will comply. Also, if you turn his request down, remember to make the laws, procedures and regs, and not you, the culprit. This will help cover you later on if things turn ugly.

Remember also the penalty you could incur for violating agency rules and, possibly, public laws. If you choose to grant him his special favor, make clear that you are doing him a special favor, that you are bending the rules for him and his client, so *he owes you*. In fact, this IOU is part of the package. Make sure you document this, so if you get into trouble, then he will, too.* This gives him a strong incentive to use his influence among his friends the legislators to squash any tendency to question or investigate your action.

Best of all is to have your own lobbyist, someone who can push your agency or its cause in Congress, or the State House, or City Hall. Often, your outside

---

counsel performs this rite, but better yet is to have a certified, card carrying lobbyist on your payroll—and best of these is both of them. Most agencies, if the budget is big enough, can hide lobbying funds. If you can find him, a lobbyist becomes a member of your Power Team. Or if you're real smart, you can work it so that a piece of your budget is earmarked for a specific lobbyist as part of someone else's payoff. If so, he will usually be likely to put in a few good words on your behalf with the boys in the legislature.

There's no fixer like your fixer.

---

*   Once you've done so, *keep all such CYA documentation in your personal safe deposit box, NEVER on the premises.*

See also COST ACCOUNTANTS, DALEY, GOVERNMENT MONOPOLIES, INSURANCE POLICY, POLITICAL FAVORS, POWER TEAM, and SAYING NO.

LOCK THE DOOR

soon be back on the street and, if so, rest assured that his first act will be to try to retrieve his former job. This, you don't want . . .

There are two time-tested ways to prevent his return:

- When he departs, fill the opening as quickly as possible. It's hard to return to a job that has been filled.
- Second, and far more important, after he leaves, document his screw-ups. All of them. Make it clear he caused all the problems that made his departure a cause to rejoice and celebrate. This way, even if he asks his wire to find him a new position in his old agency, it will be much harder, if not impossible, to place him in your shop.

It is best to keep any such documentation inside the agency, so the departed cannot easily find out about it—*don't make no waves*. One thing is certain: since your nemesis will neither be around to argue it, nor to muster his defenses, your documentation can be unusually candid and explicit.

A friend related in passing to my colleague Art and me that his boss (whom we'll call Boris) left to take a similar job in industry. Boris had been bad news, both to work for and for the agency: his incompetence jeopardized the flow of federal funds into agency coffers. I asked about the company Boris went to, venturing that his new employer must be pretty hard up to scrape the barrel to hire the likes of him. "No, no," my friend corrected me, "It's a tightly run company, highly respected in its field."

"Well," chimed in Art, "if that's true, Boris will be out of work in six months, and he'll want his old job back. Have you documented his miscues?"

"No. I only clean up the mess. Like the guy with the shovel who follows the elephant act . . ."

"Write up his screw-ups; bring them to light, because otherwise Jack (Boris' boss, whose loyalty to his people was notorious) will bring that turkey back on board. And you know it." My friend needed no second urging. During the next few days he immersed himself in an orgy of documentation, writing memo after memo. Needless to say, the departed Boris played a starring role in these epistles.

Six months later, Art reported, "Have you heard the news? Boris is out on the street. His company fired him."

"I'm not surprised."

A day or two later, I happened upon Jack in the men's room. "I hear Boris is out on the street."

"Yes. I was sorry to learn that."

"Do you think he'll come back here?"

"I can't use him now.

To illustrate an obverse twist to locking the door, here's a cautionary tale. Clyde, an executive director whose competence was severely challenged, departed under a cloud at the invitation of his board of directors. He left behind an agency in shambles. Such was his local reputation that nobody, or at least, no nearby agency, would touch him with a barge pole, much less hire him. But eventually, time and two thousand miles distance found Clyde ensconced as executive director of another agency . . . for a short while.

Then he was abruptly terminated. Seems that the board of directors at his new habitat had undergone a change of heart regarding his suitability to run their agency. How come? Well, a couple of months after Clyde arrived, they received an envelope thick with news clippings that detailed the problems that had accompanied his presence at, and prompted his departure from, his prior employer. A phone call to confirm and then history repeated itself . . . only before things got screwed up.

This sad tale illustrates the perils of leaving an unhappy staff. The moral is; that if you leave your agency on someone else's timetable, know that there can be a severe downside to leaving behind a thoroughly alienated staff. Whose actions you no longer control.

See also CAMEO APPEARANCES, FORMER EMPLOYEES, LEADERSHIP, LOYALTY, MEDIA FRENZY, PATRONAGE, and REVENGE.

LONG-TERM

Second, the duration of my present job, until I quit, retire, or move on. At that point, and unless I have done something criminal, all my actions, my decisions and judgments, good or bad, sound or merely expedient, become my successor's. This rule holds regardless of one's rank in the agency hierarchy. With a little luck, if my successor is someone I detest and doesn't immediately tumble to what he has inherited, he's not just stuck with my problems—they're now *his!*

See also SETTING THE TONE.

LOYALTY

Loyalty is a Smith-Barney resource which can only be accrued the old-fashioned way: it must be earned. It cannot be bought with a grant or by dispensing services. Loyalty upward can accrue only by demonstrating loyalty downward.

Many department and agency heads will tell you that they enjoy or believe that their title guarantees them the loyalty of their staff. This is bullshit. They mistake control for loyalty. Perceiving one's staff as potential scapegoats will only earn their hatred, not their loyalty. To repeat, loyalty must be earned.

My observations suggest a continuum. At the high end, a staff is intensely loyal to its Leader (note the honorific title). Leo's staff defended him faithfully and vigorously from the odd slings and arrows of rivals and detractors. At the low end, the staff are the most joyfully vigorous shooters of slings and arrows at their Appointed Superior. In the rare first instance, with the loyalty of his staff assured, the leader has the foundation to build a fortress, an alpha empire. In the other, be assured that the boss probably won't last long. Most managers, I suspect, fall somewhere in between.

If you are one of the rare government managers who have truly earned the loyalty of his staff, I commend you. And I envy you!

Since staff loyalty may seem a useful resource to have in your hip pocket, you may ask, *how can I earn it?* Reread the section on leadership. Then truthfully ask yourself these simple questions:

- Do I place the needs of my staff ahead of my own?
- Would I direct my staff to do something I would not do myself?
- Do I recognize and reward them for excellent work and not hog the credit for myself?
- Most important, do I back my staff to the hilt, come hell or high water?

In Leo's case, the answer to all of these was clearly *Yes!* If, for you, the answer is *yes* most of the time, you will be rewarded with a decent measure of loyalty from your staff. If the answer is *yes* less than half of the time, then for all practical purposes you can write off the loyalty—and support—of your staff. This is especially true if you find yourself in hot water.

See also ALPHA DEPARTMENT, CONTROL, LEADERSHIP and PERSONAL EMPIRE

MANAGED NEWS

The best news is managed news.

A lawyer-in-training is admonished never to ask a witness any question the answer to which he doesn't already know. He wishes at all costs to avoid surprises, so he should know the answer before he poses the question (One recalls a question purportedly posed to a witness, "How old is your youngest kid, the five-year-old?").

In the same way, a press relations officer wishes at all cost to avoid surprises in the evening news or morning newspaper describing what took place at the agency. The news that gets reported should be the bite-sized pieces he fed to the reporters, no less, and no more. Ideally, the press officer shouldn't even have to turn on the TV for the evening news because he already knows it, knows the tenor and substance of each story filed today by the beat reporters who follow agency matters. Even if the press officer didn't see or talk to them that day, the stories should be uniformly told, with no surprises.

This is managed news. This is what all press officers strive for, and what the competent ones consistently achieve.

See also THE MEDIA-ACHIEVING CONTROL and PRESS RELATIONS.

MANAGEMENT STYLE

AUTHORITARIAN
I call the shots: you do the work.

QUADRANT I

DELEGATIVE
Here are the resources,
solve the problem.

QUADRANT II

CENTRALIZED
Get a pencil then
report back to me.

QUADRANT IV

QUADRANT III

CONSULTATIVE/PARTICIPATIVE
How do we want to do this?

Each axis, Authoritative-Consultative (AC for short) and Delegative-Centralized (DC), represents polar opposites in decision making style, and divides the framework into quadrants. Each quadrant corresponds to a specific combination of traits, defined by the poles of each axis.

A Quadrant I manager calls the shots but is willing to delegate tasks to his staff. A man who uses his hierarchy, he represents the ideal for a mature agency), where (hopefully) the staff are smart and competent enough to perform the tasks they are given, but somebody needs to make the decisions, and make them decisively. People like him end up becoming agency heads.

Quadrant II represents a managerial style ideal for offices where the work is repetitive and best suited to women or low-intellects who cannot decide things on their own, so that every aspect of their work needs to be followed up. Or, the boss is weak and insecure, cannot bring himself to trust any of his staff to do anything on their own and feels a congenital need to oversee every aspect of their work. If he doesn't start out with employees as described above in this paragraph, that's all he'll be left with—if he's left with any at all. For one who plans to ascend the career ladder by blaming, this is the boss to latch onto: his innate paranoia will guarantee the blamer an attentive audience.

In the Quadrant III style, everyone reports to the boss, but he'll listen to each of them. Bosses like this seldom advance beyond office manager or head of a small department, because they ignore or cannot reconcile themselves to the hierarchical pyramid. For someone who craves more and more power, this boss is good to latch onto: he'll let others (why not you?) make decisions for him.

For me, the most enjoyable and rewarding place to work is a Quadrant IV office or department. The input (and thus, implicitly the knowledge, expertise and creativity) of the staff are valued by their boss, and he is secure enough to give them the resources to carry out their duties. Staff here must be mature and motivated enough to be able to carry out their jobs without close supervision. My own sense is that such opportunities are the rarest, found chiefly in new organizations or in offices where research and development, or other technical work, render the more commonly encountered managerial styles not just ineffective, but irrelevant.

See also AGENCY LIFE-CYCLE, BLAME, and HIERARCHY.

MANDATE

An agency's first goal is to fulfill its mandate and defend it against enemies, rivals, and outsiders. Its second goal is to expand the mandate.

See also GOVERNMENT-A BRIEF ESSAY, THEORY OF THE AGENCY, and TURF.

MARKETING: SOME THOUGHTS

For most managers in government, marketing is a subject in which they are vulgarly ignorant. To many, marketing means *sell shoes* or *if you advertise, it will sell*. Others conceive it as speeches, ribbon cuttings and similar tailored-for-the-media hoo-haw.* None of these conceptions comes remotely close to explaining either the concept or the practice.

So what is marketing? More to the point, why is marketing important to agency managers? Very simply, it involves a practice that many agencies aren't good at: determining the needs and wants of client or target publics, and meeting those needs more efficiently than competitors. If the task is done right, this means integrating the services of, even the agency itself, into the needs, the very life, of its client public. Further, meeting these needs becomes a stated, fundamental goal of the agency, as important in the long run, because of its implications for acing out external competition, as catering to the needs (and egos) of the agency's Prime Public. But to meet and, much harder, keep on meeting these needs makes this ideal extremely difficult to sustain, because the needs of the more highly valued publics invariably become more pressing: marketing involves service-based, not the more seductive image-based, performance.

For practical purposes, marketing may include the most challenging tasks that face an agency: enticing, educating, or perhaps forcing a target public to adopt and use the programs and services provided by the agency when at the outset that public is skeptical, unenthusiastic, hostile and resistant to its program. The drive to expand turf should make the importance of marketing obvious, and enhances the likelihood it will be used by the "younger" agencies; in mature ones, a fundamental misperception of the practice, along with what it entails (i.e., ignorance) poses an enormous internal impediment to its adoption.

One strategy, which was introduced in primitive form by the New Deal and perfected in the '60s and '70s, works best with the collusion of special interest groups and advocates, on the one hand, and a sympathetic (or at least unquestioning) media, on the other, involves identifying a potential target public, pronouncing it the helpless victim of an abuse which only your agency can correct or redress, and then push hard to create agency programs to address, or redress, the abuse. Once this target public becomes accustomed to receiving its handout, slowly, progressively—and best of all, inexorably—it becomes infantilized, incapable of functioning without the program, and reduced to a reliance on it that rivals a chemical addiction. A classic example of integrating agency programs into the needs of a client public. And kicking a subsidy addiction, like high

g (............ ....g) the agency is Kotler and Roberto's *Social Marketing: Strategies for Changing Public Behavior* (New York, Free Press, 1989).

---

* However, this should not be construed to denigrate the importance of appearing at media events.

See also AGENCY LIFE-CYCLE, COMPETITION, IMAGE, *IPSE DIXIT*, THE MEDIA-SOME THOUGHTS, NOT INVENTED HERE, THE PUBLIC, PUBLICS, and TURF.

MEDIA FRENZY

I find powerfully descriptive (and hugely compelling) an analogy between the media and sharks. Both are carnivorous, both feed on dead or rotting flesh and, when they become excited, they'll even consume their own species. Both cull sick and otherwise unsound specimens for the environment; and both go absolutely out-of-control when they smell blood. Once sharks start feeding, nothing can stop them: they won't quit until the prey is devoured, bones and all. In a proper feeding frenzy, with the victim's blood and scraps of flesh seeping into the water, sharks will occasionally mess up and consume healthy (i.e., innocent) creatures, even each other. Similarly, the media frenzy often indiscriminately casts the spotlight of blame and shame on everyone around the victim—whether their attention is deserved or not—and any unfortunate who gets in the way risks being devoured. As with sharks, nothing can stop a media feeding frenzy until the carcass has been picked clean, and its bones lie bleaching in the sun.

Also, like sharks, the media really don't care about any consequences to the victim—because they are the consequence.

So woe betide the unfortunate man or agency that gets in deep enough trouble to trigger a media frenzy. Here, "gets in trouble" means having some abuse or disaster (*crisis* in media-speak) or immoral or illegal or lurid act (*scandal*) become public knowledge. The downside: an agency *per se* is difficult to criticize, so the media naturally focus on its head. If that's you, hey! too bad.

And, just like an unfortunate who swims into a school of sharks when there's blood in the water, they won't stop 'til you're history. Even the best press relations officer is powerless to prevent this. If the event is memorable enough, there will be one-month, six-month, and thence annual media revisits for years to come, wherein its significance and any tantalizing taped tidbits, will be hashed and rehashed ad nauseam. I ascribe this practice to two factors: it fills air time and columns, and a prewritten "story"—it can hardly be called fresh, can it?—precludes lazy correspondents from having to dig for fresh news. Then, too, this procedure enhances the process of indoctrination.

And all despite their pro-government bias.

The best defense against the media frenzy: don't let one start. Insulate your agency so well that nobody can ever point the finger of blame at you with the slightest semblance of credibility, even if it was your staffer who shot Archduke Ferdinand at Sarajevo.

THE MEDIA: ACHIEVING CONTROL

Like nuclear energy, the news media are at once capable of inflicting incalculable harm and being harnessed for enormous good, and it is toward harnessing them for good (i.e., the good of the agency) that this chapter is written. As it applies to the media, the goal of the agency is to ensure that all the news which relates to it is *managed news*. No surprises, no unfavorable stories. This goal is pretty much universal, though in achieving it, countries without democratic or otherwise quasi-representative government enjoy an enormous competitive advantage over us: recognizing the inherent superiority of the pen over the sword, they control the news media, directly and absolutely; they punish free-thinking (anti-establishment) expressions by demotion and, when appropriate, torture and death. These extreme sanctions, sadly, we cannot yet employ.

Still, the media are enormously important to government: they carry the good deeds of the agency to the general public, which only accentuates the importance of harnessing them.* As with nuclear energy, control can never be taken for granted; it is achieved only through constant, painstaking effort. The never-ending nature of this task underscores the unsure compact between the media and the agency. Out of control, nuclear energy can cause a disaster of unprecedented magnitude, and if the media react out of control, staff may wish they'd been at Chernobyl or Hiroshima instead of here (witness Watergate). To derive maximum advantage and minimize, or at least dampen, the harm the media can create requires that their habits and needs be learned and understood better than they themselves know and understand them. And still they must be monitored constantly . . .

Fortunately, time-tested stratagems have been devised to accomplish just this. That brings us back to our initial thrust: how to gain the upper hand *and keep it*.

---

* Central though this may be to the individual agency, it is secondary in the overall scheme of government. As an extension of government, the main purpose of the media is to indoctrinate and continue the indoctrination begun by schools—not just of adults but, increasingly, of younger members of the populace, because as public schools inexorably move down their life-cycle path, they are increasingly failing at this task.

Though they overlap, these stratagems fall conveniently into a few well-defined categories, which will be developed in turn. These include doing their work for them, rewarding those who cooperate and punishing those who don't.

Here, an aside: it is useful to distinguish between offensive and defensive communications. Offensive communications include all the predigested

of possible consequences. A squirrel may be rewarded for a valiant effort with an extra tidbit. Similarly, news releases and carefully controlled interviews give beat reporters extra tidbits of material to use. In this way, reporters become *de facto* agency employees—the challenge is *to keep them on our payroll.*

Another useful trick is to let friendly journalists know where to find second-source confirmation for controversial stories. In time, hopefully, they become used to taking the proffered goodies, and those who cooperate most fully can be rewarded with food and drink, maybe other incentives. In this way, they become accustomed to dealing with the press relations officer, and all of their associations for preferred (compliant) behavior are pleasurable. Like an addiction. Reporters who refuse to play ball get the same treatment as squirrels which refuse food from one's hand: no goodies.

In this way, offensive communications are used to bring the media under control, to co-opt them and keep them there. The strategy works: beat reporters can be made to lay off even the most high-profile stories. When the *Washington Post* broke the Watergate cover-up conspiracy, the journalistic coup of the decade, maybe of the century, Woodward and Bernstein, the writers who took the story and ran with it, were drawn from the paper's pool of national writers, not from its beat reporters assigned to the White House.

By rewarding cooperative reporters (incidentally, a great trick is to convince a reporter that all these freebies are an off-the-books job perk, just as similar inducements constitute an important perk for many agency purchasing officers), the agency seeks to create a permanent public composed of the direct recipients of the beneficence of the media relations officer. In this way, reporters will be much less apt to stand by passively if colleagues from their paper or network seek to poach on their turf, there are tricks to punish those who refuse.

One such trick, really a great trick, I call the *controlled scoop*"(because I don't know its journalistic name): a first-rate news story is tendered only to reporters who cooperate with the agency. Non-players are deliberately excluded. None who cooperate have the slightest incentive to clue a rival in on any story he may have missed; their papers or networks carry the story, and his does not. If this omission gets the rival in trouble with his editors or producers, hey, that's his problem. The controlled scoop is a wonderful leashing device. Network news anchors were all treated to (or more accurately, victimized by) this trick first-hand when Ross Perot went live in primetime on to announce he would run for president on Larry King's TV talk show. This left all the major network anchors fuming on the sidelines as mere commentators. At the networks which got skunked, the jealousy quotient must have been extremely high that evening.

Knowing that honey catches more flies than vinegar, the astute media relations officer will attempt to establish a relationship of genuine friendship and respect, or as close to that as he can manage, with the beat or pool reporters who cover his agency. Human nature being what it is, and with reporters being all too human, it's a lot harder to file a story that gratuitously screws a friend—especially if the friend is a never-ending source of goodies.

If offensive communications are used to secure and reinforce the compliance and complicity of the media, defensive communications provide the agency with the (unsought and undesired) opportunity to find out how well their offensive efforts have succeeded. Defensive communications involve stonewalling and cover-ups, changing or best of all killing an unfavorable story; they comprise a major portion of an agency's damage control program. Here, the press relations officer pulls out all the stops: like a nuclear reaction gone out of control, once the media frenzy gets started, there's no stopping it.

If, despite the best efforts of the agency to bring them to heel, a small subset of the media (a paper or TV station) persist in independent action to the point that it threatens the agency, there remains sheer brute force, the get-tough tactics. It must be emphasized that these are truly the tactics of desperation, of last resort, because once they have been implemented, word of this will get around. These include yanking a broadcast license or sending in the building inspectors to (temporarily, anyway) close a troublesome operation down. It is, I believe, the implicit threat of these, and similar actions, that keeps reporters from getting too big for their britches too often.

See also ACADEMICS, AGENCY LIFE-CYCLE, BRIBES, COVERING UP, DAMAGE CONTROL, INDOCTRINATION, INTIMIDATION, MANAGED NEWS, THE MEDIA-SOME THOUGHTS, PRESS RELATIONS, PUBLICS, PURCHASING, and THEORY OF THE AGENCY.

THE MEDIA: SOME THOUGHTS

...country where the press is "free," the news media have nonetheless become a virtual and indispensable extension of government (some assert, and I agree, that the media constitute the fourth branch of government, and for better or worse the only branch lacking any semblance of check or balance to curb its excesses), to the point where they enjoy full, though sometimes strained, membership on the Power Team.

Achieving this measure of power and influence over the media, who like to pretend that they're free—they are, nominally—is perhaps the sublime achievement of government during the last sixty years, one that must be considered in detail to be fully appreciated and one, I believe, that owes much to the concurrent rise of television. Still, government does not yet directly control the media, the key word being "directly," and this can produce an uneasy tension between the agency and the media who report its doings to the public.

And to reiterate, it renders understanding the media, how they function, their reward structure, their agenda, how they transmit their underlying messages and, most important, their weaknesses and vulnerabilities, all of which lead to their *de facto* control, not just mandatory, but central to the survival of elected officials and agency heads alike.

In that vein, here follow several fundamental truths about the media:

First, to be rewarded, reporters must play a baiting game for their advertisers: they must capture, and above all, retain the attention of readers and viewers. This leads to the Parker Paradox (modestly named for its discoverer) regarding the media: economically, any value of the news, however much it provokes, entertains, amuses, or even elucidates and informs, is secondary. The true economic purpose for transmitting the news is to provide a hook that attracts readers, listeners and viewers to their ads and commercials; advertising dollars make the news world go 'round. The more viewers the media attract to their advertisers and sponsors, the greater their reward. Economically speaking, journalists are glorified shills for their sponsors and advertisers, no more.

It follows that journalists are a monotheistic tribe: they worship one god, the god of selling more newspapers (or larger TV or radio audience share, which amounts to the same thing), and none other. No liturgy has yet been devised to further their devotion more effectively than a) to entertain and b) to create controversy. And how better to do that than to emphasize the sensational, to varnish, to slant or even fabricate the news? The more entertaining, the more titillating, the more controversial that reporters can make the news, the more viewers and readers they seduce. That's what they learn at journalism school. And that's how they get rewarded. So remember that—and forever banish from your thoughts all you've heard about how a free press seeks to publish or broadcast the unvarnished truth. That's crap.

A corollary is that almost all journalism (down to and including the garden editor's column) is biased journalism, news written to promote some agenda. Sometimes this is simply to enhance or colorize the news, sometimes for other reasons (more on that later).

Second, the ethical journalist, like the chaste whore or the truthful politician, is a linguistic construct that sounds plausible yet does not exist (in discussing plots for his animated cartoons, Walt Disney used to refer to *the plausible impossible*). Interestingly, journalists themselves, unlike others in controversial vocations, freely concede this self-damning admission. Any reporter worth his salt would sell his grandmother into chattel slavery if it meant his byline on an exclusive. Gladly. When one deals with journalists, this wisdom must be kept uppermost in mind. Always. One is never "off the record"—and, as with wild animals raised like housepets, one can never fully trust a journalist.

Third, journalists are surprisingly ignorant. Often they get important aspects of a story just flat wrong. I ascribe this to their journalism school training, which teaches how to gather, sensationalize and file news stories but nothing about other walks of life, other industries or, finally, other intellectual disciplines—and nothing about the people who work in them.

Moreover, because theirs is the realm of the written and spoken word, reporters tend to be verbal, seldom analytical. Perhaps this explains why numbers seem to impress them more than words: they seldom question statistical claims that are quoted or fed to them. In fact, journalists will readily parrot as gospel "facts" and claims so extravagant that they could not possibly be correct. One suspects that journalists never trouble to ask where the data came from, much less care how it was derived (besides, if they were told, few could understand the explanation, anyway).

Nor is their response to sudden controversy deep and penetrating: instead of unearthing quantitative, statistically significant information that bears on the issue, or even troubling to find if any exists, a few perfunctory quotes from some bozo in the street usually suffice to establish their viewpoint. This is especially true for claims dealing with economic and social issues. Seldom if ever do they

...coverage on today's City Hall event" and you'd think a single person had done all the reporting. The editorial tone, the slant to their stories is often identical, almost as if the same guy told them what to say (he may well have).

It's no different with White House news. I met a network reporter who covered the White House, and my curiosity go the better of me: wouldn't it pay, I asked, to adopt a different editorial tone in his reportage, and thereby differentiate himself, his network, from all the others, from the competition? His reply was short and most instructive: there is, he said defensively, great value in following the herd. So much for independent thought—or perhaps any thought! Still, as a beat reporter, he was getting his daily tidbit from the hand that fed him, and he wasn't about to queer this convenient arrangement by acting rashly.

My acquaintance's reply made it pretty obvious that implicit or explicit collusion (I assume the former) occurs among pool reporters, journalists who, in theory, compete against each other for audience share. The herd approach extends beyond the journalists who file stories from City Hall and the White House to the radio and TV news desk types, and their writer/editors.

Happily, herds can be driven far more easily than solitary creatures.

Fifth, image is everything, worth a hundred times a thousand words. This holds especially for TV, less so for newspapers, least of all for radio news. Take away the image, take away the picture, the action, and you substitute noise (a reporter talking) for action and rob a story of 75 percent of its punch.

Sixth, the media all face one enormous challenge: each day, every day, they must fill their allotted air time or columns of print to balance out all the advertising—few read newspapers just to read ads or watch TV solely to view commercials. This means that if news is slow, they must find or produce something to fill the void.

One time-tested trick is to revisit old stories time and again. How else to explain the one—and six-month, then annual revisits of various disasters and scandals? (Pearl Harbor, Watergate and the Kennedy assassination come to mind. If someone had videotaped the battleship *Maine* blowing up in Havana harbor, we'd see that, too.) Or standard fare, such as the obligatory story of what the president did today, even if he no more than belched heartily after a state dinner. This is news? But hey, it fills air time and columns—so it must be.

Seventh, journalism has seen some self-correction. Forty years ago, journalists made up much of the news as they wrote it, and did so pretty openly. Now they've become much more subtle—they get exposed only occasionally for making up news, and even require second-source confirmation for a controversial story (i.e., one that, if it were reported, could get their paper or network successfully sued for slander—no confirmation, no story). Dan Rather's sudden departure from CBS News stands as a conspicuous, colossal exception to this truth.

Eighth, reporters uniformly exhibit a strong pro-government bias. And transmitting this bias to their viewing, reading and listening public is a key part of their agenda. When the scandal broke involving the alleged misappropriation of funds by senior officials at the United Way of America, a charity which competes (loosely speaking) with government agencies in providing social services to the needy, a DC-area TV reporter opined live that all charitable work could best be left to the government, implying that the time had come to debate this question. God, I love it! Talk about pro-government bias!

How can this be? The explanation is complicated, and owes as much to prior government involvement with the media at many levels as it does to current involvement. Part of the media's bias toward government, I believe, can be explained by their indoctrination in school. They're taught to report for the little man, the have-not. Government is universally perceived to be THE leveler of the playing field, the little guy's best pal.

And part, I suspect, is that agency press relations officers and spokesmen give journalists a great deal of usable material, in the form of news releases, non-derogative information and juicy quotes from "informed sources," access to highly placed officials and a lot of good air time. To exhibit reportorial independence is to bite the hand that feeds them, something no rational human is likely to do, and, worse, risk losing ready access to high personages and on-the-air opportunities—they might actually have to work for their supper.

Another and more important part, I believe, derives from the fact that the media have come to know and savor the political power they wield, the power that accompanies being an arm of government. In fact, after lawyers, journalists wield more power in government than any other occupation—and they aren't even directly on the payroll. Mighty, indeed, is the pen! Mightier still the TV camera. To cite one extreme symbolic example of this phenomenon, White House reporters enjoy the use of work space on the premises to prepare their stories, provided by the federal government. Do they hop to when the press relations officer informs them of a speech or an upcoming photo opportunity? Maybe, if

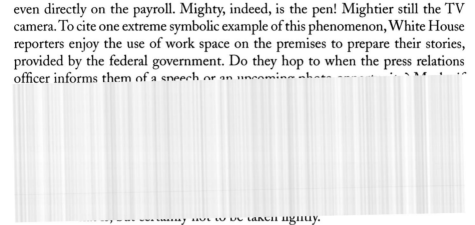

... but certainly not to be taken lightly.

And in truth, so considerable is their power it would be difficult to expand further; in fact, it would be far easier, and (no doubt journalists know this all too well) they are much more likely, to lose it. Consequently, this leaves the media in much the same position as agency hangers-on who face the same problem: they can be expected to do everything possible to retain their power, just like their counterparts directly on government payrolls. What holds for the White House press corps holds to a lesser degree for the media who cover other government bodies.

But the main part, I think, is the money. Ever the cynical realist, I place the greatest credence in an economic explanation. No doubt, all network reporters are keenly aware that the federal government gives them their daily bread, in the form of their broadcast license, and could easily take it away.

But is goes beyond that. Over the last thirty years, the *Washington Post*, which, because of its preeminence in the nation's capital is arguably the most politically influential of the nation's four leading newspapers (the other three: the *New York Times*, the *Wall Street Journal*, and the big-city daily nearest the home of each elected official), has enjoyed an extraordinary run of prosperity. Its home town has been a boom town—government has been a real growth business. It is persuasive to assume that the *Post* will find most congenial any policy initiative, no matter how well or poorly conceived, that means more government, because that a) reassures and reinforces its government-friendly image to its elected, appointed and civil-service readers, and b) more important, subtly lobbies the number one employer in its city to bring in more subscribers and readers. But this should come as no surprise; broadly speaking, the *Post* is on the payroll.

The *Post's* October 2, 1994 book review—it could be more accurately termed a rebuttal—of Kevin Phillips' *Arrogant Capital: Washington, Wall Street, and the Frustration of American Politics*, is instructive. The review, entitled "Washington: Has it Lost Touch With the People?" was penned by Representative Barney Frank (D-MA), a congressman whose credentials as a member of the book reviewing *literati* may be questioned, but whose interest and investment in continued heavy government intervention cannot. Having Rep. Frank review the article amounts to calling in the heavy artillery. While Rep. Frank certainly is entitled to his opinion, it appears in, and he presumably speaks for, the *Post*, and his opinion therefore carries the paper's explicit imprimatur. It goes without saying that Rep. Frank debunks the troubling (to Beltway insiders) thesis posed by Phillips, which, if it were left unrefuted, could signal that the *Post* is less than one hundred percent behind its home town establishment.

To a lesser degree, the same applies to the other papers.

So it can be understood why the *Post* and the rest of the media favor every government program, good or bad, that comes down the pike. Better yet, almost as one, they call for or endorse the "government regulation" of just about everything—the amount of cheese on a pizza, martial arts instruction, child day-care providers, securities price fluctuations, even phone sex—everything except, of course, accuracy or truthfulness in news reporting.

Finally, journalists are human: they'll give a break to someone they like, and systematically screw, or try to screw, someone they dislike. As it relates to their coverage of government, this means someone they dislike or whose agenda runs counter to theirs. They tried, unsuccessfully, to screw Ronald Reagan, and probably did so with greater success to Gerald Ford, George Bush, Sr., Alexander Haig, Dan Quayle. They hare set out to skin and skewer George Bush, Jr. They never quite seemed to know how to treat Lyndon Johnson, but they boosted Jack Kennedy, Jimmy Carter, and Bill Clinton, some more consistently—and successfully—than others.

"Reactions" are how the media pass judgment. When the president belches, they'll find someone to react favorably or unfavorably, never at random, and always in a way that promotes their agenda—which can be discerned by the quote they finish up with. And when they glibly talk about the reactions of others, that means, here is our interpretation, the spin we put on the event—and they are extremely good at imparting spin to a story.

And there you have it. Or at least enough to know what keeps the knights of the keyboard tilting at windmills. (Better they tilt at someone else's windmill, not yours.) The wise agency head will do well to learn and understand all this. For in knowing what makes the media tick lies the key to controlling them.

See also ACADEMICS, AGENCY EMPLOYEES, GOVERNMENT AS GOD, IMAGE, INDOCTRINATION, INSIDE THE BELTWAY, INTIMIDATION, MANAGED NEWS, THE MEDIA-ACHIEVING CONTROL, MOONLIGHTING, POWER TEAM, PRESS RELATIONS, PUBLICS, and THEORY OF THE AGENCY.

..., complete with music and a catchy rhythm and lots of attractive female models. If you can't use video, give a slide presentation. Employ lots of nifty computer graphics, the more the better. Best of all, if your budget permits, hire an outside vendor to produce the presentation and to set it up.

Why?

Simply, television seems to dull, even wipe out, a viewer's critical faculties. Viewers seem to be mesmerized by the moving images and, thus mentally transformed into peanut butter and jelly, they become infinitely more susceptible to your sales pitch. Music, a catchy rhythm, attractive models—all these capture their attention and clog or otherwise occupy the maximum number of sensory input channels in the mind of a viewer, buyer or assenter.

This tactic also works well at board meetings and other assorted group séances. The delivery of a multi-media presentation is still in its primitive phases. I look forward to the day, which is not far off, when the insertion of subliminal messages becomes integral to this process.

Then, we can truly talk about the science of making a presentation.

See also CITIZEN PARTICIPATION, MARKETING, PUBLIC MEETINGS, and TURF.

MEETINGS

There are two good reasons to hold a meeting.

The first: to ensure enough subordinates present when verbal commitments are given so nobody can accuse you of saying something you didn't say—or don't want to be quoted on.* If you said the wrong thing, your subordinates can say you didn't, thereby nullifying the other party's accusation. This works only at a gathering of two parties: when more than two parties are present, others can testify without fear of rebuttal as to what was actually said.

The second: to convey the appearance of progress, even when none has been made. "A meeting was held October 10 to discuss the issue . . ." sounds impressive.

Otherwise, meetings are a waste of time.

A friend discovered the following wisdom concerning meetings at the agency photocopier. One wonders whether it was left inadvertently or deliberately. Its spirit demands it be included:

"ARE YOU LONELY?
TIRED OF WORKING ON YOUR OWN?
DO YOU **HATE** MAKING DECISIONS?
HOLD A MEETING!!!
You Can
See People
Feel Important
Draw Organizational Charts
Impress Your Colleagues
Eat Donuts
ALL ON COMPANY TIME!!!!!!
M E E T I N G S . . . the practical alternative to work"

See also BUREAUCRACY, IMAGE, *IPSE DIXIT*, PROGRESS, and REVISIONISM.

MEMENTOS

These mementos of days gone bye, when the staffer was in the mainstream, are standard office decor in the nation's capital, and probably in state capitals and around city halls, as well. They say, "Look, when I worked with (or perhaps for) this great and powerful man, I wielded considerable power and enjoyed his esteem," and indeed, these mementos can reveal a great deal about his patron. And they tell a lot about their owner.

Examine the picture closely. If the picture is merely a standard, posed 8x10 glossy of the great man, bearing his signature, it probably tells you that the man on whose wall it hangs was a low-level functionary. If it shows the office holder salmon fishing in the Canadian wilderness with George Bush or next to Jack Kennedy aboard the Kennedy sailboat or on horseback next to Ron Reagan, with the president's arm around him (signifying possession—this is my man), then he really knows the Great One, and has a much stronger wire.

Now check the inscription: if it says something on the order of "To my best pal and Great American, John Blitz, with grateful thanks—LBJ," then that too may be a clue as to how well wired the person is now—who his allies are and, possibly, how highly they are placed.

Finally, consider the administration. As time goes by, the clout of past administrations fades. If he's an Eisenhower man, chances are he'll have fewer clouted friends than if he's a Reagan man.

Mementos tell a lot about someone. They may identify a wounded tiger. And certainly if you must engage him in a turf battle, you now understand why a visit to his office is in order.

See also INTELLIGENCE, PICKING FIGHTS, and WOUNDED TIGERS.

MEMO WARS

One way to wage war by memo is to send a copy with multiple addresses to all except your rival or the victim. His copy you hold for a few days. If at all possible, spring it on him just before a big meeting that covers the issue for which he is being zinged. This gives him next to no time to respond, much less prepare his defenses.

And if he calls you on receiving a memo today dated five days ago, lie—tell him it was a mistake; the mailroom fouled up; so, so sorry, etc.

See also BLAME and PROMISES.

... to keep the staff informed must be balanced by their need to know. If you are an insecure manager who needs to keep your people in the dark as much as possible, or if they really are out to shiv you, then you will rest easier by not making them privy to all departmental business that gets written up.

Hey, take heart. As manager, you can ensure your troops are informed only to the extent they need to know—which you determine, because you control the flow of information to them (and if you cannot, stop here and go on to the next topic).

Here's how a friend does it. Each week, like clockwork, his secretary brings him the department's circulating file, and on the spot he prunes any memoranda he doesn't want his staff to read. Memos to file, CYAs, anything he feels in his best interest that should go unseen, aren't.

It's that simple.

Soon after he became department head, an insecure (though perhaps you should judge for yourself) manager took it upon himself to write a memo to his department file (not, he apparently thought, to any human being) describing the shortcomings of his staff. A lengthy missive, his memo went into great detail and spared no one: this guy was never around, that one drank too much, another was surly and under-qualified, a fourth was lazy and shiftless, and so on down the line, for every professional in the department.

Since the memo described only (perceived) staff shortcomings and conveniently overlooked any positive attributes, an unbiased observer might question the balance of both the document and its author. The memo was duly (and, one must conclude, unthinkingly) placed in the department's weekly circulating file.

This led to the following scene, to which, I admit, fate truly smiled on me by making me a neutral—and inactive—party:

One day, late after lunch, when one staffer (whom the memo accused of perpetual absence and alcoholic overindulgence) returned and greeted his colleagues breezily, "Hey, what can we do to make the afternoon pass faster?" another (the lazy, shiftless one) casually retorted, "Hey, Mick, check out the circulating file," and handed his colleague the reading matter.

"OK. Sounds as good as anything else."

A few minutes later, there issued from over the partition separating Mick's cubicle from the rest of us a host of angry sputtered curses. "That lying son of a bitch! God damn him!!!!" and more, and then, much more ominously, "I'll fix that bastard!"

A week later, fate smiled on me again. Cut to the agency library. I was searching for information in the archives, when I chanced to overhear the aforementioned department head commiserating with a crony.

He was saying, "That son of a bitch Mick. He didn't like what I wrote about him in the circulating file. He called his friends on the fifth floor of city hall, had them run my name through the police computer, checked me out in the patronage records, and they discovered info on file that didn't tally with my resume. Not only that, but he has lunch with those bastards each day, and tells them what a prick I am!"

He went on about how tough life is. "Someone else copied the memo and gave it to his patron on the board. Now the board and City Hall are giving the chairman grief about me, and I'm in trouble with the chairman." The man deserved his fate. He could easily have spared himself all his troubles. If only he'd had been smart enough to prune his department's, *his own department's, circulating file.*

See also DALEY, PAPER TRAILS, PICKING FIGHTS, PAPER TRAILS and SHREDDER.

MENTORS

...time and energy trying to hang on to their
goodies and perks; few are overly anxious to teach their bright, ambitious eager
beavers and Young Turks hard-learned tricks of the trade that could be used
against them. No, showing you the ropes, training you to protect yourself in the
clinches, is the last thing on their mind.

In that vein, this manual may be the closest you will come to having a real,
live mentor—and for that I am truly sorry, because a mentor (I was fortunate to
have had one in industry) can be a wonderful, positive experience.

And if that sounds like a self-serving plug for this manual, it is.

• A CAUTION: this observation is statistically insignificant.

See also LEADERSHIP and STATISTICS.

METEORIC RISERS

Occasionally, someone rises far more swiftly through the agency's ranks than could be expected through the normal progression of promotion. When that happens, it is a pretty good bet that he owes his rise to some aspect of performance that isn't covered in his job description. Assuming that the agency's circumstances haven't drastically changed (e.g., war hasn't been declared), then three possibilities could explain a rapid ascent.

One: the swift riser supplies a commodity that is not normally available—drugs or sex, for instance—to someone at the top. Sex is the more likely bet, because drugs are readily available on the street.

Another: the swift riser supplies something else, something intangible, that fulfills a psychological or emotional void with the agency head or whoever has and exercises the power to promote him. Maybe the head needs a whipping boy, or someone to make his tough decisions for him, or a yes-man; whatever the need, the incumbent supplies it.

A third: the fast riser enjoys one or more highly placed patrons who help expedite his rise through the ranks.

Seldom does competence alone provide the thrust behind a meteoric rise.

Rapid promotion is less likely to occur in the federal bureaucracy, with the tightly controlled civil service strictures regarding promotion, than at agencies outside the federal sphere.

See also DRUGS, PATRON, SCAPEGOATS, SEX, and YES-MEN.

MISSIONARY WORK

...ng

... ongoing struggle to

..., of course, is exclusively intended for

... empire.

As with scientific advances in other fields, revolutionary advances in the demand for government are increasingly hard to achieve. The strategy that offers the most likely short-term gain and long-term payoff is to seek small, measurable, incremental, marginal turf additions, thereby gradually increasing agency activity and building a constituency, all of which, hopefully, will lead to the expansion of the agency's mandate. Here, the mandate catches up with current activity. This stratagem can be pursued through stealth. It also helps having a talented empire builder within (if his presence and activity can be tolerated); someone capable of nursing a fledgling program along until it coalesces into a critical mass and takes on a life of its own.

Less likely to produce a major short-term payoff, but harboring good longer term possibilities for a young, ambitious staffer, are areas which now fall outside mandate realm yet could offer real possibilities within the next ten to twenty years. It is emphasized that great risk, and no certain payoff, accrues to one who pursues these. They include, in no particular order:

- Religious Activities Oversight Control (licenses religious leaders and practitioners; insures that religious organizations refrain from competing directly with government agencies; certifies, approves and regulates all religious dogma, claims and liturgy.
- Human Nutritional Regulatory Bureau (monitors, subsequently regulates, the amount of food each person ingests).
- Sexual Practices Regulatory Commission (regulates the frequency and type of sexual contact between all citizens).

- Federal Commission on Birth Control and Parenting (insures that all would-be parents meet federally approved guidelines, and licenses all births under penalty of seizure of offspring).
- Intolerance Control Commission (issues guidelines regarding intolerant and/or hateful speech, then thoughts).
- Consumer Spending Control Commission (regulates the amount and purposes of all consumer spending to ensure that expenditures are earmarked for socially useful purposes).

On a grander scale, other possibilities include new social wars on intolerance, overcrowding, and environmental degradation. With a little imagination and a lot of moxie (both commodities short in supply in the agency), it can be seen that the long-term opportunities for agency growth are both plausible and limitless.

Two quick notes. One, if you can't understand the reasoning behind these possibilities, then this avenue is probably not for you. Two, fields that employ intimidation as the primary enforcement mechanism may harbor the greatest promise for career advancement and longevity.

See also GOVERNMENT-A BRIEF ESSAY, GOVERNMENT AS RELIGION, INDOCTRINATION, INTIMIDATION, PERSONAL EMPIRE BUILDING, SPECIAL INTERESTS, STEALTH, and TURF.

MISTAKES

.... Admitting blame will be taken as a sign of weakness; in an organization that feeds on power, weakness, or the appearance thereof, should be avoided at all costs.

So if you feel absolutely and uncontrollably compelled to admit mistakes, your best bet is to confine your admission to yourself.

Unless you are a leader.

---

* I'm assuming you are interested only in insulating yourself from blame, not in leadership. If you aren't, ignore this, and reread the section on LEADERSHIP.

See also BLAME, IMAGE, LEADERSHIP, and SCAPEGOATS.

MISTRESSES AND OTHER LOVERS

It's OK to have 'em and put 'em on the payroll—somewhere else.

That way, you spare your lover—and (more important) yourself—the cynical snickers of the entire agency workforce. Because when the chairman's mistress graces the payroll, everyone eventually learns about it.

A set protocol governs this: it is understood by the host agency that making a place for someone's mistress is strictly a favor for her sponsor, and, as with any favor, it is expected to be repaid in turn. When she reports "for work," the mistress can do as much or as little work as she desires; normally, little or no serious effort will be expected of her. If she's actually willing to work and proves competent, good, that's an unexpected bonus. More likely, she'll sit there, primping and talking on the phone all day. When she chooses to show up.

Such people are worth cultivating as a potential source of information. Most often, they'll have no one to talk to, and in their loneliness, they may welcome the chance to converse with a friendly colleague. Most others, who know how the mistress/lover attained her position, won't give her the time of day because they resent how her presence skews hiring and promotion.

A most common fellow who held a seat in the state legislature sponsored a lady friend on our payroll. She'd arrive dressed for work in a long mink coat, sit down, pick up the telephone and file her nails. I say *common* because one is judged by one's companions: more than once, she was overheard, with little regard for decorum, loudly petitioning for a raise, "Listen, motherfucker, GIVE ME MORE MONEY!"

Evidently, shyness was not deeply repressed in her makeup.

See also ELECTED OFFICIALS, INTELLIGENCE, and POLITICAL FAVORS.

MOCK ALPHA DEPARTMENT

...mock-alpha department.

Although a mock-alpha department may not be able to do anything right, the agency head and senior staff act as though it can do no wrong. As though it were the hub of agency activity, whether it truly is or not. Perhaps this occurs when the agency head and the alpha department head enter a mutual defense pact to cover each other by warding off outsiders and trouble from each other. This phenomenon needs more study.

The difference between an alpha and a mock-alpha department can be exceedingly fine*, and although I cannot verify this, I suspect that it depends on the stage in its life-cycle that the host agency finds itself.

---

* Leo's department on occasion came extremely close to mock-alphadom. In fact, were it headed by anyone other than Leo, who was competent, his department would have speedily lapsed into mock-alphadom—or lost its alpha status outright.

See also AGENCY LIFE-CYCLE, ALPHA DEPARTMENT, and LEADERSHIP.

MOONLIGHTING

By moonlighting, I mean receiving compensation for two jobs at the same time. To my way of thinking, it's OK (by which I mean lawful) to work an evening or weekend job, and indeed there are many documented cases of, say, policemen who moonlight as security officers or clerks or others in low-paying government positions working as bartenders. In such cases, there is no apparent conflict of interest, the public is not ill-served by an agency employee who receives supplementary income (increasingly, it may well be agency employment that fills this role), and presumably there is no drop-off in the quality or quantity of work that the moonlighter performs on the public payroll.

The second kind of moonlighting is riskier and carries a much higher payoff—it would have to, to compensate the moonlighter for the added risk he incurs. This involves being paid twice for working at the same place—once by the agency and once (maybe more often) by an outside employer. Extra compensation can take the form of a payoff for providing access to sensitive, confidential or non-public data, or for expedited or preferred treatment. When an offender occasionally gets caught, his crime (this is, after all, a felony) receives much media attention.

One form of moonlighting that, I suspect, is much more common and much harder to detect, involves providing from one's desk for-hire services to an outside party while receiving a salary and benefits for simply "being there." Writing articles for journals and magazines. Books and the like.* (Organizational behavior mavens term this practice "bootlegging," and it probably centers around government workers doing their college or graduate papers on agency time). I say much more common because I have known a surprising number of people who did just this—my boss, co-workers, me (I never said I was perfect; besides, this manual is about how governments really behave, not how they're "supposed to").

---

* *Mea culpa* ... sort of. Although this book was not written on government time, the germ of it certainly came to me when my salary was a small line-item in an agency's budget.

To the best of my knowledge, none of us got rich, though some cleared a few extra bucks, but to a man, each of us succeeded in accomplishing something worthwhile, at least as much so as the work we were nominally assigned. Why, or perhaps better, how could this be? My answer goes back to the senior staff of the agency: it is their job to ensure that the employees are productive and

MORALE

In public agencies, morale varies widely from department to department. How can you tell which shops are happy and which are not?

Easy.

In happy departments, secretaries exhibit a cocky arrogance which says, in effect, you have to come to us if you want to get anything done.

In unhappy departments, signs of unhappiness abound:

- Prominently featured on the cubicle wall of one staff professional was an outsized poster of a fungus with an inscription in three-inch-high letters, "I feel like a mushroom. Everybody keeps me in the dark and feeds me bullshit!"
- Another professional ostentatiously kept a "Wall of Fame," a poster board which featured the name plaques initially presented to newly hired professionals, of colleagues who had resigned during his tenure on the payroll.
- The entire professional (versus managerial) staff of one department placed an ad in a trade publication which (roughly paraphrased) read, "Staff of fifteen qualified professionals in major, nationally known regional agency seek appointments elsewhere . . ."

When low morale pervades an entire agency, one can expect to encounter the following additional symptoms:

- Heavy absenteeism and turnover.
- Many overweight staff.
- Constant, uncontrolled leakage of unfavorable information to the media.
- Underground newsletters that lampoon unpopular managers.
- Widespread moonlighting.
- Attempts to unionize the work force.
- Widespread, often open sex, alcohol and drug use.

When morale is reasonably high, these phenomena rarely occur.

Staff morale is seldom, if ever, a priority of agency or department heads, not even in the military units I served with. At best, it's a red-herring, strictly for external consumption; at worst, it's a bloody nuisance

MUZZLE THE TECHIES

I suspect that because others lack their extensive training, knowledge and apparent sophistication, many technical professionals—economists, engineers and planners—suffer from a surfeit of arrogance that often impels them to write or, worse, voice opinions that cause you, their boss, extreme discomfort.

At a public hearing I heard a PhD techie lecture his former board on how they should "define their role." Perhaps techies resent or naturally look down on the technical ignorance of elected or appointed officials. Maybe they see themselves as the high techno priests of elaborate, sophisticated computer models which gin up all the right, and (to them) the only, answers. Or possibly they just tire of having political solutions imposed over the elegant, mathematically correct answers generated by their computer models. Whatever the cause, techies may succumb to an urge to lord their superior knowledge over the elected and appointed dunces who must live with, or prostitute, their output. Additional illustrations:

- In response to a question regarding elasticity of demand (namely, "What the hell is that?"), a staff economist responded to his big-city mayor, "Everybody knows that. It's straight out of Econ 101." Meta message: "You ignoramus!"
- A PhD planning director—a modeler—for a major metropolitan planning agency responded to a simple question from one of his board of directors concerning his pride and joy, an integer-dynamic model ("What is it?"), with an answer that would only cause a PR-man nightmares, "You should know about that." No, he really shouldn't.

In neither case did the snappy retort answer the question, which in both cases was entirely proper and legitimate: most lay people neither know nor care about elasticity of demand or integer-dynamic models or similar technical mumbo-jumbo. Instead, both answers highlighted the ignorance of senior officials in a public forum—how else could one learn of them?—and resulted in the loss of that most important commodity, *face*, to the person questioned. These replies also halted, or delayed, two promising technical careers.

But it goes beyond that. Techies often communicate with laymen (non-techies) with extreme difficulty. It's not that techies can't speak or write, it's just that they seem to encounter infinitely more difficulty using plain English than calibrating their computer models. I assume that somewhere there's an engineer who can write clear expository English; I've just

- Send a techie out alone only to technical conferences and symposia and other techie gatherings. There, he and his peers can swap technical knowledge, and tell each other how smart they are and how dumb their non-technical masters are, and nobody else will care.
- Otherwise, if his public presence is required in mixed company (technical and lay people); send him with a keeper, a non-technical layman. Ditto for any public meeting at which non-technical reporters are present. Make sure both understand unequivocally that if a technical question requires any response beyond a simple *yes* or *no*, the keeper delivers the answer.

See also CITIZEN PARTICIPATION, FACE and PUBLIC MEETINGS.

NATIONAL INCOME ACCOUNTING: A REBUTTAL

Government economists classify the salaries of most government employees in the National Income Accounts (which measure economic activity) under the same heading they use to account for handouts to farmers and other welfare beneficiaries: "Transfer Payments." This jibes perfectly with the Theory of the Agency, presented later.

By this definition, government workers do not create wealth for the economy (the country), neither via the goods and services they provide and certainly not through the money they give away. Instead, they transfer wealth and, in doing so, they constitute an economic drag on the economy, part of the overhead burden borne by the tax paying public.

There is potential danger in this definition, however, because it also implies that it could be cheaper to support government workers on welfare than on an agency payroll, since to do so could mean, to the wealth producing taxpayer, shifting them to a lower carrying cost.

That prompts the following rebuttal:

Government programs and policies, together with the employees who carry them out, collectively constitute a massive national social insurance policy. Just as our massive national defense effort is intended to insure against the nation becoming embroiled in a major war, so our national social policies, dating from the Depression, are intended to guarantee us internal peace: freedom from the revolt of the public.

See also THE PUBLIC and THEORY OF THE AGENCY.

...............g a family patron cuts down the cost of finding one otherwise.*

In other strata of government (state, county, municipal), I suspect any strictures against hiring friends and family are a bit less tight.

There's much to be said for nepotism. The Arab bromide about blood being the best protection comes to mind.

Those who oppose the practice are only jealous that their own family are not comparably well positioned to benefit them.

---

* One's spouse is best placed in just the way that one's lover or mistress is—in another agency.

See also HIRING CRITERIA, MISTRESSES, NETWORKS, PATRON, PATRONAGE, and PERFORMANCE REVIEW.

NETWORKS AND NETWORKING

Here, a network refers to the full range of one's acquaintances. If one includes the Internet, it affords potentially unlimited access to resources, especially information.

Networking simply means tapping someone else, gaining access to his knowledge and expertise, even his network. This affords the bold and the aggressive access to extraordinary numbers of people. A working constraint: if one is perceived to have taken advantage of colleagues, he can forget access to their network.

A network naturally lends itself to specialized areas: friends, information, favors, mutual aid, even getting things done in the agency. The best network of all gives one connections to high places, affording access to intelligence and, perhaps more important, protection.

Networks tend to be more old boy than old girl, though this does not preclude female members. The Power Team is a great start for building one's own network, but by the time one gets an agency up and running, one is (or should be) already well plugged in somewhere.

One last note. A productive network is an enormous competitive asset. A good card player never shows his hand: if you have a good network available, keep quiet about it. It seldom pays to advertise your connections, because someone may figure out how to use them against you.

See also EXPEDITERS, GENDER DIFFERENCES, GETTING THINGS DONE, INTELLIGENCE, POWER TEAM, and REVENGE.

...... the word on Iran, only you cannot quote me . . ." The "word on Iran" will be attributed in print to "a high ranking source in the Administration." Also known as signaling, this technique delivers its message neatly and tidily, and leaves no marks. No one will question either the message or the medium via which it is transmitted, and the reporters blessed with this confidence are pleased to take this nugget and run with it because it gives them a scoop.

The other purpose of newsleaks is much riskier, messier, and more difficult to carry out. This is the equalizing leak, the purpose of which is to neutralize, even take out some one who threatens a staffer or the programs he works with, and serves as the focus for the rest of this chapter.

The Watergate affair was sustained by equalizing leaks. The Clintons are masters of this technique.

If you would leak information this way, precautions must be heeded and key conditions must be noted.

First, for a leak to be successful, it must have news value: it must sell newspapers and compel the attention of TV and radio audiences. Otherwise, it won't be printed or broadcast, and your effort will avail you naught. If you cannot judge the news value of material you wish to leak, then stay out of the game, because unauthorized leaking is a high-risk undertaking that could land you in deep trouble.

A leaker must take special care not to be identified as the source, since, by definition; to leak material is to make waves. When he divulged the Pentagon Papers, it was all too easy for those who knew the material to trace its source back to Daniel Ellsburg.

And if the reporter who receives leaked material enjoys extremely tight relations with your agency's press relations officer (as is most likely the case in state and local news), or if he believes in that quaint practice, "balanced reporting," he may well ask his designated agency contact to supply the in-house version of the truth, and then change the story you were hoping to see printed—or even decline to print it. At the worst, he might divulge his source. Result: endgame for the leaker. *If you are exposed, expect speedy termination of your employment with no appeal.* Moreover, all that folk wisdom about reporters never revealing their source is true . . . only when doing so pays the reporter. Rest assured that if it pays a journalist to finger a leaker, he will.

And know that a good press officer, when he learns of a leak involving his agency, will go out of his way to uncover the source: damage control is a key piece of his job description, and a damaging story is much easier to control before it goes public than after. If the press officer can uncover a leaker, he saves himself enormous future headaches and gains huge brownie points with his executive director to boot.

Second, news itself is a commodity, an economic good with a tangible dollar value at several points in its processing and dissemination chain. While most people think it is bought and sold at newsstands, it is equally true that news is bought from the media by sponsors who may pay top dollar for the right to broadcast TV and radio news and by advertisers in newspapers and magazines.

The market for news extends to other venues as well. As a lowly paperboy growing up in New Bedford, Massachusetts, the 19th century business mogul, Jim Fiske, one day sold all his papers carrying the story of a whale oil shortage to the town whale oil baron, who then cornered the market on whale oil, and both pocketed a handsome windfall. In some agencies, news can be bought and sold if the press officer enjoys good relations (again, part of his job description) with the beat reporters covering the agency. More recently, Joseph P. Kennedy, Sr. reportedly spent "lavishly" among the media to create favorable spin for his son's election to the presidency: one assumes that few, if any, reporters told the senior Kennedy to keep his money (one further assumes that Old Joe was a shrewd enough businessman to have placed his money where it would reach the most readers and viewers and do his son the most good: among the national and big city media, not among the small-town dailies, which suggests that media at the highest levels can be expected to augment their salary).

This point cannot be overemphasized. For as little as a free lunch, or a few drinks (what real reporter wouldn't jump at that? No, Virginia, not all government bribes benefit agency personnel). For a chance at an exclusive interview with the executive director or a prominent member of the board, a reporter may alter or sit on a story involving the agency.

Your safest bet: *never trust a reporter;* instead, assume he'd sell his soul for a chance to sell more papers or for a scoop. He may think nothing about fingering you.

So when you leak, never identify yourself, and take precautions to cover your tracks. Here are a few time-tested stratagems:

- Never, never, never call a reporter from the office. The payphone is the preferred instrument of communication.
- Never give your name to a reporter. If he demands a name, use someone else's, preferably that of an enemy or someone you don't like, or one of the janitorial staff, or maybe the chairman's ...

department or otherwise draw attention to you.

- Unless your leaking campaign is a group venture (not recommended), *tell nobody*—not your best buddy, nor your secretary, your spouse, your girl/boyfriend, nobody—what you've done.

If you follow these simple guidelines, you may enjoy the benefits of leaking with less risk to your job and reputation.

See also BRIBES, THE MEDIA-ACHIEVING CONTROL, PRESS RELATIONS, REVENGE, and WHISTLEBLOWING.

NOT INVENTED HERE

It is not uncommon for technologies and procedures which have been adopted by, or have even come into wide use, variously, at corporations, at other agencies, even in whole branches of government, to be resolutely and studiously shunned or ignored by decision-makers who could, with a single word of assent or a few strokes of a pen, save their agency tons of funds, increase overall efficiency by light years, and (last but not least) more fully engage the faculties of their staff. What prevents this?

Some possibilities:

- The new procedure may involve, or derive from, a technology or a system with which the decision-maker is not familiar. Rather than rely on underlings who know it, which can be extremely threatening to managers who insist on calling all the shots, their safest bet is to keep the newfangled technology at arm's length—out of the agency. Besides, what agency head publicly wants to admit ignorance?
- Sheer institutional ossification is another. "We've done just fine for fifty (or one hundred) years without this, and [even though other agencies may have embraced it decades ago] we don't need it here."
- A variant of the above: to adopt a new procedure implicitly admits that we're not at the cutting edge, and this admission could be grounds for criticism. Better to do nothing that could invite blame (sin of omission) than act positively and positively invite blame (sin of commission). So nothing gets done.

No matter how you slice it, it all comes down to "Not Invented Here."

A diligent observer may note that in some agencies, not invented here creates tension with following precedent, which means mimicking the practices of early adapters, and he will be correct. He will also be correct in assuming that *not invented here* usually wins.

See also BLAME, ISMS, MANAGEMENT STYLE, and PRECEDENT.

...least long enough to earn their pension. This means that

- a politician will do almost anything to get elected.
- an appointee will do almost anything to get his patron reelected.
- civil servant will do all in his power to reach retirement with a blemish-free record and, more important, an intact retirement benefit package.

Similarly, the minimum short-term objective of all government agencies is to receive a funding authorization equal to last year's plus inflation. The minimum long-term objective of all government agencies is to gain a multi-year authorization stream that grows proportionally with inflation and the size of the public it serves. Beyond that, it seeks to enlarge its existing turf.

This means that incursions from other agencies must be repulsed: an agency must, at a minimum, defend its existing turf. This also means that a steadily shrinking service public (e.g., WW II veterans for the Veteran's Administration) presents a real problem.

Any action by individuals or other agencies that threatens these objectives can expect to be dealt with promptly and severely—if a critical mass of competent staff is on hand to resist.

See also MANDATE and TURF.

OFFICE HUMOR

- Rule 1. Always laugh at the boss's jokes, no matter how idiotic, tasteless or even politically incorrect they may be.

- Rule 2. See Rule 1.

- Rule 3. Never laugh at any joke that makes fun of the agency or, especially, its head, unless you're among real friends. Ditto, for your boss. Even then, keep your mirth as much inside as possible; curb any residual desire for a long, loud belly laugh. Particularly if you hold a position where you have much to lose.

Otherwise, you leave yourself open to charges that you do not support the establishment (*Don't make no waves*).

See also CORRECTNESS and LOYALTY.

government), agency office politics take on a much richer meaning than in most private sector organizations. Moreover, if one starts as an entry level staffer and hopes (realistically) to move into senior staff, then sooner or later he must come out of the closet and declare his party affiliation.

If you are a political neutral in such a charged arena, you have no call to bemoan the fact that the raises and promotions go to those who belong to the "winning" team.

See also GOVERNMENT-A BRIEF ESSAY, PATRONAGE and POLITICAL APPOINTMENTS.

OFFICE STOOLPIGEON

Many, perhaps most, government offices harbor a stoolpigeon, someone who runs to inform when this one called the boss an asshole, or that one returned from lunch drunk and two hours late, a third openly masturbates at his desk, and so on.*

The stoolie exists because the boss is insecure or paranoid, and believes (sometimes with good reason) that the troops are out to get him.

Regardless of their feelings for the boss, everyone comes to know and despise the stoolie. Sometimes it is the boss's secretary, but it may often be someone else.

If, as the manager, you're insecure or paranoid enough to encourage this practice, you're better off having someone report weekly or bi-weekly on happenings around the office—unless, of course, something hot demands immediate attention.† This way, the stoolie will be less obvious, and subtlety is key: unless you openly hate and distrust your troops, you don't want your fink to be known: you want his identity kept under wraps.

---

* Pop Quiz: As boss, which behavior(s) should concern you enough to redress it? If you answer with anything but the first, you get the booby prize—openly insolent, disrespectful attitude towards the boss, and by implication, the established power structure, cannot be tolerated.

† Should your stoolie belong to your Power Team? Not by my lights, unless you and he go back a long, long way, and you can be absolutely sure where his loyalty lies. My bias: one who willingly peaches on his peers would turn on you in a heartbeat. And he'd betray you when you need his services in the worst way—when your job is on the line. But if you want one, your best bet is a mole: someone buried deep in the organization who has no known connection to you. With your mole, contact is minimized—he never calls or speaks to you at the office, and he communicates only if something it behooves you to know is shaping up. You may want to contact him occasionally, say, once a quarter, to receive an independent, unvarnished sense of how favorably the rank-and-filers perceive you, and not the predictable "everything-is-rosy, the staff all love you" pap from your circle of yes-men.

If you truly fear your staff, a proven ploy is to have one obvious stoolie and a mole, someone who briefs you quietly on things that nobody would think of uttering in the presence of the known stoolie.

One clue to the identity of a mole is someone who never joins in or only speaks guardedly when the boss's short and remarked

for you.

One evening, a few weeks after he joined the department found a bright, conscientious new colleague, whom I'll call Roger, working late, or at least, after the others had left, to complete an assignment. Uncharacteristically, Feliks, our boss, also happened to be running late this evening, so Roger knocked and went in to present his work.

Feliks glanced out the door, saw that nobody else was around, and asked Roger to come in and close the door behind him.

Feliks didn't even bother to glance at the cover sheet of the folder Roger brought him. Instead, he looked at Roger and asked, meaningfully, "Is that all?"

"Is that all? Yes, it's all there."

"That's not what I meant."

"Then what do you mean?" Roger was genuinely puzzled.

"Do you have anything else to tell me?"

"About what?"

"About anything in the office I should know."

"What sort of things?" A certain suspicion was beginning to form in Roger's mind.

"Things you think I might want to know."

"Are you asking me to inform on my colleagues?" Roger was incredulous. Yes, that was exactly what Feliks wanted. Roger, young and idealistic, and still a man of principle and fair play, probably cost himself a two-step pay increase as well as a bright future in the department by refusing to bear witness against his peers. Many others would have responded differently in Roger's place.

I learned of this exchange from Roger a few months later over a beer in the bowling alley. My first thought was that this incident confirmed my evaluation of

Feliks, underscoring how insecure he was. Just think, a boss who tries to recruit one of his staff to spy on the others. To spy on me, for God's sake! An older, more reflective and mature assessment of this incident is that, although Feliks may not have been too smooth in the way he went about recruiting Roger, his was the wise precautionary action of a thirty-year hanger-on veteran of turf wars in Stage 4 and 5 outfits. As it turned out, Feliks's instincts were on target, though ironically they betrayed him at the same time. He was quite right to fear his own people. But he was also dead wrong: besides being an incompetent recruiter of informants, Feliks wasn't too good a judge of character, either. It was his chosen confidant (read designated office stoolie), Paul, who shivved him in the back, repeatedly badmouthing Feliks and his performance (in truth, Feliks left Paul a great deal to badmouth) even as Paul had Felix on the lookout for phantom bogeymen behind other desks in his department. Feliks had trusted Paul completely: until Paul elbowed him aside, he never had a clue to Paul's perfidy.

As for Roger, he eventually moved to Buffalo.

I suppose that if there's a moral to this tale of office intrigue, it's that you can never trust an informant too much, so you'd better recruit someone to keep an eye on him. The Russians have developed the best system, one that uses three people, each to watch the others, on the theory that a third person will preclude collusion between the other two. In the parlance of political science, a triad provides more stability and security than a dyad.

The absolute worst: a department secretary who took it upon herself to take attendance—openly—at 8:30 each morning, at 1:00 PM, when the lunch hour ended and at 5:00 PM, to report on those late or missing. Her boss made no attempt to curb this behavior, which led him to be despised as much as his self-appointed stoolie.

See also AGENCY LIFE-CYCLE, ISOLATION, LOYALTY, POWER TEAM, SECRETARY, SENSORY DEPRIVATION, and YES-MEN.

to problems, and not necessarily pressing ones at that. Without shame, they treat dollars as if they were cost-free and limitless (which to a fed, they are, since—in theory—the Federal Reserve can crank up its press and print the funds to cover any and all federal financial obligations).

How else to explain the hundreds of millions "invested" in the design and construction of a bus that "kneels" specially to accommodate wheelchair passengers, when the handicapped could be transported in off-the-shelf vehicles and custom-delivered to their chosen destination at much lower cost? Or the billions tied up in the Air Force's C-17 transport? Neither program was undertaken to "solve" a pressing national priority—wheelchair passengers constitute a minuscule fraction of total bus riders, and the C-17 was developed to replace off-the-shelf aircraft that still perform admirably for commercial airlines, Air National Guard units, third world military forces, and drug importers. Both programs seem to have escaped fiscal controls and taken on a life of their own. Both programs, moreover, endured enormous criticism for their excessive cost, yet both ultimately reached fruition.

Outsiders (critics) call this "the bureaucratic solution." How could this happen? How could a program escape fiscal controls or compromise? Why the absence of fiscal discipline, the seeming willingness to throw money around yelling "Whoopee?"

Agency staffers who brought forth these programs would argue that the public got its money's worth, the "best solution." The optimal solution. *Their solution.*

Who's right?

My answer: In a sense, both are.

To explain, certain conditions must exist for a program to escape fiscal control, surmount critics and take on a life of its own. First, the agency charged with the program must enjoy a run of budgetary prosperity—budgetary losers seldom prosper, and the inventiveness borne of fiscal scarcity is thereby rendered impotent and inoperable. Authorizations for all, or most of, the major projects and programs that the agency seeks to implement encourage the program managers to throw away their fiscal blinkers: they view funding as a never-ending cornucopia of cash flows which must be expended each year so that next year's authorization request can be duly jacked up. This is how they define fiscal responsibility, and more important, this is how they get rewarded.

Consequently, there is little conventional sense of fiscal discipline (except to the budgeters, and their game is tracking expenses, not analyzing alternative financial or operating scenarios). Opportunity cost, the quaint private sector notion that project funds could be put to better alternative use, is an alien concept (at a recent public hearing, when the subject was broached, a female county commissioner responded, "Hee, hee, opportunity cost? What does that mean?"), as are such standard number-crunching exercises as a cost-effectiveness evaluation or an internal rate of return analysis. Hurdle rates (another quaint private sector notion that if a proposed capital expenditure doesn't promise to yield higher returns than could be realized by investing the funds in financial instruments, scratch it) are likewise unknown. *Thank God*!

Second, those in charge must be ambitious or committed idealists, single-issue true believers who are honestly convinced that their solution is not just vital to the public interest, theirs is the best—and only—solution. Moreover, they know, better than the public, what is best for the public and, thus, in the public's best interest—even when the public disagree, desiring neither the bus nor the airplane. Hey, if that weren't so, then why do the public delegate all responsibility for the decision, and its consequences, to the agency? Even today, if you polled the staffers who gave us the kneeling bus and the C-17, they'd doubtless tell you—in all sincerity—that no waste is involved: theirs was simply the best solution for the problem.

Finally, and most important, the project must enjoy the backing of a necessary and sufficient number of powerful legislative allies (who are easily seduced by the prospect of telling the voters back home that they have "created" all those jobs which they are bringing back to the district)—or face half-hearted, disorganized opposition, insufficiently strong to derail the program—which amounts to the same thing.

With all these conditions satisfied, a project takes on a life of its own. At the agency, any remaining internal opposition crumbles, and the prestige of the agency—and its head—becomes inextricably bound up in its implementation.

Optimal solutions occur seldom, and, because most solutions are just compromises, an optimal solution must be experienced first-hand to be fully appreciated. Given their rarity, having a project achieve optimal implementation despite strident opposition—and without regard to its ultimate cost—is among the most rewarding and exhilarating experiences in government service: for the lucky player, taking part in such an effort ranks as the high water mark of their government career. Perversely, the more vigorous the opposition, the more exhilarating the experience. If you're lucky, you will play a part in at least one such program during your career.

OVERWEIGHT STAFF

Excess weight is a sign of frustration.

So when a greater than average number of severely overweight people populate an office, you can be sure it harbors a frustrated, under-performing staff. This is a sure tip-off that the office is mired in the late stages of its life-cycle. Think of these implications when you deal with its manager.

Also, think about what it tells you about working for him.

See also AGENCY LIFE-CYCLE.

disclaim otherwise, with the slightest credibility. For this reason, compared to written promises, verbal commitments are next to worthless, and this explains why the written record is the only official mode of communication, intra—and inter-agency. Once the commitments surrounding an issue have been agreed to and set down on paper, the written record assumes a status that borders on scripture.*

It becomes at once logical that its enormous power and importance place creating, altering and destroying the written record high among the supreme and sublime arts of statecraft.

This brings us to paper trails.† Just like in an old western movie, a trail can be you greatest ally or your worst enemy, depending which side you're on. The written record can confer great protective powers. Sometimes it points the green weenie of blame with laser accuracy. Sometimes you want a paper trail, sometimes you don't: not all paper trails are happy trails. There are proven ways to deal with both.

If you don't want the trail to lead to you, or through your desk, you can refuse to accept the paperwork and give it back to the originator (this works only with internal issues: those with external exposure are not so easy to duck). By "give it back," I mean physically return it to the originator and tell him to keep it.

When you deal with someone slippery, you may have to lay your trail (i.e., cover you actions) more subtly. Instead of sending a formal transmittal memo to an addressee, a handwritten note on the order of "John, Here's the info you requested on Issue X. Bob 5/24" can do the job just as well. That innocuous little

---

* Conversely, for unofficial, off-the-record give and take, the spoken word is the only word.

† The term "paper trails" is a misnomer. Perhaps a better name would be audit trail or any record permanently sight recorded—electronically or on paper.

note contains a great deal of information: it describes the content of the work, and reveals the sender, recipient and date sent. For important work, a photocopy of the note should be part of the sender's file, date-time stamped, if possible, to validate the date and time of transmission. If appropriate, a copy should also go to your insurance file. If the work went to the boss, and the date-time stamp sits on his secretary's desk, then be indirect: use the stamp when she takes her break, or use the stamp in the mail room.

E-mail poses a different challenge. Still, it records when a memo/message is sent, and many systems feature a date-time receipt, giving a sender the exact time an addressee theoretically reads his e-mail. I say "theoretically" because many supervisors can have their secretary delete their e-mail messages and correspondence, and claim they never saw it. Those who understand all too well the implications of the date-time receipt may direct their employees to dispense with this feature. (My response: continue to use it, even if it means incurring the ire of the boss, until I am directed in writing to cease and desist from this practice. I add that this action is recommended only when there an extreme adversarial relationship exists between boss and staffer. To do otherwise is to stir up unnecessary waves.)

Added protection accrues from transforming the spoken word to the written word. Memoranda describing what is said at meetings and during conversations, timed and dated—all these make good fodder for *anus protectus* files. Best of all is the degree to which this lends itself to creating a document trail where none would otherwise exist.

If creating a paper trail is a valuable craft, then erasing a paper trail must be equally so. A friend would periodically review his department's files and systematically purge any paper that in his view contained even the slightest potential to shine the spotlight of blame on him. A friend from south of the Mason-Dixon line eloquently summarizes this process: "What ain't there cain't hang you."

It can be seen that a shredder is as useful an implement around the office as a date-time stamp or, better analogy, a photocopying machine. The operant rule: better they skewer you for destroying, or appearing to destroy, evidence, than you suffer the consequences had the evidence been freely available.

From the above, it is clear that paper trails count for a lot; that with a little creativity, a trail can be created where none apparently exists, and that it is easier (it means making fewer waves) to create a trail than to erase it.

See also BLAME-FREEDOM FROM, GOVERNMENT AS RELIGION, INSURANCE, MEETINGS, OFFICE STOOLPIGEON, PROCESS, PROMISES, REVISIONISM, SHREDDER, SIGNOFFS, and SECRETARY.

The administrators and bean counters who invented all these reports did so less to show progress is being made (to them, "progress" is the completed paperwork itself) than to ensure procedural compliance. Failure to complete and submit the routine paperwork will only get you gigged for not performing and brand you an administrative incompetent.

And, for another, handing in the routine paperwork may be your department's main—perhaps its only—contribution to the smooth functioning of the agency. Besides, gun decking is pretty easy.

Heads of departments that employ a low-output strategy explicitly fasten on routine paperwork as a substitute for real accomplishment.

At my first agency, our control-freak chairman hit on the bright idea of having department managers submit a weekly summary of work accomplished by their departments. Subsequently, this was circulated to the staff (which then numbered fewer than sixty) so all could know what was going on throughout the agency.

Over a four-week span, the submission by the department charged with preparing our annual program was instructive and amusing:

Week 1: "Invite staff to audition for public hearing slide show narrator."
Week 2: "Audition staff who volunteered to narrate public hearing slide show."
Week 3: "Write thank-you letters to all staff who auditioned for slide show."
Week 4: "Appoint myself narrator for the slide show."

One wonders if the winning narrator wrote himself a thank-you letter in Week 5.

See also BLAME, GENDER DIFFERENCES, and KILLING THINGS.

PARTNERSHIPS

When someone develops a shiny new initiative, or resuscitates a moldy old one, and there's no money in the till to pay for it, the idea of *partnership* may crop up. In fact, it does so with increasing frequency these days as a much preferred alternative to privatization. Partnership just means that the cost burden for the initiative is transferred from ordinary tax-payers to a corporation which seeks to incur favorable publicity. The company pays the freight and reaps favorable PR, and an agency, or, for the more ambitious partnerships, a consortium (coalition) of agencies, provides the service (i.e., runs the program).

If you run a partnership program, it may pay you to assign as corporate liaison someone with private sector expertise, since companies have a funny way of wanting to know, in ways that would never occur to agency staff, where and how effectively their sponsorship dollars are being spent.

Once they have committed to the program, the corporate sponsors are largely stuck with it, since they are vulnerable to threats of adverse publicity if they try to pull out. In such circumstances, the media will be your unquestioning ally.

In other words, business as usual, except that a company picks up the tab.

See also THE MEDIA-ACHIEVING CONTROL and PRIVATIZATION.

whose sponsorship can place you in a nice, cushy, well-paying slot, shield you from slings and arrows of rivals, even, perhaps, from disciplinary action in the event you mess up.*

A patron can do all these things and more: he can be a valuable source of intelligence; he can attack your rivals; he can serve as your walking insurance policy. Hyman Rickover could never have built his extraordinary empire without patrons.

A caution: some who enjoy the sponsorship of a patron assume that because they have a well-connected friend, they are free to use (abuse) the system for their personal ends. In this, they're wrong. Few patrons reach their exalted station by backing wave-makers, and if you act like one, they'll drop you as though you were radioactive. Most patrons are not pleased to learn their banana has actively abused the system—it means that he's made waves and they've backed a loser—bad combination, that. Moreover, they will be exceedingly reluctant to expend scarce political capital to bail you out, especially when you've become identified as their boy.

Once you've settled into that cushy job, your obligation to your patron is not ended. Far from it. Rather, you have become part of a network (some might term it a mutual aid alliance) that transmits favors, information and protection, and an important part of your responsibility to your patron and his network is just beginning: your obligation is to perform reasonably well, so it won't appear he backed a loser, and inform him of news that could harm or benefit him. That way, you win, and he wins. My inclination (if it meets with his approval) is to dine or enjoy cocktails with a sponsor every four to six weeks, and to use the opportunity to inform him of developments that could be of interest.

---

*   Especially in regional and municipal agencies, competence alone is seldom enough to secure a senior appointment. A patron is a must; finding one if you lack one should rival assembling your Power Team on your initial agenda.

Where do you find patrons? This is the hard part; potential patrons don't openly advertise that they're in the market for new sponsorees to collect. My advice: find a winner, and help him get elected. If you played a strong role in a winning effort, he'll have to reward you—or he won't remain in office too long. That way, you help him accomplish something positive, and vice versa. (Oh yes, unless the action violates election laws, it goes without saying that if your patron runs for reelection, your butt is out stumping for him.) The worst tie to a patron: you hold something incriminating on him. Then, he'll want to see you fail; hell, he'll want to see you dead. Everybody hates a blackmailer.

One final note: if you think one patron is good, think what two in your corner can mean.

A remote acquaintance, who held a senior career position with one of the federal welfare agencies, acquired the status of cult hero in our home. Out of sheer awe and deepest respect, we clept him "The Shark." Shortly after a new administration came into power, the Shark was summarily informed by rivals that he was being fired. But those who would depose the Shark didn't know their man. A Washington veteran, an insider's insider, the Shark knew just what to do. He quickly called two extremely senior senators, one on either side of the aisle, who served on his agency's oversight committee. Together his patrons informed the secretary of his department that if the Shark were fired, his department could expect to see next year's budget gutted, because they would both personally see to that.

Needless to say, the Shark's tenure on his agency's payroll remained secure. Four years later, when the next administration came to town, the Shark managed to ensure that his tormentors were themselves fired, proving again the adage that if you set out to get rid of a rival, carry out your plan to completion lest he come after you. Or have a first-class patron in your corner.

See also COMPETITION, DALEY, INSURANCE, INTELLIGENCE, NETWORKS, PERSONAL EMPIRE BUILDING, POLITICAL FAVORS, POWER AS A CORRUPTING INFLUENCE, POWER TEAM, REVENGE, and WOUNDED TIGERS.

..., education, experience, background and skills (or lack thereof) merit-based employers cannot afford, at least not at the pay scales they are knocking down at the agency; and dweebs, one-dimensional, party-affiliated ideologues. Each will be discussed in turn.

Incompetent patronage hires and promotees owe their hiring and promotion solely to connections and favors, not merit.

By definition, they perform their assigned job less than well. They typically exhibit measurably less competence than their merit-oriented peers (after all, if they were truly competent, they would be earning their fair market value in the private sector, creating instead of transferring wealth). Instead, many of them take themselves (or their job title) way too seriously, and inject themselves into vital decision making and key assignments and just plain crap these up. Just as bad money ultimately drives good out of circulation, so too does their presence also skew any sense, any appearance, of merit in an agency's hiring and promotion, and hastens the outflow or demotion of staff actually capable of performing work. More often than not, incompetents are rewarded for these results with employment security, salary raises and promotion.

Too many patronage placements in key jobs are a sure sign that an agency is heading into advanced stage trouble. Toward the end of the life-cycle, when hiring becomes almost solely a function of patronage, a knowing (unbiased) observer may be treated to a Mummer's Parade of retreads, incompetents and losers who just can't hack it elsewhere.

The other species of patronage worker, so far as I can determine, is limited to Washington, DC and a few major state capitals and cities. In these places lurk professional cause-driven dweebs who live to right some real, perceived or invented social ill.*

---

*   An excellent tip-off to a committed idealist is a crusader bent on *saving*. *Save our Schools! Save the Kids! Save the Whales! Save Some Bay! Save the Snail-Darter!* On reflection, the reader can doubtlessly come up with other interests that merit crusades in their behalf.

When their party loses the White House or State House, they are duly swept from office and take refuge on (what are for them) the sidelines; in think tanks, on sympathetic university faculties, and at similar resting places. Here they write books and papers and provide commentary to anyone who will listen about how badly the incumbent administration is screwing their pet public, and how great their program is (or was), usually in that order, while they wait with impatient eagerness for one of their own to recapture power so they can return to *make a difference.*

When they are on the agency payroll, their holier-than-thou self-righteousness and sense of mission imbue then with insufferable arrogance. My experience suggests that such people will bend the rules, lie, cheat, steal, and connive, and justify (or at least rationalize) their actions on the grounds that the ends they seek justify any means.

Their Achilles heel: those procedures.

Both species are as much a part of the agency littoral as cockroaches in ethnic restaurants.

If you see one, you know the species, know who—and what—you're dealing with.

See also AGENCY LIFE CYCLE, ETHICS, JOB POSTINGS, and RULES AND PROCEDURES.

...here to deadlines, how much supervision you require, your reaction to setback and willingness to assume added responsibility, how well you function as a "team player," additional skills you have mastered since the prior review, whether your performance has risen, fallen or remained the same since then, and so forth. These and similar criteria comprise the boilerplate on standard performance review forms.

And some managers, particularly those at departments and agencies early in their life, would almost certainly use these measures to assess your performance.

But, contrary to what you might expect, managers in more mature organizations often employ alternative criteria to review your performance, criteria which have little to do with how much you've actually accomplished or how well you did it. Such people assess performance in terms of your willingness (or lack thereof) to not make waves, to not show them up, to not force them into decisions they'd rather avoid, to get along with others outside and especially inside the department, your observance of standing Mickey Mouse rules and procedures, even if these interfere with the work you are expected to perform.*

The colleague I cited previously was guilty of this. He finished all his work on time, brought extra federal dollars into the region, paving the way for a genuinely useful work program to move ahead. To an outsider, he seemed the very personification of a dedicated, competent employee. But my friend sneered openly at colleagues for their foibles and shortcomings, and often he had to be

---

* Many staffers themselves fail to understand these alternative performance criteria. Typically, when their agency announces the promotion of someone incapable of correctly spelling its own acronym, they are incredulous. In truth, they either don't understand the criteria on which promotion is based, or even when it becomes patently obvious, the truth is so painful that, like present-day Germans who do not wish to confront "the Jewish Issue," they ignore or deny it.

admonished to sign in and out—in short, he only performed his assigned work, he did not contribute to the smooth running of his department. His unquestioned brilliance threatened his insecure department head. Worst of all, he intensely disliked the department manager and foolishly made no secret of his feelings. Unfortunately for my friend, it was this—his nonexistent contribution to getting along with others, not what he contributed to the department or his success in sucking money from the federal government (which was, after all, the *raison d'etre* of his department)—that his department manager valued most.

Conversations with competent employees elsewhere in government convince me this phenomenon is much more widespread in review and promotion practices than one might imagine.

So be forewarned that *performance* can be a many-valued term, and it can take on radically different meanings to different managers. It will pay you to quickly learn what the term means to your department manager. Do it right and make yourself a nice piece of extra change—and save a great deal of heartburn.

Or go work in an agency less—or further—advanced in its life-cycle.

See also AGENCY LIFE-CYCLE, GIVE YOURSELF A RAISE, and UNDERSTANDING THE GAME.

.... ous, long past the service's mandatory retirement age, outlasting, on active duty, anyway, all but his youngest critics).* More recently, I think that David Kessler of the US Food and Drug Administration came as close to any Capital Beltway insider to being a true empire builder, although in state, county and local governments, there may well lurk substantial numbers of their lower case brethren.

What lessons do these titans hold for aspiring emulators?

Both Hoover and Rickover are enormously instructive, starting with the similarities in their respective careers. Each remained in office long past the federal government's (nominal, in their case) mandatory retirement age. Each ruled his domain autocratically, squashing internal discussion and debate regarding the long-term direction of their respective empires so effectively that serious questions relating to the strategic direction of their respective agencies surfaced only after both were long dead. And, on the surface, each appeared to enjoy broad-based legislative support and weathered sometimes strident controversy and criticism.

Each departed from standard agency personnel practice by hiring from the top. From the beginning, Hoover sought out college-educated lawyers and accountants, not the uneducated semi-literates who then populated the municipal police forces, to fill the ranks of FBI Special Agents (not mere "agents"). As for Rickover, he personally selected every officer who came into his Nuclear Power Program; many he handpicked only after a most grueling personal interview. In the process, he skimmed the cream of the Navy's officer

---

* While such justly famous empire builders as Franklin D. Roosevelt, Joseph P. Kennedy, Sr., Sam Rayburn, Lyndon Johnson and Richard J. Daley deserve mention here, their fine work, which depended on their continual re-election (in the case of Kennedy, on that of his children and grandchildren), falls outside the scope of this publication.

corps, bringing the service's best brains and leading technocrats into his program. Among his recruits was a future US president (talk about a 24-karat patron!). By assiduously cultivating his image among his recruits, each titan attained within his agency the status of a cult head. More important, each could count on the support of the best and brightest men in their field in inter-agency turf battles.

However, it is not the similarities, but the striking differences between their careers, that I consider most instructive. Consider the strategy each titan employed to sustain his term in office, the means by which each obtained the legislative patronage and support (in Hoover's case, non-opposition) he enjoyed. Hoover employed a two-pronged strategy. He used the media skillfully. When his special agents cornered a gangster, they kept a lid on things until Hoover, who just coincidently would be accompanied by an army of reporters, showed up to personally demand the felon's surrender. Great smoke! The media ate this up. So did the public. Then, through the extraordinarily far-reaching intelligence net he constructed, Hoover gathered damaging information on enough members of Congress, his oversight, that none dared try to dislodge him: he was a master, perhaps the master, of intimidation. Enemies and (putative) friends alike probably hated and feared—and certainly respected—Hoover, but to tackle him was to risk waves large enough to cost an erstwhile tackler his next election, a risk no politician ever runs: also remember, to the public Hoover was a popular icon, practically a hero.

Rickover approached this task differently. He owed his promotion and longevity to the sponsorship of senior, extremely powerful legislators who were friends of the service, his program and, thus, him. It's hardly coincidental that the Navy has named a recently built aircraft carrier—its largest capital ship and most visible symbol of sea power—for Carl Vinson, a key Rickover sponsor. Rickover's strategy was deceptively simple; he mastered the patronage game, and he was lucky enough—or more likely smart enough—to latch onto patrons who, like he, planned to remain in office for as long as they were able, and whose chances of being unseated were exceedingly slim. Rickover looked to Congress, not to the Navy's high command, for promotion, and thereby bypassed the service's procedures for advancement. Was he successful? Well, he ended up with four stars—as many as the Chief of Naval Operations, the senior most admiral in the Navy—even though he never held a seagoing command.

It is significant to note that when their respective terms finally ended, the two publics held hostage to their career longevity, Congress by Hoover and the Navy's high command by Rickover, took swift steps to ensure that nobody else could replicate their empire-building accomplishments. Congress closely and warily watches the FBI director, and none of the admirals in the Pentagon ever wish to suffer another Rickover.

In contrast, Kessler at the FDA enjoyed no such advantage. True, he mastered intimidation and his agency uses it exceptionally well, but only on corporate miscreants, not as Hoover did on senators or congressmen. Nor, to the best of my knowledge, had he forged many ties to the people in Imperial Washington worth sucking up to, the senators and ...

... tobacco campaign was touched by genius; by its timing, Kessler gave his incumbent president, a member of the party that did not initially appoint him, an election year issue on which to crusade, and guaranteed Kessler tenure through the next four years.

Sadly, Kessler resigned, and by doing so may have killed his chance to return to appointed office: he made many, many enemies along the way. Corporate enemies, enemies with deep pockets who boast the powerful friends in Congress he lacks and have an enormous vested (economic) interest in continuing his absence from office.

But enough idle speculation. More to the point, how can one achieve this exalted status? Well, a law degree may help, especially if you or your agency is an intimidator; both Hoover and Kessler earned law degrees, and both the FBI and FDA employ intimidation often and effectively, as did their heads. Also, none of these titans are women.

However, I find it more enlightening to recall that both Hoover and Rickover took the helm of new programs. Hoover's FBI owed its origin to a rival agency, the Secret Service, that had fallen into congressional disfavor, and when Rickover arrived to assume command, the Navy's nuclear power program was a fledgling effort, full of promise, but the technology was largely unproven. As Stage 1 agency heads, both men were able to populate their agencies with staff they chose, not stiffs they inherited, and grew them with their respective agencies. With their carefully selected staff, with no resident deadwood to root out and no entrenched baronies to obstruct them, each man was free not just to write on but to engrave his own *tabula rasa*. This enabled, each built Stage 2 organizations and retarded their advance beyond Stage 3; in other words, they created alpha agencies that endured for decades. Had they taken command of fully mature agencies, with their inevitable and inherently entrenched interests, it is unlikely that either builder could have risen to the heights of power, eminence and longevity he ultimately achieved. Incidentally, this factor underscores the brilliance of Kessler at the FDA, where he enjoyed no such advantage.

Since agency startups are relatively rare, an analogous means to start your own empire is to take on a task or program that everyone else ignores or looks down on at the outset as a throwaway. This is bound to assure you a measure of independence: nobody will believe you have turf worth taking, so they'll tend to leave you alone. Or, a program that involves cutting-edge technology may offer possibilities; critics tend to be few, because few know the technology or can sense the potential. From this point, while you are free of outside interference, if you build your department, your agency, and its constituency—your power base—with care, pick the right staff, keep your eyes and ears open and build your insurance portfolio as the opportunities present themselves—which they will, and assiduously cultivate your image and the right patrons, if you can complete these few simple tasks well, your immediate supervisors and your peers, once they figure out what you've been doing, will be able neither to stop nor unseat you. Then you, too, may outdistance and outlast your rivals, and ensure your position for as long as you want.

See also AGENCY LIFE-CYCLE, ALPHA DEPARTMENT, DALEY, DEVIL'S ADVOCATE, GENDER DIFFERENCES, HOOVER, IMAGE, INSIDE THE BELTWAY, INSURANCE, INTIMIDATION, THE MEDIA-SOME THOUGHTS, PATRON, PICKING WINNERS, PUBLICS, REVENGE, SPECIAL INTERESTS, TURF, and URSINE THOUGHTS.

. . . . exist for two reasons:

- to preserve *the appearance of impartiality* in hiring and promotion, and
- to protect the organization, and by implication its senior managers, from any employment-related job action.

Personnel officers hold special power, partly because they are entrusted with custody of personnel files and, thus, enjoy free access to the dirt on everyone on the payroll, and partly because all authorized and other changes to employees' personnel files—including and especially yours—cannot take place without their knowledge and concurrence. This makes them party to all manner of shenanigans, such as altering personnel records and making political hires (many of whom are, to put it politely, grossly unqualified for their job) somehow appear acceptable.

If you are not member of the Power Team, treat personnel officers as a special class of vulture, never to be trusted with anything remotely resembling a confidence. Above all, never confuse the motivation of personnel officers with anything like concern for employees' well-being or fair treatment. Solely agents of the agency head, never ombudsmen for the rank-and-file.

And if you run the agency, make damn sure that whoever runs Personnel is *your* banana.

A Jewish acquaintance, after he had explained verbally and by memo that he would be absent on Rosh Hashanah to observe that religious holiday, was told by an ignorant, petty department manager that she couldn't care less whether the next day was Rosh Hashanah and he'd better get some last minute, trivial, time consuming bit of work done—or else.

This really stuck in my friend's craw. After the holiday, he called his rabbi to ask whether this action was Kosher (it blatantly wasn't) and then visited the Personnel Office to inquire into the agency's religious holiday observance policy (incredibly, it had none). Within forty-five minutes of his visit, the offending department manager called my friend in to her office and oozed effusive apologies for being out of line, under stress and a lot of other unctuous, soothing pleasantries that were clearly intended to make my friend forget her earlier intolerant indiscretion.

The point here is not the manager hustling to cover her rump and diffuse a potentially damaging charge of religious harassment and discrimination (that, you'd expect), but that someone at the Personnel Office recognized from the tenor of my friend's questions that he soon might face an unwanted opportunity to practice damage control, and with his leisure thus threatened, took prompt steps to head off the threat.

The following is presented to illustrate the real purpose of the Personnel Department—keeping the agency out of trouble *a posteriori* for the personnel policies it pursues:

A transit agency advertised for, and duly posted, the job of Locomotive Inspector. Two qualified staffers, whose current salary fell below the range for the posted position and whose expertise conformed to the posted job requirements, duly bid for the job. Both knew agency policies and procedures, and secure in the thought that their department head knew them well and respected their professional knowledge, they figured they had a leg up on any outside bidder. Certainly, they had every reason to expect one of them would land the job.

To their dismay, neither got it. Instead, it went to a funny little gnome who took three days to learn his way to the men's room. In locomotive technical matters, the gnome was equally lost. Much aggrieved, the two skunked bidders cried foul, "The job posting clearly states that the selectee must be intimately familiar with the inner workings of a railroad locomotive, and this bozo can't tell a caboose from a cow-catcher." In both assertions, they were correct.

Worse, they filed a grievance, committing their gripe to paper and in the process posing a vexing (and potentially embarrassing) problem to the agency. The ball landed squarely on the court of the Personnel Department. Jeez, what to do?

Not to worry. The following day, there came a written *ukase*, signed by the chairman himself, pronouncing the new hire an intern. A 64-year-old intern. No rules or policies violated, all but two people happy—and they were left without recourse. The Personnel Department had come through like a champ. Problem solved!

[Insiders would learn later via the grapevine that the new locomotive inspector intern's resume had come to personnel from the chairman's office, bearing the cryptic notation, "Process to Hire" over the chairman's initials. The gnome had previously worked as a building inspector in an office notorious, even in a city hall infamous for graft and kickbacks, f

..., COMPLAINTS, DAMAGE CONTROL, ISMS, JOB POSTINGS, OBJECTIVES, PATRON, POWER TEAM, RUMOR MILL, and SECRETARY.

PICKING FIGHTS

Certain people insist on picking fights. Gratuitously. Unnecessarily. Some are young and foolish, others are maladjusted or just carry a chip on their shoulder, and still others are wounded tigers.

Treat pugnacious colleagues as you'd treat fools who entertain themselves by giving themselves electric shocks—with a wide berth.

No professional picks fights gratuitously, because doing so makes waves and almost certainly creates future enemies.

You don't want that, do you?

See also WOUNDED TIGERS.

From time to time, a new or radical idea or notion really sets the ruling establishment's teeth on edge. With increasingly shrill invective, they and the media as one denounce the idea as impractical, dumb, and *unfair* (a wonderful word that ranks with "socialite" in having many imprecise meanings), the product of an evil, vicious, impractical, unfair, ignorant, dumb, uncaring and mean-spirited inhuman being of dubious ancestry.

Here holds the old law school adage, "When the law is with you, argue the law; when the facts are with you, argue the facts, and when neither the law nor the facts are with you, pound the table!" If their criticism sounds like table-pounding—knee jerk accusations devoid of substance or substantiation (critics confuse the stridence and shrillness of their tone and the persistence with which their view appears in the media for substance, even moral authority), and especially if the media denounce the idea enthusiastically—then that's a tip-off that the new idea may have real merit.

A sure clue that its proponent is really on to something is when the character, the life, and personal ethics and morality of the proponent are dredged up and damned or if a real or alleged transgression is dug up from his distant past to "prove" his inherently evil nature. The editorial and style sections of the *New York Times* and the *Washington Post* and the *Doonesbury* satire comic strip provide excellent sounding boards for such criticism. Incidentally, the public relations term for this practice is "source derogation."

As long as a controversial idea, proposal, notion or philosophy is in play (i.e., the subject of public debate), keep in mind that the one thing to avoid at all costs is to back a loser. So it pays not to denounce the new paradigm too strongly, if at all. In fact, it might even pay you to quietly support it, assuming you can find no problem with it beyond unsubstantiated denunciation. So let others rail against and source derogate, and when they do so, nod sagely (after all, you don't want to make waves, either), and say or write nothing to disagree until you are absolutely sure their criticism is on target. You may, however, note who said what: this could give you an important advantage later.

And if the idea ultimately turns into a winner, you can claim (truthfully) that you were among the first on the bandwagon.

If you are looking for a winning staffer to hitch your wagon to, your best bet is to identify a power seeking colleague. He may not (have to) be all that smart, although certainly intelligence is not cause to disqualify him, but he must pursue power competently—unerringly and with single-minded relentlessness. If one who fits this description is available, befriend him, help him, offer him information—he'll use it far better than you can, stroke him, and with a little luck, you can follow him up the hierarchical ladder.

See also AGENCY EMPLOYEES, DALEY, HERETICS, INTELLIGENCE, MARKETING, THE MEDIA-SOME THOUGHTS, MISSIONARY WORK, PERSONAL EMPIRE BUILDING, and STEALTH.

THE PIPELINE INTO

... the next, and the next still, until ... complete and the project is finished or the program, implemented. One staff acquaintance terms this prescribed series of procedures *the pipeline*, and metaphorically, the name says it all.

Some aspects of the pipeline deserve to be expanded on.

First, once a project enters the pipeline, procedures ensure that it cannot escape: it can slow down, can even stop cold, but it cannot escape. Every gatekeeper along the way, every party having signoff power, must process the paperwork within a reasonable time frame or risk being zinged for non-compliance. If there's no legitimate reason to withhold approval, if that aspect of the program for which he bears responsibility passes muster, then (in theory if not in practice) he must approve it *in writing* and pass it on. This keeps the program moving inexorably forward—there is method, proven method, behind the apparent plodding.

Second, it follows that every project, every program in the pipeline needs a driver, a program manager or project champion, to ensure it keeps moving. Absent a driver, projects may stop. It goes without saying that if he is to be at all effective, the driver must have authority to prod his charge along, which means the power to zing sluggardly or inattentive gatekeepers. The power to zing means power to blame.

Generally, I believe, offensive minded agencies and departments are not wanting for drivers. This enables them to face the world feeling that "we have the drivers; we need programs for them to drive." Such vigor usually accompanies agencies and departments early in their life: their problem is finding programs and projects.

Mature agencies, on the other hand, tend to enjoy a surfeit of projects and programs but increasingly lack competent drivers; their problem is moving existing projects through the pipeline. Often, these agencies seem not to care whether a project or program is finished or implemented; their focus is solely on turf, and for them, the trick is to position the program in *their* pipeline, from which it cannot escape—whether it subsequently gets anywhere or not.

See also AGENCY LIFE-CYCLE, BLAME, BUREAUCRACY, COMMITMENTS, PAPERWORK-ROUTINE, PROCESS, SIGNOFFS, and TURF.

..., even if the initial application is OK. Remember, he's gotta come to you for the goodies.

This way, all supplicants will know you read their application, and you condition them not to expect instantaneous approval, much less take approval for granted. This practice guarantees you more time to scrutinize non-standard or otherwise controversial applications.

Moreover, you give the grants department at the submitting agency clout internally because only they can suck the dollars from you. Implicitly, they own you one for that, and they know it. Also, if you decide to deny some, or all, of their request, they will not be so unpleasantly surprised and less likely to call in the heavy artillery, support from their congressman/senator, to reverse your decision.

The same applies to internal signoffs.

See also BELTWAY, KEEP 'EM WAITING, SIGNOFFS, and USING YOUR CONGRESSMAN.

PLOW HORSES

When a conscientious new employee starts work at the agency, he naturally tends to work diligently to impress his supervisor. If he proves competent, he can count on having his work increasingly piled on.

The tendency to assign work in this fashion overlooks one important point: if our competent employee becomes overloaded and goes unrewarded in pay and title relative to peers who watch his labors with detached bemusement, sooner or later he can be counted on to relax his pace a little and give himself a raise. Or depart for greener pastures.

While I cannot prove this, it is my impression that it takes women longer than men to realize their conscientiousness and drive are being exploited by a boss who's unwilling or unable to crack the whip on their underperforming peers.

See also COMPETENCE, GENDER DIFFERENCES, GIVE YOURSELF A RAISE, and STATISTICS.

POLITICAL APPOINTMENTS

...ying suitability, depending on hot election year issues and which party holds power. The scale shown below, slightly modified, currently holds. An appointee is assumed to be a US citizen (though legal challenges to Proposition 187 and a weak president may one day nullify this) and, further, not a major financial contributor to the party—if he is, all bets are off: though neither likes to admit it, both political parties reserve appointments for auction.

The scale, in order of suitability, follows:

1. Minority
2. Female
3. Humble roots
4. No convictions (either moral or felonious, in no particular order)
5. Homosexual
6. Single parent (illegitimate)
7. Single parent (divorced)
8. Single parent (adopted)
9. Military background
10. Wealthy family background (but not a fat-cat)
11. Divorced and remarried
12. Married (never divorced, no children)
13. Married (never divorced, with children)
14. Fat Cat (wealthy political contributor)
15. Qualified for the job (based on prior experience)
16. Able to perform job

A couple of notes. If Republicans hold the White House, the order of criteria one through fourteen is reversed. Also, the factors are additive, which means that more than one factor can apply to an appointment; in fact, the more the better.

Thus, a minority lesbian (by definition, also a female) from humble origins makes a far superior candidate to a minority male who served in the military and sports an arrest-free record (under these criteria, none of the founding fathers would come remotely close to qualifying for any slot above Deputy Under Assistant Secretary). Finally, the suitability scale corresponds amicably to our definition of an agency as a parking place for the friends and supporters of elected incumbents.

Note where qualifications and ability to perform rank on the scale. Above all, the appointing politicians want someone reliable and loyal, someone who, when push comes to shove, will do their bidding without question and who won't make things too much worse. Beyond that, notwithstanding disclaimers to the contrary, they don't care how he performs. (Many staffers, especially younger ones, don't understand this, and express puzzlement and confusion when no attempt is made to rectify problems that most obviously need to be fixed.)

These criteria guarantee that few, if any, appointees will make any long-term difference in the agency they've been chosen to run, meaning that they are unlikely to retard its inexorable progress down the life-cycle trail. More often than not, they only hasten the journey.

With a few fellow appointees, many appointed agency heads consort in an Elysian field of interaction with legislators, their appointing executive, and the media, advancing their personal agenda. Like the Bellamy family of *Upstairs Downstairs*, they seldom exhibit more than passing awareness of or interest in what goes on in the lives of the staff, which is a mixed blessing. Any loyalty is reserved exclusively for a few court favorites; as far as the rest are concerned, they couldn't care less.

Fortunately for appointed heads, most agencies have become so bound by procedure and regulation that even if the new head were a man of real ambition and ability, he couldn't accomplish much.

To the career staffer who remains at the agency while appointed heads come and go, the implications are obvious: the incumbent head is to be treated with deference, recognizing that nothing he does will likely amount to much. More important, the staffer will probably be around long after the head has moved on. If the head proves grossly incompetent, with a little luck he'll be gone before four years have passed. Remember, though, that he who sits in judgment (the Prime Public) ultimately defines competence.

See also AGENCY, AGENCY LIFE-CYCLE, HIDDEN AGENDA, LOYALTY, PERFORMANCE CRITERIA, PUBLICS, REVENGE, TITLES, and UNDERSTANDING THE GAME.

future date. Insofar as I can determine, the value of the return favor, the payoff, remains constant over time.

To refuse to return a favor, like welshing on a gambling debt, violates an unwritten (until now) code of conduct that applies throughout government, among elected and appointed officialdom alike. When word of a refusal gets around, it brands the welsher a pariah, one never to be trusted—and one who may later fall prey to revenge-motivated sanctions. There are two exceptions to this code: if a payoff could lead to a debtor's ouster from office (but in this case, his creditor is supposed to know better than to ask), and if the debtor is not in office and, thus, lacks the power to deliver.

Although I am aware of no research on this phenomenon, one expects elected officials to need (or demand) favors as elections approach. The tighter the election, the more favors they need. The consequent payoffs of the winners (losers, by definition, are in no position to pay their debts) may result in seemingly bizarre or otherwise anomalous hiring and purchasing behavior.

The story is told of a genial congressman from a backwoods Southern state. Over the years, he performed many, many favors for colleagues on both sides of the aisle, supporting this bill or that bill as requested. Wonderful fellow! But eventually back home there arose a serious challenge to his incumbency. The challenger campaigned on the accusation that the incumbent had delivered nothing to, had done nothing for, the good folks in his home district.

This fine representative of the people called in his markers from incumbent colleagues, which meant nearly the entire House of Representatives. Cheerfully, and by a whopping margin, his colleagues authorized the construction of an enormous dam in his district, a pork barrel proposal that had languished unauthorized for years. With the dam authorized, he went home and convinced the voters that he sure had done something for the district, and here was (literally) concrete, enduring evidence to that effect.

The grateful voters returned him to Congress.

———

To a taxonomist, the damned thing looked like the product of an illicit union between the San Diego Chicken and a blue feathered boa. *It* was a person in a bird suit, like Big Bird on *Sesame Street*. It spoke in a high, indeterminate pitch, much like Mickey Mouse, so one couldn't determine from its voice the sex of the person inside the suit, which the suit itself also masked. I refer, of course, to the one and (to my knowledge) only Buster the Bird.

My exposure to Buster came one day when the androgynous avian was led by the hand/wing around our offices by a low-level functionary from the personnel department. Buster was introduced by the personnel functionary, and as if that weren't enough, Buster him(?)self chirped, "Hello, I'm Buster the Bird."

Some enthusiastically, others caustically, greeted our new feathered colleague with such bon mots as "Hey, Buster, how's your pecker?" (this tableau took place in the Midwest, where subtlety is seldom encountered) to which Buster sagely paid no mind. I think my greeting was "Jeez, Buster, that suit must be hotter'n hell," to which Buster nodded heartfelt assent, and dutifully plodded on.

Metaphysicians who speculate in such phenomena could interpret Buster in several ways: some dude (or dudette) wearing a funny-looking bird suit; a pedagogical device to inform school kids about safety when they ride the bus (which was the officially stated reason for Buster's existence); and the interpretation I favor, a payoff.

I was to learn, soon after Buster made his office rounds, that we'd paid well into five figures (in late '70s dollars) for the "concept" of Buster: a Buster coloring book was part of the package. Since your average third-grader could have just as easily invented this concept, Buster had to be a payoff, a legal, lawful way to channel agency dollars to return a favor.

In a like manner, we were offered agency neckties and, presumably for working ladies who espoused the feminine look, scarves ("presumably" because I knew of no male on the payroll donning the scarf, whereas some *avant garde* ladies opted for the tie in lieu of the scarf). These we were issued FREE! Featuring the agency logo in silk and polyester, from a distance they looked snappy and businesslike, and when they were worn with a business suit, they didn't look too bad. Some rah-rah types even wore them to work. I kept my agency tie, and I still have it somewhere. These, too, were a payoff. A downtown necktie dealer who had earned a favor from someone with clout was paid off in this coin: I heard through the office rumor mill that he netted something like $15,000 for his ties and scarves.

So, too, was the agency logo a payoff. A few intersecting squiggles and arrows.

not to ask too many questions about them. At times, ignorance can be bliss.

See also DALEY, ELECTED OFFICIALS, IGNORANCE, PATRONAGE, PERSONNEL OFFICER, PURCHASING, and REVENGE.

POWER AS A CORRUPTING INFLUENCE

Lord Acton said it far more elegantly and eloquently than I ever could: "Power corrupts, and absolute power corrupts absolutely."

Lincoln agreed, "If you want to test a man's character, give him power."

Assuming Lord Acton and Honest Abe knew what they were talking about, it follows that the wielding of power in government agencies will ultimately and absolutely corrupt those who run them (by *corrupt*, I mean, to entice the incumbent to use public resources for personal ends). The logic seems simple: the longer you run your agency, or the higher you rise up the totem pole, the greater the power that the office confers on you, the more accustomed you become to that power, the more you appreciate its use, and the greater the temptation to bend it to private purposes. For many who seek high office, elected or appointed, a major motivation is to attain that power and use it to grab and hang onto as many goodies as possible.

It follows that the appointment of an agency head for an indefinite term (J. Edgar Hoover comes to mind), meaning until someone succeeds in unseating him, will almost always corrupt him, and his view of reality is likely to become increasingly distorted by yes-men and the releases of his press relations officer.

Two questions you might ask when you start work at an agency are, "How long has the head held his job?" and "How much longer is he slated to hold it?" These will give you a valuable clue of how likely he may be corrupted by his position—and what evolutionary stage the agency may be in. In that way, you may better know what cues a manager will respond to, and appreciate the criteria for promotion. Especially if you report to him.

See also AGENCY EMPLOYEES, HOOVER, PERFORMANCE REVIEW CRITERIA, POWER TEAM, PRESS RELATIONS, and YES-MEN.

possesses or controls too much wealth or wields too much power. Their suspicion extends to actors within government agencies. How much power constitutes *too much*? Within an agency's sphere of influence, enough to make relevant publics jealous or uncomfortable, which explains why Congress swiftly enacted laws limiting the tenure of the director of the Federal Bureau of Investigation following the death of J. Edgar Hoover.

In a like manner, within the agency, both institutional and individual behavioral norms have evolved to prevent any single person from gaining too much power. Both people and organizations tacitly (and often actively) collude to prevent this, even when it comes at the expense of "achievement." Collusion renders it difficult, though by no means impossible, to build an empire.

In any event, would-be empire builders take note: count on the other players to tilt the playing field against you as you efforts bear increasing success.

See also COMPETITORS, PERSONAL EMPIRE BUILDERS, and PUBLICS.

THE POWER TEAM

Wake up and pay close attention! This chapter comprises one of the central tenets of this manual. First, though, a necessary preface . . .

By accepting your appointment as agency head, you also have implicitly tendered your undated resignation to whichever chief executive or board or legislative body who appointed you. Remember, you serve *only* at their pleasure. They enjoy the statutory right to terminate your appointment, and if there is political hay to be made by doing so, termination will occur instantaneously, with no qualms whatever on their part. Any Civil Service or comparable job protection that your full-time (unappointed) staff enjoy lies far beyond your grasp. So just that quickly, you can be (or are) gonzo. Outta here. History—if your tenure was noteworthy.

The tenuousness of your appointment points up the need to assemble your Power Team. By Power Team, I refer to a cadre of people in key positions who report and are loyal solely to you. Your Power Team is the engine that keeps you in charge and provides the foundation for your successful tenure. I call it the Power Team instead of the "management team" because the two are as different in task and function as chalk and cheese.

While management is undeniably important, and a couple of key members may hold positions on both teams, it comprises only a part of your job, and maybe a small part at that: in government, power, or more precisely (and more difficult) keeping it, is the name of the game. The trick is to control as many variables as possible on order to preclude or minimize unanticipated problems.

This is not so easy as it may seem. As incoming head, you will likely inherit senior staff who owe their position to the same process that landed you in the corner office on the top floor; you haven't hired or promoted any of them. If they serve at the pleasure of the same appointing agent you do, your ability to promote or terminate them may be limited. In a like manner, you inherit the rest of the agency's work force. You cannot trim staff deadwood, so don't even think about that: the underlings enjoy civil service protection (although I think this holds less for state, county and municipal agencies, where employment and employee safeguards may be a tad less stringent). Because it's much easier to get rid of you than axe them, it follows that in hiring and firing, your administrative latitude is severely curtailed.

Still, there are steps you can take to ensure your term runs uninterrupted and (if possible) uneventfully until its end, longer if possible. And if you plan to keep all those perks that go with being top banana, it may pay you to take them.

Hence the focus on team building. In this realm, the efforts of an agency

their collective job to ensure that if any problems arise from this quarter, they take place on the watch of your successor.

All this leads to the second aspect of team building, the Power Team. Ideally, the effort that goes into building the Power Team should be so subtle and shadowy that its existence goes unknown, even unsuspected, by outsiders and insiders alike. Although its members may rank well up in the agency's management hierarchy, it functions wholly apart from management: *its sole purpose is to keep your butt in the plush chair in the corner office with the picture windows on the top floor.* The Power Team may comprise the most important component of your efforts to retain your tenure. Through its members you can monitor and manipulate every person on your agency's staff; they can project your chosen image to internal and external publics alike, and they can make and take hits on your behalf. At a minimum, this group includes your executive secretary, your personnel and press relations officers, your reporters (a direct extension of your press officer), your outside counsel (if you're smart or lucky enough to have one), your lobbyist (ditto), your mole/stool pigeon (if you're insecure enough to need one), your accountant, your inspector general, your hatchet man and your scapegoat. Each position is described elsewhere herein, and in each case, the person is as important as the position, and vice versa.

For a department or agency head who wants to build a fortress, these people collectively form the bedrock on which to build it.

Notice also that each position on the Team is prefaced not with an indefinite article but with the possessive pronoun "your." The reason behind this should be clear: these key players are *your bananas,* nobody else's. They report only to you, their loyalty (such as one finds it in government) is only to you, and it is to you that they look for protection and reward. In turn, it is to them whom you look for protection against disloyal employees and threats from outside—to identify and purge, or at least ward off or neutralize them. Oh yes, it inescapably falls to you to make them yours—their recruitment and cultivation cannot be delegated. You can hire, earmark or promote each Team member independently of personnel rules and regulations.

The Power Team may never formally meet as a group—it's not important that they do so. In fact, it's probably best that they never do so.

See also AGENCY LIFE-CYCLE, CONFIDENCE, CONTROL, ELECTED OFFICIALS, EXPEDITERS, HATCHET MAN, JUDICIARY, LOYALTY, MANDATE, PUBLICS, and SCAPEGOATS.

If your agency is awarded new or added responsibility, its mandate expanded, unlike anything it has ever done before, what you want to do, in fulfilling this mandate, is seize the maximum possible amount of turf—once you possess it, it's much harder to snatch away. After this comes the constraint: you want to blaze new trails while avoiding the appearance of doing so. You are not a pioneer, and for this task, you neither possess nor desire an ego; you want to follow established custom. As with General Motors and US Steel, "not invented here" is an excellent watchword.

Precedent is wonderful. It is flexible enough to let you say. "Yes! We are doing something new and exciting" (which may be true), and at the same time, it enables you to rest secure in the knowledge that some other agency, somebody else, has trod this path before you did.

Your first task is to survey agencies elsewhere that have faced your problem. The more agencies you survey, the better. Learn how they have approached and solved it, find out the challenges—regulatory, constitutional, even popular—that they encountered along the way. Their experience enables you to go forth and do likewise.

Discovering likely landmines and pitfalls you could encounter along the way is nice; it even may be a real labor saver. But the best reason to follow the herd is to insulate your agency (and you) from blame. If critics claim that your program is a radical, unwarranted seizure of power/turf, you can point in reply to similar programs elsewhere and state with perfect truthfulness that your practices are in full and absolute accord with the current best practices and procedures elsewhere, and (implicitly, any way) challenge them to develop a workable alternative—in other words, put up or shut up. Most critics, especially the media, will accept this pretty much without argument.

And thereby prevent a potentially enormous ape from ever climbing onto your back.

In a broader sense, following precedent can be viewed as an institutional version of the outward buckpass—the most advantageous kind. In citing or following the footsteps of others, actions, even legal decisions, can be justified on the grounds that we are only doing what others do. Best of all, by citing previous authority far removed from your turf, you shift criticism and blame outwardly, to parties far removed from you and your agency.

Sometimes, precedent can be employed as a crutch, a prop to preclude the need to rule or adjudicate a thorny issue on merits. When the Supreme Court, for example, admits allowing itself to be guided by foreign appellate rulings, it not only employs the outward buckpass, but judiciously sidesteps the apparent need to make a constitutionally driven decision.

Precedent can be used to expand turf. "They do it this way in (pick one) Ohio/the United Kingdom/Senegal/tribal custom/the Koranic Codes."

In summary, an elegant, subtle, powerful weapon—the value of precedent can neither be overestimated nor overemphasized.

See also BLAME-FREEDOM FROM, BUCKPASSING, and DECISIONS-MAKING AND AVOIDING.

examination of the agency's publics clearly reveals that those most influential, and therefore those most important, are external.

Perhaps most, or maybe all, of the information about the agency that these publics, including legislative overseers, receive comes to them via the news media. This means that dealing effectively with the media is *the* key task of my external relations officer. Naturally, this makes him a key member of my Power Team, and then some. He is the agency insider's insider: he has to be, because if he is to deflect criticism from the media, then he'd better know where the agency is vulnerable. To do his job, he gets *all* the resources he could reasonably ask for, and he briefs me twice a week, more often if necessary, on media relations.

The PRO functions as the agency's sole authorized contact with the media, the *only* agent who transmits our message to the outside world.* His goal is to ensure that all the news relating to the agency which appears in print or gets transmitted over the airwaves is managed news.

This topic deserves amplification. The point of contact for most information exchanges with the news media takes place between two professionals, one from the media (the beat reporter) and one from the agency (the PRO). Each has been carefully selected for his job, and for both, the trick is to keep this contact between themselves. The beat reporter doesn't want other reporters horning in on his by-line or air-time (journalistic ethics), and PRO seeks to remain the sole conduit for information going outside the agency. His job is to restrict the flow of information to those whom he has cultivated (socialized)—no in-depth briefings for outsiders except in unusual circumstances—and, just as his opposite numbers in the reporting pool seek to exclude others from poaching on their beat, he wants NOBODY else from within feeding information to them.

An ideal press relations officer, says a friend, is paid to have no honor. She might have added more accurately that he's also paid to abandon his conscience—a basic, inescapable (and unwritten) piece of his job description. Beyond this, he should begin to build friendly, lasting, long-term relationships with the fourth estate. He curries favor with beat reporters by producing as much of their material for them as possible, thereby sparing them from having to do so, and, as he secures their appreciation and trust (keeping in mind the adage regarding journalistic ethics), he will keep them up to date on goings-on in the agency, including material not yet in the public domain.

My press relations officer will monopolize the time and attention of all journalists on the premises. Nobody else on the agency's payroll goes near them, much less talks to them—not my lieutenants, not anyone else. Including and especially me. I've not been trained to speak to the media, and I never want to see myself on the six o'clock news responding poorly—they'll have me endorsing drunk driving—to an off-the-cuff query carefully formulated to make me look bad and sound venal, corrupt or stupid. Remember, the media can, and when it suits their purposes, won't hesitate to quote out of context. Smart agency heads swiftly grasp this point: egotistical ones never absorb it.

Along the way, my PRO will learn the sexual preference of those he deals with. He will have the budget to reward those who cooperate by indulging them (what better leverage over them in a pinch?). He will have socialized them to expect at least one free meal a week and drinks daily (reporters are renowned for their consumption of alcohol), when that fits their schedule.

By all these means, he deftly places the beat reporters on my agency's payroll and keeps them there. His goal is to curtail, to compromise their journalistic independence as much as he possibly can, and to transfer their loyalties away from their newspaper or network, away from their readers or viewers, to him, to the agency, and thus, to me. *In effect, they're now on our payroll. The importance of this process, and its continued success, cannot be overemphasized.*

In return, I expect him to be privy to their stories before they are filed and to be able to delay, change the focus of, or squash outright any piece that portrays my agency or me unfavorably. A good press officer can take a lemon of a story and spin it into lemonade. Of course, if (God forbid) a media frenzy occurs, all bets are off. But his job is to prevent that from occurring.

It's also understood that although he speaks for the agency, the PRO does not speak for its head. This subtle distinction ensures that if he misspeaks, he can claim he was misinformed. And *he* takes the hit. If I voice some horrible, idiotic bozoism on videotape, I could claim so, too—except who'd believe me?*

I also want my media man to learn promptly if our beat reporters receive information from unauthorized sources within the agency, together with the name

his ire against the agency in print or on the air. One way to prevent this is to treat a reporter as a knowledgeable insider and, in effect, grant him *de facto* membership on the Power Team. From here, he has a greater stake in what happens at the agency, and he will be more inclined to treat unfavorable breaking news involving the agency sympathetically—or not at all.

As agency head, the loyalty of the PRO is to me *and only me.* The sensitivity of his position confers him with a singular ability to cause the agency—and therefore me—grievous harm and renders any other arrangement untenable.

One day the beat reporter from a big city daily who covered our agency exercised independent action and actually dug up a story. Were it published, it would have portrayed the agency most unfavorably.

Fortunately, our PRO had done her groundwork well, having previously socialized the reporter to show her the story before he filed it. Which he did.

---

* Caution: Danger can accrue from pairing an able press relations officer with a weak agency head, especially if the head believes all the good things he reads about himself. After all, it appeared in the newspaper, didn't it? Under these circumstances, the natural temptation of the press officer is to exploit his advantage (press relations officers are human, too, and a power void doesn't last long) and focus more effort catering to (stroking) the ego of his boss than cultivating the news media. When an agency head begins to confuse stumbling through mud puddles with walking on water, you can be sure he heads an agency whose press officer is stronger than its head. This distorted sense of reality can lead to major problems later.

"You're not going to print that," she told him, just like that.

"Yes I am."

"No you aren't. Instead I'll give you something else, of equal interest. It'll be your exclusive and under your by-line. But you can't print this."

So he didn't.

But, ten days later, under his byline, his paper carried an exclusive interview with the agency's most controversial and, therefore, interesting board member. Personality profile, interesting quotes, great fluff—a saleable human interest news piece. This was the *quid pro quo.*

This incident illustrates the work of a fine PRO. Everyone was happy; the chairman and the agency were spared unfavorable press; the reporter filed an exclusive story that pleased his editors; the reading public never knew what it missed but still received something to whet its interest; the relationship between reporter and press officer remained close and productive; and presumably, his supply of food, booze and other incidental favors continued uninterrupted.

This feat of PR legerdemain occurred only because of the careful, prolonged cultivation of the beat reporter by our PRO. It could not have been pulled off otherwise. Also, and note this well, she never tried to con the reporter, never tried to pretend the story he unearthed had never happened or that he had got it wrong. Instead, she hustled to substitute a story of equal news value for the story he didn't file, and she guaranteed him an exclusive, which in an important sense validated his earlier effort. In that way, the working relationship between press officer and reporter (alternatively, between agency and the media) continued to be (from the agency's perspective) highly productive, characterized by good will and mutual respect.

––––––––––

Twenty years ago, the Commander-in-Chief of the Navy's Pacific Fleet was asked to resign. Why? Because in the aftermath of a *foreign* civil rape trial of three of his most junior enlisted men, he foolishly remarked to reporters that the guilty sailors could easily and more cheaply have procured the services of a prostitute. While his assertion was factually correct, it couldn't have been more politically incorrect. The ensuing howls from the media, women's groups and elected officials over his thoughtless pronunciamento truncated his career.

This was totally needless—and stupid. If he'd only let his PRO talk to the media about this piss-ant matter, his career would have survived intact.

––––––––––

A newly appointed agency head, whose engineering background bore at best tangential congruence with the field his agency occupied, found himself described by an agency press release as an expert in his adopted field. A man of flawed ego, he readily believed what his PR Department said about him. So thereafter, he billed himself as an expert—even though his exposure to the field was less than three years, and only in an engineering capacity.

During a particularly nasty winter, the press officer at a Midwestern transit agency showed up early Monday morning in the agency's hastily constituted Snow Operations Center, where two professionals kept tabs on morning rush-hour snow delays. A popular radio station called in to ask for an hourly status report.

"Ooooh! That's my job," said the press officer. "*I'll* talk to them. Give me the phone." She snatched the receiver from the hand of one of the staffers.

"Are there any delays on the Northern commuter railroads?" asked the radio deejay. Live. A reasonable question, exactly the sort of query the Snow Office had been set up to answer.

He might as well have asked a wino for an informed opinion on an obscure conundrum in theoretical astrophysics: the press officer hadn't the foggiest idea of the answer. In fact, she barely knew what he was talking about—where the railroads came from, and ran to—because she had never troubled herself to find that out. "Oh, umm, errr . . ." was the best she could manage. The two staff pros, no doubt thinking, "Well, babe, if you want to do our job it's all yours!" just looked straight ahead. No help from this corner.

"How are trains running on the Western railroads?"

She didn't exactly hit this one out of the park, either.

"Well, how about the Southern lines?"

No answer. An interminable silence. To station listeners and to the deejay, that agency didn't really seem on top of things that morning.

No agency can long endure this incompetence in such a key post. The job requires someone who knows what to say when a reporter thrusts a microphone into his face; who can answer the easy, straightforward questions (like these) with straightforward ease; who knows when to dissemble, when to play for time. In short, the job demands a pro.

Not surprisingly, following this and similar incidents, this lady received her walking papers. Saddest of all, when (to the relief of everyone but her) she was finally sacked, she burst into tears—she really had no idea how poorly she had been performing.

See also COMPETITION, CORRECTNESS-POLITICAL, MANAGED NEWS, THE MEDIA-ACHIEVING CONTROL, THE MEDIA-SOME THOUGHTS, MEDIA FRENZY, NEWSLEAKS, POWER TEAM, PUBLICS, VACUUM, and YES-MEN.

no agency wants competition from that quarter; in fact, it wants no competition at all. It seeks to reserve solely for itself the power and perks that go with running its program. Ours is a government monopoly.

Research has uncovered two reasons (incentives may be a better word) to privatize. Since privatization inevitably means loss of funding, it is not surprising that the first is fiscal: funds grow scarce relative to expenditures—spending has outgrown the current revenue stream, or revenues or authorizations have taken a hit, or both. Either way, trouble . . . and the P-alternative crops up.

The other reason is a second P—patronage: when elected officials run out of agency jobs in which to park their friends, their incentive to maintain the agency's authorization stream drops considerably. This poses a much bigger problem, because it means that the agency's Prime Public no longer has any use for it. However, this is much less likely to take place, because no politician can ever have too many patronage jobs to reward his friends and followers.

There may be a few catches to privatization:

- First, if the services which some would privatize are so badly needed, companies would have provided them in the first place.
- Then, after a company contracts to supply privatized services, what incentive does it have to constantly seek to improve them? After all, having just bought it, the company now holds a government-conferred monopoly for this service, and it will almost certainly begin to act like a monopolist.
- Worst of all, once a company becomes entrenched in its franchise, it will be difficult if not impossible to dislodge. It will speedily learn to manipulate the system for its own ends, developing many of the skills and perfecting many of the techniques listed herein to become, in essence, a corporate hanger-on—or a government agency in corporate guise. Moreover,

dealing with (read controlling) companies, especially those that develop advanced hanging-on skills, may prove to be most difficult, as a career staffer in any regulatory agency will testify.

So privatization is an idea which should be fought, opposed, resisted, and stonewalled at every turn. Its backers within should be mercilessly purged from government service.

A far better idea is partnerships.

See also AGENCY, AGENCY EMPLOYEES, BUDGETS, COMPETITION, CONTROL, CUTBACKS, ELECTED OFFICIALS, GOVERNMENT MONOPOLIES, HERETICS, INERTIA, PARTNERSHIPS, PATRONAGE, and TURF.

the rules and, most of all, this means process. What private sector denizens would term the actual *results*, the bottom line, are to agency employees mere by-products of the process, not the end in itself.

This focus holds for the legislation by which consensus is achieved politically and through which the agency's legislative mandate comes into being; it holds equally for interagency projects and programs; it even holds internally among all departments which must interact (cooperate) to bring a program or project to fruition. Once they have received the go-ahead, process is part and parcel of program management—fill in the forms and move 'em along to the next station. The focus even extends down to distributing benefits to recipients—all process. Where the few exceptions exist among agencies and departments, the underlying tendency, the overwhelming tendency, is to convert them to process as soon as possible.

By definition, finding, building and obtaining consensus, gaining a written working agreement to which all parties and participants assent, is slow and tedious. If the agreement is not in writing, it's worthless. When you cut the crap, this activity is the quintessence of statecraft, of governance, the sublime *raison d'etre* of government. All agency work is process, there is nothing else. So if you are impatient, looking for the proverbial quick fix, you would probably be happier working somewhere else.

For government agencies, process isn't just the bottom line; it is the only line.

See also AGENCY LIFE-CYCLE, BUREAUCRACY, HIERARCHY, MANDATE, PAPER TRAILS, PIPELINE, and PROMISES.

"PROGRESS"

Two thoughts:

Claimed with far greater rapidity and frequency than actually occurs.

You will never get in trouble by claiming it.

See also CODE WORDS, *IPSE DIXIT,* and PROMISES.

has imposed on corporations, Leavenworth would overflow with former senators, congressmen and mayors, dog-catchers and presidents. Campaign promises really mean "tell 'em what they want to hear," no matter how convoluted or impractical or stupid the idea. Besides, the best politicians invariably leave themselves an out.

No, you discount the promises of elected officials. An important exception: when they are made with great emotion, usually anger, out of a desire for revenge. Then, hope and pray that you are not the object of their wrath—*Don't make no waves.*

What of promises of appointed officials? Verbal promises and commitments made by agency heads and staffers are likewise made only to sound good—or convincing—and are intended to be kept only when it suits the needs of the promisor. Why? Because they're not in writing, they're not on the record and thus, are subject to denial.

Treat all promises by anyone in public service with the expectation that they'll be broken, and you'll never be victimized by a broken promise. If there's any question about someone's word (i.e., if his actions diverge from his promises), one would do well to recall the old saw that deeds speak, if not louder, then far more eloquently than words—though paradoxically 96 percent of the time words are accorded more credence. One exercise that can be most revealing is to list for each issue both what someone promised and what he actually did (if the public subjected elected officials to this scrutiny, the ranks of incumbents might be severely diminished. Fortunately, this seldom happens).

Counter-intuitively, you may get into trouble if you keep your promises. If you consistently deliver on your promises, you'll probably stand out from your peers, but then you risk becoming the object of sanctions for making them look bad. It follows that it is best to avoid making promises altogether ("don't make no waves"). That way, nobody can later accuse you of breaking them or seek to punish you for delivering on them.

It follows that if you extract a commitment from someone, get it in writing.

If you must promise something, do so without great fanfare and give yourself plenty of leeway to carry out your commitment. The most advantageous promises to make—and to honor—are to parties outside the agency, since they are less likely to punish you for delivering. Also, if you can, make it a point to deliver. Many promisors don't.

The best promise of all is the one you never made!

See also COMMITMENTS, ELECTED OFFICIALS, GRESHAM'S LAW, PAPER TRAILS, and THE PUBLIC.

cannot perform effectively) because doing so relieves them of one of life's basic requirements: responsibility for their actions and, increasingly, their lives. More and more, Americans seem disinclined to take responsibility for the most basic things in life; they shrink from it and happily slough it off on their government. Maybe they confuse relief from responsibility with freedom from responsibility.

In any event, demand for relief has increased steadily since the Great Depression; since then, government at all levels—federal, state, county, municipal, regional—has been a growth business.

Despite their demands, Americans resent the inevitable intrusion of government into their lives. Certainly, their feelings toward it are generally devoid of gratitude. Once they get used to sucking the government tit, the weaning process is as difficult and painful as kicking a drug habit, maybe more so. I believe its "clients" love and hate government for this. They love it for feeding their addiction—everybody loves Santa Claus, even non-believers. Yet for its attendant long-term cost in self-esteem and self-reliance, they also mistrust it—deep down, junkies despise their connection because they know all too well what he is doing to them.

But it goes beyond that. Citizens who are self-sufficient (i.e.,—those whose tax payments net out higher than the transfer payments they receive) resent or envy those getting a free ride as much as they hate government for supplying the vehicle. Most of all, they deeply resent having to pay for both.

This leads to the following thoughts regarding the general public:

One, they *want* to be governed. Increasingly, they want to be told what to do, so they can avoid responsibility for the most basic aspects of their lives. It follows that agency employees get to choose what's best for the public; that's what they get paid for. The public may not like this; in fact, they may resent it and hate and vilify staff who serve the public (and run their lives), but that's too bad: they can't have it both ways. Besides, power seekers are drawn to a vacuum.

Two, they *need* to be governed. And only agency staff (with an assist from academics and the media) really know what's best for them. The thought of an ignorant public (Exhibit 1: look whom they elect to office. Exhibit 2: the mindlessly screaming people in the street spotlighted on network TV morning shows) exercising the slightest shred of self-determination presents a truly frightening specter.

Third, the public deserve the government they get and get the government they deserve. Voters who again and again elect indifferent representatives to office have to be themselves indifferent to the services they receive, and they should be thankful (to their agency benefactors, of course) that they receive any service at all. As an agency employee, there is little you can do to change either of these facts of life—although many try.

Fourth, hopefully many of the public already grace the rolls of your agency, which means that you control them. Treat the remainder more deferentially than other agency publics since they represent an opportunity to add to your rolls. This gives you a special interest group who can be guaranteed to remain in your corner, regardless of how the agency performs in carrying out its mandate. And finally, recall that the public, although they are fickle, suspicious, ignorant and ungrateful, and forever seeking something for nothing, pay the bills—your salary—through their taxes. Because they exercise ultimate power of the purse strings, it does not pay to stir them up unnecessarily, even if they seem indifferent to the services they receive—or, more likely, take for granted. Therefore, even the most disgruntled, hostile citizens should be handled with kid gloves, accorded the utmost courtesy and respect—unless, of course, your agency separates them from their cash, like the IRS or municipal parking authorities.

See also ACADEMICS, AUTHORITY, COMPLAINTS, ELECTED OFFICIALS, GOVERNMENT AS GOD, GOVERNMENT EMPLOYEES, THE MEDIA-SOME THOUGHTS, NATIONAL INCOME ACCOUNTING, PUBLICS, SPECIAL INTERESTS, THEORY OF THE AGENCY, TAXES, TURF, and VACUUM.

From time to time, an important and lawfully mandated (and therefore unavoidable) public meeting or hearing will arise, one that gives host to a potentially incendiary issue, threatens the credibility of the agency and, worse, the tenure of its head. Such meetings are incomplete without a roomful of vehement, vocal protesters and the ever-present media, who feed off controversy and therefore constantly strive to create and intensify it.

As agency head, you know that at the least your agency stands to take a major PR hit, squarely on the chin. At the worst, it could ignite media frenzy. What can you do to protect your agency and, more important, yourself?

A time-tested tactic has been devised to meet this threat to diffuse, or at least dampen pyrotechnics and thereby head off unfavorable publicity.

First, you will have set the stage long before. For starters, designate and set aside at your agency one single Official Public Meeting Room, in which you stage all public meetings, public hearings, board meetings and the like. The day before the potentially incendiary meeting, have your janitorial staff prepare the Official Public Meeting Room for its regularly scheduled bi-annual painting: gather the furniture in the center of the room and cover it with drop cloths, have tarpaulins over the floor, and start—but don't finish—slapping paint on the walls. They can finish painting tomorrow, the day of the meeting. Don't fool around with latex-based paints that dry in two hours, either. Instead, use a strong-smelling, oil-base paint, the kind you thin with turpentine and takes two days to dry; it will give a pounding headache to anyone who breathes the air within for more than five minutes. This way, if an outside busybody actually enters the room, the paint fumes will overpower him and he can testify that yes, the room is out of service and no, it cannot be used today. On the day of the appointed meeting, turn loose the janitorial staff to finish the job. This will preclude the use of the agency's Public Meeting Room for the day.

Now, the meeting will have to be held in a smaller room, one with limited capacity for the public and the media. And you still cannot be accused of denying access to the public. Before the proceedings start, pack the seats with staff who have been carefully vetted—sanitized—and briefed to act absolutely neutral, to do nothing and say nothing, no matter how incendiary or abusive any protest might become. Seemingly bored participants make poor visual images on the evening TV news. Have your staff already seated all around the room so that a) blocks of protesters cannot cluster together when they enter and b) little available space remains for attendees from the public or the media (you have to let a few in for form's sake).

Finally, have a certified city building inspector, along with city policemen, present to take attendance for fire code purposes. When the building inspector rules that the capacity of the room has been reached, nobody else enters, and the presence of the policemen guarantees that his rule holds: the fire code must be observed. No exceptions!

If this process is handled correctly, you and your board can control the meeting, or at least prevent things from getting completely out of hand. Demonstrators will be seated randomly around the room, so that the critical mass necessary to achieve an effective visual image is denied them. In this way, noisy, disorderly demonstrations and recriminations will be kept to a minimum, there will be few(er), if any, juicy sound bites to record, and few reporters present to report it. This does not preclude protesters from gathering outside—if they have obtained a demonstration permit—but it keeps massively damaging pictures and news tape of demonstrations inside your agency's offices, in the presence of you and your board, out of the newspapers and off the evening radio and TV airwaves.

Which is what you want.

See also BARRIERS, CITIZEN PARTICIPATION, CONTROL, CUTBACKS, DAMAGE CONTROL, THE MEDIA-SOME THOUGHTS, and MEDIA FRENZY.

Control, 3rd ed., Prentice-Hall, 1976) with whom it directly or indirectly interacts. Okay, what's the big deal?—why bring this up? *Because for any agency, the relative importance of each public orders, in turn, all agency behavior, all its output.** Which makes this another A-List chapter.

With that in mind, these publics are listed in descending order of importance (i.e., of their power and influence and, therefore, potential to harm) the agency head and, secondarily, the agency.

- The Legislative Oversight Committee, which controls agency funding. He who controls their purse strings controls their hearts and souls. This public also includes committee staff, since individual staff members can have as much influence as a committee member. Because this is where an agency's purse strings are held, this public deserves your maximum attention and the utmost respect.
- The Board of Directors. Directors owe their position to raw political clout, not their sunshine personalities. They are appointed by, and should therefore be considered and treated as a special subset of, the chief executive or the legislature. Often, they place their own people on the payroll, and if the agency head is weak, they may deal directly with staff, circumventing the normal hierarchy, even directly calling internal shots—down to and including employee performance reviews (and thereby pay raises) and contracts.
- The Full Legislature. This body passes (and can modify) the enabling and authorizing legislation that justifies an agency's existence. Its members must (and believe themselves entitled to, and because they control the purse strings, they should) be treated with all the respect and deference

---

* Whether agency behavior is ordered in a way the framers of its mandate planned is irrelevant.

that their station in life entitles them. This public also includes their zit-popping staff aides. Together with the oversight committee and board (if any), they comprise the agency's Prime Public.

- The Power Team. Collectively, they only serve as the foundation for the successful tenure of the agency head. It is through them that all other publics are dealt with. One could easily (and arguably) rank them first in this listing. Their importance is self-evident.

- The Media, who gather, report and transmit news concerning the agency to the outside world and constitute an extension of your agency in their own right. Because of their power to focus public attention and galvanize the public into action, they alternately need to be stroked and brought sharply to heel.

- The Financial Community, if the agency has bonding authority. It supplies funds to carry out the agency's mandate, determine the agency's credit rating (and, thus, the cost of funds borrowed), and when its members collectively pass financial judgment on the agency's fiscal performance, the consequences can affect not just the agency but the entire economy.

- Vendors. They can bestow great favor and favors on key internal decision-makers. Often, they are tightly wired in to individual, often key, legislators, inner sanctum members of the Prime Public.

- Special Interest Groups Opposed to, or Regulated by, the agency. These include consumer lobbying and industry trade organizations, and regulated companies and industries. They are bound to have a following in the legislature, the size and strength of which depends either on the number of parties who stand to gain (or lose) or the amount of money that stands to be gained or lost from the agency's actions. Because they can mobilize armies of voters or swing huge campaign contributions to compliant or against resistant politicians, which confers them disproportionately large influence within the legislature, these groups must be recognized and dealt with carefully, and every effort must be made either to cultivate or neutralize them.

- Friendly Special Interest Groups, which lobbied the legislature to authorize the agency in the first place. Unlike the group above, this crowd is in the agency's corner and, as the countervailing force (in the legislature) to their opposing peer groups; every effort should be made to keep them there. With them, the agency should strive to achieve the closest possible hand-in-glove working relationship: they are to be stroked and cultivated for all you're worth, fed inside (non-public) information. Why? Because as zealous *outside* true believers, they function as your unpaid lobbyists. Any and all effort they expend on your agency's behalf translates into money in your budget.

- Other Agencies with which cooperation and rivalry take place. Either way, their existence cannot be denied, and dealing with them—keeping current turf and seeking new turf—will necessarily consume agency resources.
- Members of the Public loosely opposed to the agency or its programs. If

more important, loyal body of alumni cannot be overemphasized.
- Officers of the Employee Union. They must be coddled, and they and their demands must be treated with far more respect than their rank-and-file. Like the media, they can be bought off or otherwise controlled.
- The General Public. In the final analysis, it is through their desire or, more likely, their somnolence, that the agency was created in the first place. Their good will and sufferance, or their continuing indifference, which amounts to the same, allow the agency's continued existence.
- The Professional and Clerical Staff. They are, in the final analysis, a fungible commodity, and their position on the payroll leaves them more susceptible to direct control. One constraint: if they leave, they become former employees, at which point they pass beyond agency control and pose a threat far more severe than when they were on the payroll. The order between this public and the one preceding reverses when the work force is unionized.
- Key Department Managers. If they owe their jobs to patronage, they are almost certainly connected to legislators, also. You sure don't want to lose their loyalty and support. If you do, you're as good as dead.
- The User or Client Public, the subgroup the agency was created to serve (versus regulate). But since the agency is almost certainly their sole service provider, they can wait their turn, thank you. Besides, they're already getting their payoff, so what more do they want?

In one sense the list is misleading: by distinguishing between internal and external publics, it implicitly draws a sharp line between the two groups. However, broadly speaking, many external publics hold an important position on the agency payroll, and they can become players in internal politics and other power games (for example).

By far the most important public is the Prime Public. Except for the Power Team, it exceeds in importance any other by a factor of at least three. The importance of assiduously cultivating this most important of publics cannot be overemphasized.

One might question the placement in the list of two or three publics, and they may move up or down, depending on the relative influence of current pressing issues (for example, if a strike looms, then both the union hierarchy and the employees rise in importance; if the agency must go a-borrowing, then the ranking of the financial community rises commensurately). But over the longer term, I believe the list is accurately rank-ordered and substantially complete.

Finally, assuming this ranking accurate, it should be noted that external relations constitute a far more important, and fruitful, focus than internal relations. This may explain why the most talented senior staff often hold positions in Media or Government or some other field of External Relations. While my observed sample is too small to be statistically significant, preliminary evidence suggests that the most talented agency heads reserve this all-important task for themselves.

Second source confirmation on the accuracy of this ranking comes, aptly enough, from a state social service agency in the following memo, which has been modestly altered to mask its origin:

"INTER—OFFICE MEMORANDUM

From: Departmental Customer Service Coordinator
To: All Departmental Staff
Subject: Customer Service

"A clear understanding of who our customers are . . . is necessary to properly assess the effectiveness of our customer services [*sic*] . . .
[Our customers] are listed below . . .

Our Own State Social Services Agency Staff
—District Office
—Central Office
Competing State Social Service Agency Staff [rival agency that provides complementary services]

Local and Regional Service Agencies
Local, State and National Elected Officials
Consultants [vendors]
Social Service Management Associations [trade associations]
Citizens' and Special Interest Groups
General Public [this agency's client public]"

Each "customer" is listed (no doubt unconsciously) in order of its perceived importance not merely to the writer, a first-level professional staffer, but to her entire department. Note which Customer comes last. In fact, placing the General Public at the bottom of the list seems almost an afterthought.

Assistant Secretary for Clandestine,
Hot and Steamy Affairs
Washington, D.C.

MEMORANDUM

TO: All CHSA Personnel
SUBJECT: Our Congressional Relations

In my recent memo to Bureau personnel, I stressed the importance of maintaining good relations with Capitol Hill. That includes, obviously, senators and members of Congress, but also their staff.

In the event that you didn't see the memo, I remind you how important the Hill's impression of us is. All our hard work can be shattered if we are seen to be less than helpful or cooperative with a staffer.

The Hill is very important to us. Perceptions are frequently reality. I realize that some . . . staffers may be rude. But I expect you to continue to be professional and do what you can to assist the caller in his/her request. If you are not lawfully able to do what the staffer wants, I ask that you explain why as carefully and politely as you can. *If a request is becoming contentious in your judgment, please alert one of the deputy assistant secretaries or me* [Emphasis added]. We will be better prepared to support you if we are aware of the issues in advance of a call from the principal.

I appreciate your continuing efforts to be responsive to the Congress . . ."

Note that contentious requests for service are bucked swiftly up the hierarchy, presumably with notification for those bypassed to managers to come later, if at all. This suspended formality eloquently states the importance accorded congressional staffers. One presumes that similar exhortations appear often at the other offices.

The critical importance of this imputed hierarchy can be neither overstressed nor overstated. One federal bureau head who stubbornly and stridently articulated an unpopular, doctrinaire position on a current hot issue (and, much worse, in the process alienated and offended his agency's funding subcommittee) was rewarded with legislation (a federal law, an Act of Congress) specifically forbidding him from using the executive dining room in his own agency.* Surely, this made him the laughingstock of his agency, and the loss of face he had to have suffered with his agency's rank and file can only be imagined.

A word to the wise . . .

To staffers who mistakenly believe that their government position confers them a higher rank than the general public, one can only expostulate, *consider the evidence!* The Military Airlift Command casually exempted itself from the safety standards to which the Federal Aviation Administration holds commercial airlines, which in part explains the transport plane crash that killed Clinton Administration Commerce Secretary Ron Brown. In 1996, five full years after the fact, the Department of Defense admitted that combat personnel who had participated in Operation Desert Storm had after all been exposed to chemical and/or biological warfare agents which had been released into the atmosphere following the demolition of Iraqi arms bunkers.

Nor is this phenomenon by any means limited to military agencies. A few years ago the headquarters of the U.S. Department of Transportation underwent a thorough cleaning to remove the fungi *Cladosporium, Basidiomycetes, Aspergillus Niger* and *Aspergillus sp.* Concurrently, "working papers" were being tested to determine whether they had been "contaminated with toxigenic or pathogenic fungi." While communications from the Power Team to the rest of the staff emphasized that no hazard existed, workers were nevertheless enjoined to clean with detergent files they removed and returned after their floor was

---

* Presumably, he alienated the staff who actually crafted the legislation—generally, your average senator or congressman has more important matters to attend to, and hasn't the time for this sort of pettiness.

cleaned out, and to repot in "clean" soil any potted plants. These seem eerily reminiscent of the precautions the Desert Storm soldiers would presumably have taken, had they known they had been exposed to chemical or biological agents. It is most ironic that the U.S. Environmental Protection Agency also

See also ALPHA DEPARTMENT, BUDGETS, COMPETITION, CONTROL, INTIMIDATION, CUSTOMER SERVICE, DEPUTIES, EMPLOYEE UNIONS, FORMER EMPLOYEES, LEGISLATIVE STAFF AIDES, LOYALTY, LOBBYISTS, MANDATE, THE MEDIA-ACHIEVING CONTROL, THE MEDIA-SOME THOUGHTS, NETWORKS, PERSONAL EMPIRE BUILDING, POWER TEAM, PRESS RELATIONS, THE PUBLIC, REVENGE, SPECIAL INTERESTS, THEORY OF THE AGENCY, and TRIANGULATION.

PURCHASING DEPARTMENT

If you want to get rich while working in government, this is the place to do it from: the opportunities for bribes and kickbacks are far more numerous and the procedures, far more susceptible to abuse here than in most other areas.

Many agency purchasing agents, I believe, consider kickbacks and gratuities a key perk of the job.

Since procedures don't always prevent abuse, the smart agency head will take steps to insulate himself from any non-standard occurrence in Purchasing.

If you choose to supplement your paycheck in this manner, a single injunction applies: *just don't get caught!* It makes life easier all around.

See also BRIBES and THEORY Y.

Most people assume that to eliminate an employee whose presence you no longer desire, you simply fire him.

But as with skinning cats, there is more than one way to go about this, and perhaps most often, it pays to find some means other than firing to terminate an employee who doesn't perform—or performs too damn well.

First, consider carefully the working constraint: an unhappy ex-employee can cause you no end of grief, and after he's gone, there's little you can do about it. Since he no longer works for you, you no longer control his paycheck, his working conditions, his work assignments, or anything else—your leverage is nil. He, on the other hand, knows your people and, thus, has information pipelines into your organization, and he can use these to exact retribution. Compared to former employees with blood in their eye, Captain Ahab's obsessive pursuit and stabbing of the great white whale seem benign as St. Francis of Assisi hand-feeding birds and squirrels. Vengeful agency alumni can stick it to an ex-boss (who may be totally oblivious to their actions) literally for years—I know; I've seen it.

To minimize risk from this quarter, when someone leaves your organization, for whatever reason, it is in your best interest to insure that his last impression is a happy one. Go out of your way to make it so.

Simple firing is in order if and only if the victim has violated the rules or procedures of the agency or the laws of the land, and termination of employment is both required by the rules and expected by everyone involved—including the victim. Neglecting to do so puts the official responsible for termination at risk for not performing what amounts to routine paperwork with all the opprobrium that failure to complete it engenders. If you haven't the stomach to carry out this rite, then delegate it to your Hatchet Man. Inform the victim that as a consequence for being caught, agency rules/government statutes, require prompt dismissal for the offense (note the wording: it is carefully chosen to take the firing official completely out of the play, making the rules, not the messenger, the causative agent for the act. No personal pronoun even creeps into the verbiage.) Why such care over the wording? Risk aversion: you don't want the guilty party to leave thinking you fired him: better to leave in his mind the notion that the system did the deed. *Don't make no waves.*

What can you do with someone in a critical position whose performance isn't merely subpar but costs your organization—and you—points that neither party can afford to squander? Or, someone too competent who shows up everyone else in the shop? To fire the offender requires an enormous amount of effort and paperwork, and unmistakably signals to the party (unless he's extraordinarily stupid and out of touch) that you're out to sack him, an action that can only turn him into your enemy—more of whom you don't need; you have too many of them as it is.

A tried and true alternative is the Up-and-Out Procedure, by which the underperformer is promoted into an outside position in which his lack of competence becomes apparent to everyone, and if action to terminate his employ must be taken, that burden falls on someone else's shoulders. This is a variation of the Outward Buckpass—pass the problem person out of the agency and saddle him on an outsider. But your skirts, or kilts, are clean. Make no mistake: you are out to float your turd in someone else's punchbowl, so best the offender be floated into a punchbowl outside your agency. That way, neither your boss nor any other internal manager can blame you for inflicting your cull on him.

This method works equally well with super-competent employees, people who outperform all others in the shop (up to, and including, an insecure boss) and thereby show them up. Such people can cause enormous dissension because their less competent peers view them only as a threat. Assuming the work will still get done (only slower), the super-competents, and you, are far better off when they are no longer around.

A variation on the Up-and-Out ploy: arrange for someone marginally competent whom you no longer desire or can't afford to have around, but do not wish to risk firing outright. Burdened by his added (and, perhaps unfamiliar) responsibilities, the victim's nonperformance will quickly become apparent to everyone, and his rivals and subordinates (whose security will be threatened by his incompetence) can be counted on to tear him apart much more swiftly and effectively than you ever could. He then can be (reluctantly) terminated with little risk to you. Note, though, that you merely *arrange* his promotion; you do not promote him. That job falls to your Hatchet Man. When the incompetent must be notified of his impending demotion or (much better) termination, your Hatchet Man draws this assignment, too. In this way, your skirts are clean—you neither promoted the incompetent nor fired him. If other benign possibilities, such as early retirement, or any other means of engineering for the undesired presence a happy, gentle landing, do so.

Another less benign option: ice him in the agency's Siberia—transfer the offender to the Omega department. Here no one can reasonably expect to see or hear from him again.

Perhaps the most brutal way to signal an employee that his presence is no longer desired is to systematically strip him of perks and duties. If the former won't get him to leave voluntarily, the latter almost certainly will. You can exclude him from meetings, you can reassign his work to others, you can reduce or eliminate his

Street Journal (not, incidentally, in *Public Administration and Development*), entails sending an unwanted presence to the agency shrink: the manager of a Tennessee Valley Authority nuclear plant sent an engineer who questioned a proposed new security procedure to the agency psychologist. The engineer, who was subsequently fired on grounds of unfitness, relates that she was subjected by the shrink to a series of hostile, adversary interviews. ". . . she was questioned about church attendance, how much she missed her husband when he traveled and whether she had ever had more than $100 of unpaid parking tickets . . . ." (The *Wall Street Journal*, March 20, 1996).

For this procedure to work best, your agency needs a shrink on retainer or on the payroll, and just as with your Personnel Officer, the shrink must be *your* shrink. In fact, your personnel officer must be party to these proceedings, and it may pay you to consider the shrink a distant member of your Power Team.

The beauty of the technique: the unwanted employee bears the burden of proving he isn't unfit. Also, with a little luck, the word of a shrink should be sufficient to bypass most employee job protection safeguards. Because this technique seems so extraordinarily promising and powerful, why limit it to nuclear workers?

One final thought: if you set out to get rid of somebody, follow through and make sure he is dead (organizationally speaking, of course), and I mean with a stake driven through his heart—gone and off both payroll and property. Too often, such people are merely demoted, and they sulk around, stalking the halls, looking for work to disrupt or plotting revenge. Wounded tigers are only trouble.

See also BLAME STRATEGIES, BUCKPASSING, CONTROL, DEVIL'S ADVOCATE, FORMER EMPLOYEES, HATCHET MAN, HERETICS, INTIMIDATION, ISMS, PAPERWORK-ROUTINE, PERSONNEL OFFICER, POWER TEAM, PUBLICS, REVENGE, SAYING NO, SHOWING UP, and WOUNDED TIGERS.

QUESTIONING

Government employees believe, or profess to believe, that the job they perform each day is founded in good works, that the *raison d'etre* of their agency is therefore rooted in good works, and that their stated desire to do good justifies the continued existence of their jobs, their programs, of the agency itself. Regardless of what actually gets accomplished.

To question this belief out loud is to cast aspersions on one of the most tightly held, sacred canons of government service, much like a minister or rabbi publicly doubting the existence of God. And on the same order.

Thus, one can be extraordinarily, even criminally incompetent, but it's OK because his motives are pure. And somewhere along the line, presumably (though, alas, not positively) some good has been accomplished, someone has been helped, and the resultant effort has *made a difference*.

This thinking also holds for an agency mired in Stage 5 or 6 . . .

Anyway, that's what people like to think. And thinking thus gives them great comfort.

So, regarding questioning, don't. Or at least, not out loud: keep any questions to yourself. To do otherwise is to risk being branded a heretic. It is well to recall how the Catholic Church reacted to Luther, or the Jews, to Jesus . . .

See also GOVERNMENT AS RELIGION and HERETICS-PURGING.

propounded by their ivory tower teachers. When their ideas, and they, seem too radical, too far out, that testifies eloquently to the quality of their indoctrination, but there's a downside.

Committed idealists are strictly self-appointed; they need to be reined in. Firmly. It may pay to treat them like techies—muzzle them. Often, they are so far out in front of the public and the elected officials, to say nothing of their staff colleagues, that few are prepared to listen either to them or their ideas, much less have these turned into policy. This can only lead to losses*, and by now you should know that it doesn't pay to back losers.

If you are a committed idealist, despair not: in three decades, sooner if you're lucky, most of the opponents and critics among the populace and elected officialdom will have died off, and your policies may yet reach fruition.

---

* The backing and appointment by a senior elected official of too many committed idealists can only result in the radicalization of his administration, the estrangement from the mainstream of his political party, a field day for his critics and a potential bonanza at the polls for his rivals at election time.

See also ACADEMICS, INDOCTRINATION, MUZZLE THE TECHIES, and RADICALS.

RADICALS

By radicals, I mean fanatic extremists and zealots whose beliefs lie so far outside the mainstream that their very presence on the payroll could discredit the agency.

Marx happily communed with radicals; Trotsky actively recruited them; Lenin distrusted them and had them closely watched; Stalin shot them.

Clearly, Stalin was a Stage 6 agency head.*

The dividing line between committed idealists and radicals is a fine one. Idealists are OK, though I wouldn't want to build my agency around them, but I'd avoid flaming radicals like the plague. If you find a radical on your payroll, there's more than one way to handle him: purge him, or place him in a slot that precludes any exposure to outsiders.

---

*   A passing note: Stalin ruthlessly used his Power Team to root out and purge radicals. In fact, Stalin used his Power Team as well as anyone I know of. What J. Edgar Hoover represents in First World government, Stalin surely embodies in Second World government.

See also POWER TEAM, PURGING, and SCREENING PROSPECTIVES.

appointed district manager for her agency. He had, from all reports, capably performed the same the job out in a rural area.

But this was an urban, big-city post, and it was much more complicated and demanding than the position he left in the outback. The number and quality of his rivals increased many fold. External relations and the interaction with elected officials, tasks which only required and received lip-service back in the boondocks, were critically important here, and these he neglected. Some time after his arrival, he began to become aware that he had gotten into deep water. Still, he struggled manfully with the job, which he performed in a quasi-competent manner. He decided, or tried to decide, issues on their merits, pushed and promoted reasonably competent lieutenants into key staff and line slots, and while work slowly fell behind, he did the best he could.

Finally, it became apparent to him that he was in hopelessly far over his head. He could not win, could never hope to. And with this realization he metamorphosed right before my friend's eyes. The quality of his appointments changed. Competent performers were passed over in favor of incompetents who would not threaten him with competence or excellence, and of yes-men and sycophants who would stroke his ego and not make him feel uncomfortable. Decisions he initially struggled to make soundly, he now made on the basis of which would pose the least threat or simply avoided. Then the support of key department managers began to flag.

As things become increasingly worse, he is now awaiting replacement by some unfortunate who will have to pick up the pieces (if that can be done) with a staff increasingly riddled with people in key slots who are unable to perform—which is why they were selected in the first place.

I include this observation because I had always assumed that when a key managerial position is filled by someone who was elevated beyond the limits of his effective capabilities, he simply performed at a constant linear (unsatisfactory) level. My friend's observations suggest this assumption may be wrong:

performance may start out reasonably well only to worsen progressively as time goes by. Whether the lower limit of competence is found, or, if the incumbent is moved back into a less demanding position, whether he can recover and again produce satisfactorily—these are not known.

But they'd make excellent subjects for research.

competition into something predictable and orderly. Regulate who can buy certain products and services. Regulate who can sell, and how they advertise, and how they record profits and losses. Regulate the amount of cheese on a pizza, the practices of child day-care providers, and the amount and chemical composition of the smoke that goes up the chimney. Regulate all these and a whole lot more.

The news media overwhelmingly and indiscriminately favor regulation; certainly they employ the term mindlessly and often; they never say what they mean when they use it (perversely, if politicians would protest being held accountable for their promises, imagine the squeals and howls if the media were held accountable by federal "Accuracy in Media Reporting Regulatory Authority," which would only seek to hold their reportage to the same standards of truthfulness and accuracy as, say, the Federal Trade Commission holds their advertisers and sponsors?)*

By now, gentle reader, you may be wondering if you've been set up, and indeed you have. For a civics lesson:

Q. Name a fail-safe way in which a politician can favorably respond to pressure from a strident, vocal special interest and still politically isolate himself from the consequences of his action?

A. Create a Regulatory Authority to manage the problems (not necessarily solve them) and issues, and monitor events in the arena. In other words, *regulate* them.

---

* The media do this as a matter of course with lots of words. For instance, who, or what, is a "socialite"? An airhead who throws a lot of parties? One of the idle rich (e.g.,—the late Howard Hughes)? Or merely someone who gets written up for being seen at parties and other social events?
I don't know, either.

To my knowledge, the regulatory commission is a distinctly American invention, a brilliant extension of the political genius that created our federal system of government. Politicians in countries that employ other systems of government would do well to adapt it to their ends, too.

The creation of a regulatory commission imbues its creators and, later, its overseers with a number of significant benefits:

First and foremost, for doing its bidding, a legislator receives the grateful support of the special interest that sought regulation, which translates into the next all-important installment of gratitude in his never-ending quest for reelection: campaign contributions, votes and, probably more often than we'd like to imagine, under-the-table gifts.

After the Regulatory Commission has been created, our legislator gets the interest group off his back. Better it hound the Commission than him for favors and preferential treatment. With the Commission around, he can safely (without fear of losing votes) respond to complaints and entreaties by telling his petitioner, "Call the Regulatory Commission. They handle these matters now." A legislative version of the Outward Buckpass.

And cushy commission jobs make terrific rewards and payoffs to a politician's friends and supporters. The more a job pays, the more likely it will be filled by a political placement. So if he uses his influence wisely, a politician can place a friend in a high-paying, low-risk lifelong commission job: I suspect it's possible to vege out for life at the FCC (my version of heaven: appointment to a state boxing commission).

By now, even politicians have begun to understand that soon after their creation, commissions ossify to the point where at their best speed and deliberateness, they make a slug seem faster than a greyhound. Thus, they make wonderful targets for media-oriented, anti-commission rhetoric. Commission-bashing reassures their special interest that its boy in Washington holds uppermost the needs of his friends and signals the voters back home that he won't let any Regulatory Commission push them around. [By the way, never think that abolishing the commission enters our legislator's mind. For one thing, the interest group that demanded it in the first place might be ungrateful enough to blame him for its demise and throw its support behind his opponent at the next election—*don't make no waves*. For another, it's far too valuable serving its second real purpose, as a political punching bag that garners the slugger votes back home.]

Oh, here are the political disadvantages I've discovered in voting to institute a Regulatory Commission: none.

What are the implications for working at a commission? Balance two competing interests (the group you regulate and others who gain from their being regulated) and safeguard a third (the primacy of the regulatory authority).

Difficult decisions can be hedged, compromised or deferred (i.e., not resolved). Job security is excellent.

The push to regulate is one of the best friends to agency job security. Do all in your power to encourage it.

Island Railroad) filed for bankruptcy and subsequently went out of business; the company's assets were duly liquidated. A liquidated Rock Island effectively rendered moot the Commission's final decision; in fact, it practically rendered moot any need to even publish the decision.

As a case study in decision avoidance, the Rock Island merger case represents a truly brilliant piece of regulatory work by this, the first federal regulatory agency.

See also AGENCY, AGENCY LIFE-CYCLE, BUCKPASSING, DECISION AVOIDANCE, THE MEDIA-SOME THOUGHTS, and PATRONAGE.

REORGANIZATION: TWO KINDS

Reorganization, the reorganization of an agency, is a highly paradoxical process.

There are two kinds of reorganization. And when any agency is reorganized, regardless of how, you can safely bet that its reorganization will be presented to outsiders in general and the media in particular as the first kind. This is when an agency is slimmed down. Senior staff are reshuffled into slots where either they can perform more effectively, or at least more productively, or moved aside where they don't get in the way and can no longer louse things up. Procedures are streamlined, some may actually be eliminated. These changes could even move an agency back a stage in its life-cycle. All reorganizations are presented this way.

Then there's the second kind. It is characterized by the creation of additional well paid positions, usually reserved for friends and relatives and creditors of elected officials whose strategic place with the party in power opens doors to their employment. Seldom is anyone let go, so another layer of staff come aboard. This may create an additional round of reviews and signoffs. Reorganization of this sort only advances an agency towards or deeper into Stage 6.

Most reorganizations fall into Category Two. "Reinventing Government" could well go down in history for replicating this process on a grand scale—if it hasn't been long forgotten.*

Which leads to the paradox: Most agency reorganizations billed as Type 1 turn out to be Type 2s.

---

* Since from all accounts the Clinton Administration had to live with the phenomena detailed elsewhere in this manual, it was not exempt from their effect. And so, gentle reader, it is left to you to judge for yourself whether government was truly "reinvented."

See also AGENCY LIFE-CYCLE, *IPSE DIXIT*, THE MEDIA-SOME THOUGHTS, and PROGRESS.

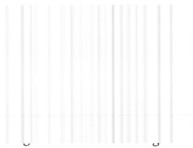

composed equally, and inseparably, of authority—having discretionary command of the resources to do the job, and responsibility—being accountable to one's superiors for how it is done. At many agencies, it doesn't quite work this way.

All too often, one charged with doing the job (awarded responsibility, or maybe more accurately, had it crammed down his throat) without being awarded the authority or the resources to carry it out—authority and resources seldom are crammed down a subordinate's throat.* When this happens, it signifies either a Downward Buckpass or a reluctant delegator, a boss who cannot bear to let authority (i.e.—power) slip beyond his grasp.

If an underling can take some job, do it well and carry it to the point that it begins to assume a measure of importance in a department's or agency's scheme of work, then unless he is masterful at retaining his turf, his authority (but seldom his responsibility) often will be taken over and micro-managed by a glory-starved or insecure boss. Invariably, such a boss can neither bear to see his subordinate recognized nor permit his subordinate, dealing with elected or appointed outsiders, to be accorded his due measure of respect and, more important, credibility with these crucial external publics.

When things go badly wrong, then the reverse is likely: responsibility is swiftly re-conferred by a reluctant delegator on the subordinate, or the subordinate is fingered as his scapegoat. Failing that, there is stampede for the exits; responsibility now is shunned like contact with a carrier of venereal disease. When the Blue Ribbon Panel or the Inspector General comes sniffing around to find out who was in charge, "ain't nobody here but us empty desks."

---

* Along with being awarded resources, the most liberal (complete) definition of authority includes backing the delegate (and thus your awardee) when he encounters unwanted resistance he cannot control—resistance outside the department, for example.

Clearly, Harry (THE BUCK STOPS HERE!) Truman was an anomaly.

See also BUCKPASSING, ENFORCEMENT, LEADERSHIP, MANAGEMENT STYLE, PUBLICS, SCAPEGOATS, and TURF.

Revenge is among the most powerful motivational forces I know in government service. More powerful than getting ahead, more powerful than fleeing failure, immeasurably more powerful than helping others or *making a difference*. Occasionally, more powerful even than avoiding blame. When someone asked a senior congressman (I think Dan Rostenkowski) why he constantly sought to expand his power base, he replied, "So I can get back at all the sons of bitches who stabbed me in the back."

Ah, yes, revenge. How wonderful it is to contemplate! And how sweet it can be!

But return now to reality. In contemplating repaying a disloyal bastard in his own coin, keep in mind that active revenge is a psychic luxury few can afford—even though many actively keep after it. Untempered, the desire to avenge real or supposed disloyalty corrodes the human spirit and consumes a man with anger and bitterness. It can cost him severely—his friends and allies, his effectiveness, even his job. The Arab proverb, *living well is the best revenge*, reflects a well-reasoned, well-seasoned wisdom.

But living well is not so easy as it seems: although many shrinks make a good living trying to convince their clients that they would be emotionally better off letting go their anger and hostility, it remains far more difficult to release these than embrace this wisdom. Still, one is best advised and served by releasing his anger toward the perpetrator, or at least allowing it to cool down. Besides, a schmuck's actions have a funny way of rebounding against him, and with a little luck, the perpetrator will screw himself far more effectively and thoroughly than an avenger can. Being the miserable son of a bitch that he probably knows he is, he has to live with himself.

In their *jihad* to avenge a wrong, the sagest revenge-minded agency employees follow the advice of Brother D-Day (of the film *Animal House*), "Don't get mad. Get even!" Getting even is best done when the quarry can't fight back (kick him when he's down). One tried and true way is to wait until he gets into hot water. Only an emergency can be counted on to galvanize a staff more quickly than a disloyal colleague who has run into trouble. Thus, an excellent gauge of how many enemies someone in trouble has made can be determined from the number of knives that collect in his backside after the onset of his problems, when he's unable, or less able, to defend himself. These usually come under the heading of additional troubles that suddenly beset the embattled one.

Not only, to quote an old adage, is revenge a dish best eaten cold, but getting even is best done when it is carried out covertly. When retribution comes as a bolt out of the blue, the quarry is less likely to know where his misfortune came from, and less likely to visit the same on you—again—later on.

Practically speaking, one who runs roughshod over his colleagues can expect most of them to harbor thoughts of revenge. In fact, the threat it poses constitutes a prime rationale for getting rid of (versus demoting) a rival or an incompetent.

My working model of revenge: if I happen to be sighting in the target scope of my loaded elephant gun, and by happy coincidence a sworn enemy crosses my field of vision, when he comes smack in the crosshairs, I am willing to squeeze off a couple of rounds to test the accuracy of the scope.

Note well: This assumes sheer dumb luck on my part, sheer coincidence; not me relentlessly stalking the victim.

See also BLAME-FREEDOM FROM, DALEY, EMERGENCIES, FORMER EMPLOYEES, INTIMIDATION, PURGING, and WOUNDED TIGERS.

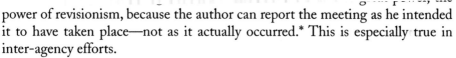

power of revisionism, because the author can report the meeting as he intended it to have taken place—not as it actually occurred.* This is especially true in inter-agency efforts.

Moreover, once the minutes have been circulated for review, it is much more difficult to have them changed or amended—especially if your department didn't write them or if they report as fact its diametric opposite.

From this, it follows that as much care and attention should be given to reviewing as to writing the minutes of a meeting, especially if your department didn't originate them. Otherwise, you may find yourself in writing and on the record obliged or assenting to commitments that you never made.

By producing the meeting minutes, their author may also confer himself another source of power—especially if he or his department weren't initially responsible for the project or program. If he quickly distributes the meeting minutes with his imprimatur, he has not only aced those nominally responsible, but he has effectively taken control of the process, and he may take over the whole project. Clearly, a powerful offensive ploy. The countervailing defensive ploy: if you are charged with running any program, *you* swiftly produce and distribute all meeting minutes, and thereby insulate your preserve from this manner of poaching.

Best bet: make it your responsibility to produce the minutes. This may be a minor pain, but it is nothing compared to the annoyance of fighting a perpetual battle over their content with someone you cannot control. And if they have a problem with the minutes, they must come to you.

---

* Revisionism, Marxians teach us, is to be hated and feared. Unless you are the revisor.

See also CONTROL, CREDIT STRATEGIES, *IPSE DIXIT*, PAPER TRAILS, PERSONAL EMPIRE BUILDING, and TURF.

RITUAL

Ritual fills the corridors and offices, even the work programs, in each and every government office. It encompasses many little acts most take for granted in day-to-day office protocols. Little things like modes of address. Employees greet the agency head with either "Good morning, Sir," or, if they're far enough down on the totem pole, "Good morning, Mr. Chairman." He will greet them in turn: "Hello, Jim" to a close subordinate, "Good morning, Smedley" to a subordinate further down whose name he knows, to just "Good morning" to the clerical people. Clerical staff don't even rate a name, and interpersonally incompetent agency heads ungraciously refuse to acknowledge their presence with any greeting at all (among government agencies, only the uniformed military require that a superior return a salute or greeting). The subordinate initiates the greeting.

Similarly, in written communications, a memo to multiple addressees usually lists them in decreasing order of rank or importance. Letters to influential outsiders acknowledge their clout with such honorifics as "The Honorable," "Mr. Chairman," "Mr. President." The proper salutation of a letter from a federal agency to a congressman is "Dear Mr . . ." but to a senator, "Dear Senator . . ." Many sign a letter to a superior "Very Respectfully;" to a subordinate, merely "Respectfully."

On a few moments reflection, one can doubtlessly think of more examples. These protocols almost certainly trace their origins back to the Middle Ages, even ancient times.

What purpose do they serve in a First World government agency that has just entered the Twenty First Century?

To continually condition and reinforce, subtly, but nevertheless physically and psychologically, the levels in the hierarchy and the importance (and the power) of key outside publics, and, perhaps more important, to ensure obeisance to the people at the top of the ladder. Internally and externally, ritual is the handmaiden of power.

That, you must agree, is a timeless reason. And it explains why department heads get testy if outgoing correspondence is mis-addressed.

See also HIERARCHY, RULES AND PROCEDURES, and PUBLICS.

and procedures will guarantee their observance, then you've been living on one of the outer planets.

The staff obey the most niggling rules and procedures about the way most Americans observe the tax laws or obeyed the fifty-five mile-an-hour speed limit: they often ignore them. In the 1980s. when 55mph was mandated the national speed limit by congress, if you took a ride at 55 on an Interstate or other well engineered highway, you could watch most traffic sail past you. More important was how diligently the cops ticketed speeders. Usually (and I concede that there are exceptions—I've experienced them first hand), a violator had to be traveling at least 10 mph over the limit to attract attention from the average gendarme.

It is human nature to test posted limits. A colleague remarked when an old (and oft ignored) procedure was heavily publicized, "After three weeks nobody'll pay attention to it. If they really wanted people to observe it, they'd stiffen the penalty." Of course, he was right.

So why the procedures, why all the rules and regulations, especially when nobody observes them? After all, they only serve to divert time and energy from more important pursuits.

My answer is that these exist for two mutually reinforcing reasons. First, few are naive (or stupid) enough to believe that publishing and promulgating rules intended to curtail undesirable behavior will so result; the rules may inhibit that behavior, but they won't prevent it entirely. Still, the process of identifying and promulgating rules and regulations and procedures constitutes one of the most important fundamental tasks facing the agency and every manager. Based on an absolute lack of trust in the employees, it is an advanced, though little understood form, of institutional ass-covering that is vitally necessary to the survivability of the agency and senior staff.

Very simply, by having all those chickenshit rules and Mickey Mouse procedures, the agency and, by implication, its senior staff, are insulated from any and all transgressions of its staff from every possible source of blame, ranging from (figuratively) spitting on the sidewalk to felonious assault. Senior management knows full well that placing the up-to-date rulebook (rules MUST be printed and in the hands of, or readily available to, all employees) doesn't prevent the offensive behavior they specifically refer to. Far from it. But if the rules have been promulgated, they don't care when a violator is caught: they can point to the rules he ignored, chapter and verse. Their skirts are clean. The blame stops THERE.

An added benefit: these rules afford the means to dismiss for disobedience anyone whose presence is no longer desired.

In this way, no outsider, no competitor, no one on the legislative oversight committee, no member of the news media—nobody—can accuse the agency head and senior staff of running an agency where the climate encourages violation.

Which leaves them free of blame. And that is a big deal.

The second reason for all those rules and procedures is to ensure that in the event of a conflict each successive level of management will always enjoy primacy over the one below it. The higher-up is always right. If you seek to overthrow the established order from within or hope to cause the dismissal of an incompetent or a rival in the rank above, don't hold your breath. Procedurally, the deck is always stacked in favor of the existing hierarchy, especially the Power Team against any single staffer—or group of staffers.

And this is by design.

See also BUREAUCRACY, HIERARCHY, POWER TEAM, PURGING, RADICALS, and THEORY Y.

about .667: two-thirds of the time it's right on the money.

Pervasiveness and accuracy make the mill a valuable source of intelligence about goings-on in the agency.

Its ubiquitous presence also renders it extremely difficult to clamp a lid on internal behavior that an agency or department head wishes to keep from becoming known to the staff.

Aware that information can be transmitted as well as received through the mill, knowledgeable game players can use it to advance their own agenda.

See also CONFIDENTIALITY, INTELLIGENCE, and NETWORKS.

SAFETY NETS,
THE IMMUTABLE LAWS OF

———————

Safety nets are agency programs designed (in theory) to distribute shelter, food, clothing, funds; in short, to ensure the subsistence of those most in need. In practice, this process has been altered, expanded to cover a wide range of goods and services that far exceed simple subsistence. The aggressive eagerness with which safety net handouts are embraced and accepted—and expanded—gives rise to the laws that affect their existence.

These laws are assumed to be axiomatic:

Law 1. The Law of Marginal Add-Ons. Once an agency safety net has been established to aid, subsidize, or otherwise distribute largesse, the ultimate size of its user public will exceed the number the program was initially forecast to serve.

By way of explanation, after a safety net program has been implemented, a number of non-qualifiers, parties whom the program was not initially intended to serve, will alter their behavior or modify their status to qualify as recipients. This phenomena, I believe, can be viewed as an extension of the *theory of rational expectations*, which states that individuals or parties whom government fiscal and financial policy stands to harm, in time will come to anticipate any adverse impact and, thus enlightened, they will take steps to insulate themselves, thereby nullifying (at least in part) the intent of the policy makers, and blunting the desired result of the policy itself. In the case of add-ons, individuals who do not, but could, by altering their behavior, qualify as recipients of agency-supplied goodies, will not hesitate to do so if the perceived benefits outweigh their perceived losses from changing their behavior or status. This leads me to restate rational expectations thus: people and parties will alter their behavior or status (e.g., a full-time job holder who receives the current minimum wage may opt to cease work to qualify for welfare) to take advantage in any way—insulate themselves from harm *and seize the proffered benefits*—of announced government policies.

Corollary: it follows that once this phenomenon has been recognized, parties having an interest in obtaining more government-provided benefits will seek to influence (legislatively and through stealthy actions) the means by which goods and services are conferred so as to benefit themselves. In addition to current and prospective recipients, these parties include elected officials and agency staff.

This leads to Law 2, the Law of Width and Depth: the wider and deeper the safety net ~~the~~

~~will coalesce into~~ an interest group to protect their stream of benefits. Once the program metamorphoses thus, few politicians have the fortitude to vote against it. Best of all, the courts overwhelmingly treat the benefit stream as an inalienable property right which, by definition, is constitutionally protected from seizure (i.e., abrogation). The implications (measured in additional authorizations and job security) for the lucky agency created or tapped to carry out safety net mandates should be obvious.

As to the existence, to say nothing of the long-term impact of these laws, program proponents and its user community alike can be counted on to deny, derogate, protest and employ any and all other means to counter-argue their very existence. You should, too, even though you now know otherwise. Also, the media can be equally counted on, and readily enlisted, to publicize counter-claims and support counter-measures (e.g., protests) alike.

See also HIDDEN AGENDA, *IPSE DIXIT*, THE JUDICIARY, THE MEDIA-SOME THOUGHTS, PROMISES, THE PUBLIC, PUBLICS, SPECIAL INTERESTS, and STEALTH.

SAYING NO: HOW TO DO IT RIGHT

This chapter could be subtitled "The Gentle Art of Refusal."

First, three *don'ts*:

- When it becomes inescapably necessary to refuse a request for funds, services, resources or whatever goodies your agency dispenses, no matter how stupid, frivolous or off-the-wall a supplicant's request, never use the first person in your denial message—to wit, never say or write this:

  > "I [or We] regret to inform you that I [we] cannot approve your request of December 25 seeking ABC Agency funds to purchase an island in the Bahamas . . ."

- You don't want to be an actor here; you don't want the party whom you are stiffing even to think a human being stands behind this decision.

- Second, never mention the agency in the text of your refusal. You don't want the agency linked with the refusal, either.

- Finally, as agency head, you never sign a letter of denial. You don't want your name associated with a turndown; you want to avoid being viewed as the Grinch Who Stole Christmas, who is universally detested (you want to be Santa Claus, remember?).

Now, here's how to do it right:

- Make the law, rule or procedure that precludes granting a supplicant's boon the actor, viz:

  > "Federal law specifically prohibits the awarding of federal funds for the purchase or construction of gambling casinos and/or bordellos

beyond the borders of the United States and its territories and requires denial of your request for funds . . ."

or

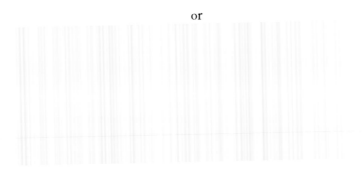

"Federal law . . . requires denial . . ."

and

"Agency policy requires . . . the denial . . ."

Get it? Personal pronouns are avoided. The agency's name never appears. These denials are as impersonal as you can make them—though no doubt with a little imagination they can be improved—yet they carry the full force of the laws and procedures you invoked.

- Lastly, have an underling sign the letter. This job is tailor-made for your Hatchet Man or an out-of-favor courtier.

It goes without saying that the rules and procedures cited must be invoked correctly, otherwise, all is in vain. But deftness here can reap rich rewards.

---

* For the definitive explanation of how to make the procedure the actor, refer to Joseph Williams's classic, *Style: Toward Clarity and Grace*, University of Chicago Press, 1990.

See also HATCHET MAN and SAYING YES.

SAYING YES: HOW TO DO IT RIGHT

If you now agree that there's a fine art to saying *no*, then you might suspect that there might be a preferred way to say *yes*. And you'd be correct.

As you have guessed, saying *yes* is the diametric opposite of saying *no*. Whereas nobody likes the carrier of bad tidings (the Romans, never ones to mess around, executed them), everybody loves the bearer of good news: even non-believers love Santa Claus.

Thus, when your agency awards a goodie, you, as its head, now become the actor: you want to be the person who delivers good tidings. After all, when you're Santa Claus, it can be just as blessed to give as to receive. You want to mention the agency, *your* agency, and you embrace the first person personal pronoun to communicate your happiness over, and support for, your supplicant:

"It is with the greatest personal pleasure that *I* inform you that your request for funds has been approved in full . . ."

As Santa Claus, *you* sign the good news letter. Use the active voice. Better yet, call the supplicant personally, especially for a major award. Call a hoo-haw news conference to announce Christmas in August. If practicable, notify interested members of the Prime Public (especially legislators) of the award so that they can attend the festivities and be photographed—that way, they implicitly owe you one at authorization time. Make your supplicant joyful. Make everybody joyful!

An impersonal *yes* buys you nothing. A personal *yes* message brings you great favor.

See also MARKETING, PRESS RELATIONS, PUBLICS, and SAYING NO.

of, the misdeeds of others, usually higher-ups, thereby sparing important agency *kahunas* from the slings and arrows of rivals and Blue Ribbon Panels, and, more important, allowing senior staff to save face. Indeed, many artful senior staff owe their present exalted station in life to the existence of a scapegoat. If blame must be assigned and borne, then best that someone else bear it.

Two kinds of scapegoats may be encountered on the agency littoral. The most obvious, and most commonly encountered, is the unfortunate who gets stuck with the blame even though someone else was at fault. When that happens, colleagues lower their eyes when the victim passes in the halls, and when his name comes up, voices in the office drop down to whispers. Too often, they know the real story. *Poor bastard, he took the hit for someone else.*

The second kind of scapegoat is encountered less often, and if the 'goat can stand the heat, he may have the most secure job in the agency. Most smart bosses (and make no mistake—some bosses are extremely canny) know that because they are human, they may be prone to an occasional error, even though they never admit it. To bear responsibility for one's errors would be unthinkable: doing so could give their rivals ammunition to use against them; even worse, it could lead to a loss of face.

So someone acts as the resident scapegoat. When things go wrong, he gets the blame. Or if something isn't done properly, the agency head ostentatiously chews out the 'goat for his alleged sin. But aside from bearing the public opprobrium for his alleged misdeeds, he suffers no apparent consequences for them—and you can be sure he will never be canned. On the contrary, he rates a two-step pay increase when salary review time rolls around.

When this happens, you can be sure that the resident 'goat and the agency head have a quiet implicit pact: the 'goat takes the fall in his boss's place and reaps the rewards for so doing. And in the process, he becomes an important figure to have around, perhaps an honorary member of the Power Team.

Unless your psychological makeup allows you to play the role of staff tackling dummy, or perhaps a living sacrifice (not recommended), it's best to avoid being resident scapegoat. In the other instance, careful record keeping and adherence to the principles laid down here will normally preclude having the green weenie aimed at you.

See also BLAME-FREEDOM FROM, BUREAUCRACY, FACE, IF YOU ARE BLAMED, INSULATION, and TASK FORCES.

screening them for too much competence, ambition, independence, intelligence or other qualities which, if they are present in a prospective employee in too great and obvious a degree, will guarantee tension between a weak, hanger-on boss and his eager new worker and result in the worker's resignation or dismissal soon after hiring. Or, a manager knows whom he wants to promote and now must go through the public advertising, internal job posting, interviews and all the other mandatory formalities and window dressing that perpetuate the illusion that a real search has been conducted.

Two excellent tactics have been devised to meet these needs; doubtlessly there are more. The first, which a friend clued me into, entails a pre-hiring screen, one suited equally well for a truly open position (whose future incumbent has not yet been chosen) and a slot for which the future hire is known and so renders the whole process cosmetic.

Let my friend's experience describe this process: He had applied for an important, sensitive staff opening, prominently advertised in a local newspaper. His experience and credentials were relevant, so he was invited in for an interview. He hadn't previously worked at the agency whose staff he sought to join.

What he encountered was an interview in name only—he later termed the meeting "an inquisition." He did not meet his prospective boss. Instead, when he walked through the door, he was presented with a list of four varied and exceedingly complicated hypothetical work situations and given twenty minutes to study them. He was then ushered in to meet a battery of questioners, one from Legal, one from External Relations, one from the Budget Office and a fourth from Personnel (presumably to insure the procedure was carried out according to internal agency guidelines). My friend responded orally to questions pertaining to the four work situations. As he spoke, his questioners furiously scribbled reams of notes. At the end of the session, he was courteously told that he'd soon be informed whether he would be invited back for a follow-up interview.

His rejection form-letter arrived the next day.

The beauty of this technique: not only is the interviewee blind-sided by something for which he is completely unprepared, but he hasn't the slightest idea against what criteria he is being evaluated. It is as blame-free and stacked against a candidate as any procedure could be—four witnesses, four words, against his one if he later complains or sues. And you can be sure that the battery of questioners can—and will—attest that his responses were sub par, that he left uncovered this or that issue, and commit to the record any and all other failures and shortcomings, real or otherwise. Moreover, heretics and independent thinkers can be uncovered; a candidate's brain can be picked, so if a loser has good ideas, these can be employed to benefit the interviewer or the agency. An interviewee cannot, of course, examine the responses or evaluations of rival candidates because these conveniently fall into the category of confidential personnel matters; he can't even see his own. No passed-over candidate can ever learn what the interviewers wrote or reported: in the final analysis, he has no way of finding out whether his questioners wrote down his responses accurately, or even truthfully.

If you get bushwacked by this technique as an interviewee, assume the future incumbent has been selected, that it won't be you, and you are without further recourse; there's nothing you can do about it.

If your agency does not use this screening ploy, I strongly urge you to consider adopting it.

A second technique is much less elegant. It features a probationary period for new hires, lasting from six to twelve months. During their probation, they are exempt from the standard Civil Service or comparable employee protection and so can be dismissed for cause without the usual appeal procedures that tenured, full-time staff enjoy.

In theory, this policy is intended to give the agency the opportunity to identify and slough off non-performers and gross incompetents.

In practice, and equally valid, this policy is employed by weak, insecure managers to cast out any new employee whose superior knowledge, training, education, intelligence, creativity, initiative, competence and professionalism threaten, or appear likely to threaten, them.

[If you are hired under the latter auspices, you are on probation until the period expires. Expect to be closely observed for signs of independence, creativity, initiative, and competence, not only by your boss (and perhaps his boss), but by peers and rivals as well, none of whom want a super-competent colleague around the office to show them up. Passing muster requires that you kowtow obsequiously to your new supervisor. For the duration of your probation, assume the guise of a beta employee. Possible exception: if you absolutely must say anything, limit it to "How pleased/honored/excited [pick any combination] I am to be here." Laugh at your boss's jokes, no matter how stupid, idiotic or tasteless they may be. Be prepared to fetch, sit, roll over, and play dead on command. If your boss proposes the dumbest idea you ever heard, either praise its originality and cleverness (if you have the stomach) or else shut up and give non-verbal assenting cues—nod your head, smile encouragingly.

A friend, battered and bruised, ruefully relates the following saga.

There were three months left in his probation at a federal agency when George (my friend) undertook, naively and on his own initiative, though with the blessing of his boss, to survey morale throughout the agency. A natural mistake for a beginner. Energized by his task, George designed a survey questionnaire, and boldly set forth into offices, corridors and closets to probe employee morale. Staff at all levels were fair game for his queries, and one presumes that the employees whom he approached responded gamely; at least, he obtained sufficient cooperation to complete his survey accurately.

After he had gathered his data, he tabulated it and incorporated his findings into a report. Tables, graphs, ratings for individual departments, the whole megilla. Predictably, his researches disclosed that some departments enjoyed pretty fair morale; at others, morale suffered badly. George's boss, apparently delighted, pronounced his effort the best piece of staff work he'd seen in ten years. *Terrific!*

A few days later, the report was distributed for comment at a weekly meeting of department heads. *The next day,* George was summoned into his boss's office and given two weeks' notice. Summarily. After that, off the premises. No explanation, no appeal. George appealed anyway (here, he had nothing to lose) to his boss's boss, but to no effect. *Sorry! My hands are tied. Procedures are procedures. Nothing we can do. So long!*

What happened? After all, organizations don't usually fire someone out of the blue. My friend was just doing his job, and to judge from his boss's reaction, doing it well.

But that was the problem. His report threatened and, worse, embarrassed (*face*) one or more senior department heads within whose fiefdom morale was extremely low. George, bless his heart, unwittingly had created tsunamis! Given this, the response was predictable and certain: the displeased department heads reacted swiftly and without hesitation, employing the implicit veto that accrues to their rank and seniority to remove him. Because George was still on probation, he could be—and was—terminated for cause. On the spot.

Parenthetically, note the nonexistent support George received from his boss when George's job was on the line. Also, compare the speed of the agency's response here with the speed it responds to, say, *customers*. Finally, note that neither the quality nor the quantity of George's work was at issue—at least, not insofar as a layman might judge: one presumes his survey and report bore all the hallmarks of competent workmanship and were not chock full of errors or otherwise shoddily prepared. Yet that was the problem, all of it.

Ironically, since George was never told why he was being fired—he was merely given notice—he'd never fully understood why he had been terminated, had never put it together. He went on to pursue his career in another agency. Many career agency employees don't understand The Game. As for George—well, now he's older and wiser.

See also ALPHA DEPARTMENT, APPOINTED OFFICIALS, CONFIDENTIALITY, CUSTOMER SERVICE, DALEY, FACE, HERETICS, MORALE, OFFICE HUMOR, PERFORMANCE REVIEW CRITERIA, PROMISES, THE PUBLIC, PURGING, REVISIONISM, UNDERSTANDING THE GAME, and VOLUNTEERING.

In choosing her, I first want someone who is hardworking, professional and proficient at the standard secretarial skills. She, and no unctuous staffer, functions as my assistant: she keeps my tickler files, follows up on assignments, schedules my appointments and ensures I make them; in other words, someone who acts as my shadow and keeps my ass out of trouble. But I want more, much more: someone tough, wise and street smart. Someone whose loyalty toward me is unquestioning, who will support me (like a surrogate wife) through thick and thin, who would put my interests above all others—including the agency's. Someone whom I can trust, totally and implicitly, when my job is on the line, someone who will never stab me in the back and who will safeguard me from those who would. Someone whom I can ask about things going on in the department and get an honest answer. And someone, the only one, who can—and will—tell me, when it's so, when I'm full of shit and need to back off.

Beyond that, I want someone who (though I will not tell her so and it certainly won't appear in her job description boilerplate) will, if it becomes necessary, lie to protect me, also cheat and steal. I want someone who will unobtrusively keep her eyes and ears open among my staff, listening and watching for signs of infidelity, as well as for wholesale disregard of my or the agency's rules. I neither care nor want to learn about niggling rule infringements; I do not want an obvious fink or an office stoolpigeon, because I want people to feel free as possible to speak their mind in front of her, and if she plays the obvious stoolie, nobody will. I also want someone who can unearth goodies (dirt) about other department heads from their secretaries, but give nothing of substance away about her boss—me—unless I authorize her to do so.

Good or even great looks are optional, even irrelevant, as is sex with her, though my ideal secretary would be someone with whom I could feel secure enough to share intimacies. Besides, the smartest managers who succumb to, or indulge in, extra-marital or extra-curricular sensual pleasures do so off the premises and with somebody who does not grace their agency's employee rolls.

And for doing all this, you'd better believe I'll take care of her. In fact, her happiness and well-being are among my most important daily concerns.

The ideal secretary: Rosemary Wood, President Nixon's secretary during the Watergate proceedings. Those who criticized her involvement in the alleged cover-up (she allegedly erased the tapes that could have convicted her boss of criminal conspiracy), I suspect, were jealous that their own secretary might not do the same for them. When the chips were on the table, Ms. Wood protected the boss to the best of her ability. If you're lucky enough to have someone with half Ms. Wood's capabilities, and especially, her personal loyalty, consider yourself many times blessed.

A district manager at a large state agency was promoted into his job from another district. The job was a stepping stone to a senior slot up in Capitol City. He was selected over a division head from within his new district who had also bid for the opening and not only thought herself eminently qualified for, but (ominously for its new holder) entitled to, the post. Needless to say, the selection of an outsider massively displeased her, and her subsequent vengeful, disloyal actions reflected her displeasure.

Soon after his arrival, the district manager made a bad situation worse: he alienated his own executive secretary through interpersonal incompetence.

At least once a week, the spurned, would-be district manager lunched or went shopping with her new boss's executive secretary, the lady who screened his calls, opened his mail, kept his appointment calendar; in short, who, by acting as gatekeeper for his office knew almost as much, in some ways more, about his job than he did. One assumes that over lunch, the secretary passed on to the disloyal division head, who thoughtfully picked up the tab, a lot of information the district manager would have preferred be kept under wraps.

Incredibly, the district manager was unaware of the liaison between his rival and his secretary. In due course, the liaison led to him taking hits, some below the waterline, hits he otherwise could have avoided. How badly this allaiance hurt his career cannot be ascertained; suffice it to say that it sure didn't move him any closer to Capitol City.

On the contrary, with his Power Team built on quicksand, one can see that his career has come to a complete halt, even in a slow moving agency in a sleepy state.

A classic example of a manager's executive secretary not being *his* secretary.

See also ASSISTANTS, LOYALTY, OFFICE STOOLPIGEON, PICKING FIGHTS, SEX, SUCCESSION, and WOUNDED TIGERS.

nothing less than sensory deprivation.

Senior staffers who pursue this foolish practice would do well to recall that totalitarian regimes employ sensory deprivation as torture, the purpose of which is to reduce a prisoner to a gibbering idiot.

Sensory deprivation can be played both ways. Know that many game players would *manage* their boss, or his time, just to reduce his exposure to rivals. By monopolizing his time, isolating him, one can minimize the time that one's rivals could spend with him.

This, too, is sensory deprivation.

Either way, the result is the same.

I'm told that when he was Secretary of State, Henry Kissinger spent an inordinate amount of time in the president's office. When someone asked him about all the time he spent there, he responded, "I stay there so other cabinet officers [i.e., rivals] can't see the President."

In the early 1950s the FBI suspected that the British Government had been penetrated at the highest level by the Russian intelligence service. Its urgent letters warning of treason, which naturally carried the highest TOP SECRET clearance, came across the desk of Burgess or MacLean (I can't recall which), highest level assistants and double agents. All such letters were summarily destroyed. The resultant delay in receiving the warning gave the Burgess/MacLean/Philby team additional years to pilfer and transmit secrets.

Sensory deprivation.

See also ASSISTANTS, COMPETITION, DEPUTIES, POWER TEAM, SHREDDER, and YES-MEN.

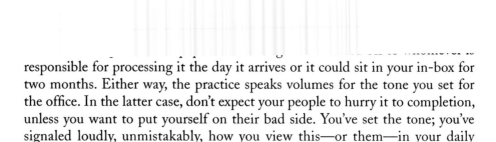

responsible for processing it the day it arrives or it could sit in your in-box for two months. Either way, the practice speaks volumes for the tone you set for the office. In the latter case, don't expect your people to hurry it to completion, unless you want to put yourself on their bad side. You've set the tone; you've signaled loudly, unmistakably, how you view this—or them—in your daily scheme of things.

At mid-afternoon one payday Friday, the workload was light, the boss was out of town, and so two of us decided to celebrate this happy coincidence at the bowling alley bar downstairs.

Whom should we encounter on arrival but the entire mail room gang. A quick glance revealed that they had been there awhile.

Said my friend by way of greeting, "Hi, guys. You're off to an early start on the weekend."

Replied one who clearly was feeling little pain, "I seen the chairman af'er lunch. He so drunk he cou'n't even stan' up straight (our August Leader, Chairman Harmon, it will be recalled, was known to abuse alcohol daily). "'F he c'n do it, so c'n I."

Touché! Who could argue?

From the halls of state government comes the following tale, one at once so bizarre and picturesque that it cries to be related here.

One day *it* simply appeared. Perhaps its owner allegedly smoking dope during her lunch hour influenced its arrival, but periodically it would return, talking, squawking, and making a mess—along with a most distinctive statement for the department it hung out in.

It was a parrot which one of the secretaries sometimes brought to the office. Other staff protested its appearance to the department head, citing the bird as a distraction and, no doubt concerned over the image it conjured up, claiming (not unreasonably) that its presence signified a rampant lack of professionalism for the entire office. Much aggrieved, the secretary defended the company of her feathered friend on the grounds that it got *lonely* if it were left home (though how the creature communicated loneliness must remain a mystery—maybe it came through during her lunchtime smoke break).

Incredibly, but on reflection not surprisingly, the department head took no action in this matter. Without written procedures to guide her (somehow, the constant presence of feathered companions in state offices never occurred to the unimaginative rule writers back in Capitol City, so there was no written procedure to cover this contingency), the department head, a textbook Gold Star girl if ever there was one, was powerless to decide this perplexing conundrum. Wishing not to anger her secretary, the department head did the manly thing and vacillated, deciding nothing.

So the creature stayed. It shed feathers, scattered birdseed and crapped on the carpet. Sometimes, it adorned its owner's shoulder, perching there unfettered for an hour at a time while she typed, fielded phone calls and filed her nails. Once a visitor innocently opened the door, and the bird, which happened to be loose, flew off down the hallway frantically pursued by the secretary and a couple of staffers she hastily enlisted. The bird's presence was, to put it charitably, graphic and vivid, and it set a most idiosyncratic tone for the department. Certainly the winged companion left an indelible impression in the mind of visitors and staff. One fellow swore the bird constantly masturbated, but no other observers were sufficiently attuned to avian sexual behavior to confirm this assertion.

In time, the bird became almost as much an office fixture as the coffee pot. Until one fateful day, when the division director actually left her office to visit the nether reaches of her empire and came across the bird, perched on the shoulder of its owner. To the chagrin of the secretary (and the relief of everyone else), she declared with finality that the creature must go.

The chairman of the first agency I worked for, which was a brand new start-up, decided to welcome new employees. As he rose before the assembled new hires, who at this stage numbered less than fifty, a shirt tail flapping from his unzipped fly irresistibly drew all eyes to his crotch. Afterwards, no one remembered what he'd said, but decades later the open fly still sticks in the minds of all who were privy to this tableau.

Setting the tone . . .

SEX AT THE AGENCY

Among our most basic, natural biological drives, sex ranks right up there behind food and water, and for some it is as much a part of daily life as eating, sleeping, and drinking. With the other drives mostly satisfied, it's perfectly natural to presume that while they're in the office, people think of sex as much as, perhaps more than, drinking and visiting the bathroom. Certainly, many (especially male employees) think more frequently of sex than they think of work. One wonders whether the need for power, often encountered in government, represents a displaced or repressed sex drive. If so, maybe it explains the drive for sex in the office.* Alternatively, perhaps the high that some derive from power becomes a sexual turn-on, an aphrodisiac—power, raw power, carries with it a primal, carnal fascination that defies description. But no matter whether you consider it a primary motivator or secondary reinforcer, sex, or the drive to get it, is in its own quiet way as much a part of the agency littoral as buck-passing and finger pointing.

The primary motivation for office sex is power: access thereto or use thereof. Either superiors make it clear to subordinates who conform to their sexual preference that pay raises, promotion and other desirable outcomes can be obtained faster—or only—on the office couch, or subordinates seek to speed or skew the pay and promotion process by trading sexual favors for preferential treatment. Either way, it comes down to the same thing: sex for power.

To someone well advanced up the totem pole who, sexually speaking, happens onto a good thing, the best strategic move is to transfer one's paramour to another agency, thereby escaping potentially damaging rumors and finger pointing.

Occasionally, the sexual urge overflows one's thoughts and manifests itself in other ways.

---

* An observation: to so engage is to play with fire—which may turn some on all the more—since the penalty for getting caught in the act far exceeds any harm done to the public. Be forewarned.

- Sometimes, two (who knows, maybe more) employees engage coitally at the office or elsewhere on the premises. Some are turned on by the moment, others by the thought of raw political power. One recalls Rep. Buddy and his wife Rita Jenrette plumbing the physical world to untold

- Employees who listen to phone sexlines, tap in to cybersex, and read *Playboy*, *Penthouse* or *Hustler*, or jerk off at their desks, bespeak other, deeper-seated problems: ennui, boredom, not enough to keep them busy, and uncaring or insufficient supervision to prevent this. For those so engaged, sex provides an escape, and it usually marks an agency deep in its last two evolutionary stages. If you work in an agency in these stages of its life, one thing is certain: sex sure beats work!

See also AGENCY LIFE-CYCLE, GENDER DIFFERENCES, HIERARCHY, MISTRESSES, MORALE, and PERFORMANCE REVIEW CRITERIA.

SHARING TURF

Remember when you were a child being admonished to share (*It's nice to share . . .*)?

Forget it.

Consider instead the law of sharing turf:

"To share turf is an open invitation to lose it."

He who voluntarily shares turf invites his colleagues and rivals to poach.

Ergo, *never share*. Trade, maybe; share, never.

See also CONTACT, JOINT EFFORTS, TURF, and WHO'S IN CHARGE.

to show him up (which you obviously are) and will act against you accordingly.

See also FACE.

SHREDDER

If your office or agency doesn't have one, get one. Crank it up and use it. All the time and as a matter of routine.* In this way, its use will not cause idle gossip or supply grist for the agency rumor mill.

If your office already has a shredder, use it. Often. In this way, your presence over it will not be cause for idle gossip or grist for the agency rumor mill.

Because of its potency as an engine of damage control, the shredder ranks with the photocopier among the leading tools of statecraft. One does well to remember that the penalty for shredding evidence usually is less severe than the penalty which could accrue had the shredded evidence been delivered intact into the hands of a Blue Ribbon Panel.

A caution: make it a matter of daily routine (on second thought, make that office policy) to burn all paper shreds from your agency or office each day. From unburned shreds the Iranians who captured the US embassy in Teheran reconstituted extremely damaging papers relating to US support of the Shah. It took the *mullahs* well over a year to paste the shreds back together, but then, time was on their side. Time is always on the side of any party who thus possesses the shreds.

A friend works in a field office of a government license bureau whose daily routine entails extensive contact with the license-seeking general public, many of whom are brusque, rude and demanding. On occasion, their brusque rudeness is returned in coin by the clerks at the office, who are, after all, human. My friend reveals that faxed license requests that are accompanied by gratuitous complaints of staff rudeness or noncooperation end up in the shredder, which, by happy coincidence, sits beside the fax terminal. He personally (and cheerfully) invokes this procedure daily, and he believes its use has become almost universal, whether

---

*   One possible use is on excess paperwork.

through individual initiative or because of collusion he cannot say—the other clerks at the office employ it, too.

Several years ago, former national security advisor Sandy Berger was reportedly caught while removing from the National Archives pre-9/11 material that might incriminate him or his boss. An embarrassing though clear-cut case of not shredding in a timely manner. Far better to shred *a priori* then *a posteriori*.

See also DALEY, DAMAGE CONTROL, THE PUBLIC, RUMOR MILL, and SURPLUS WORK.

SIGNOFFS

A signoff indicates assent or approval—in writing.

To be able to sign off on a project confers the signor with the ultimate in procedural power—the power to postpone, prevent or preclude. At most agencies, to refrain from signing off is equivalent to casting a presidential veto—and is equally effective. To proceed without all required internal signoffs is unthinkable: it would mean that internal consensus has not been reached, that concerns remain unaddressed, or questions, unanswered, and if any part of the enterprise in question founders or, worse, becomes the object of public controversy, the non-signer can show he never approved, and can escape blame . . . while implicitly casting it on those who opted to proceed without his assent.

Like a presidential veto, the decision to withhold a signoff is not taken lightly, since by exercising it too often or without valid cause, a dissident risks becoming perceived not to be a team player.

This brings to mind an amusing illustration. My department had produced an extremely important and sensitive letter (it meant millions in additional federal discretionary funds), a draft of which had been duly circulated, per standard procedures, to the appropriate department and division heads for review and signoff. After the signoffs had been duly collected, the letter went out.

Apparently it contained details that, on second thought, gravely concerned our head of finance, a squirrelly, fractious fellow who cordially disliked my boss. These concerns he raised at the next weekly meeting of department heads. My boss, who couldn't locate the draft with the signoffs in our departmental files (which were abysmally organized), asked if I had it. I didn't, but later, in rooting through the agency's central files, I chanced upon the original, complete with the initialed approvals from every department head—including the head of finance.

I presented the initialed draft to my boss. On seeing it, his face broke into a smile. "Asbestos!" he exclaimed happily.*

I couldn't have put it better!

SOLE-SOURCE PURCHASES

Sole-source purchasing simply means dispensing with the formality of competitive bids for goods and services.

Often there is a sound reason behind a sole-source purchase. A favored supplier may be the only supplier, or his product may be far superior, or he may be geographically (his plant is located in our city/county/state/country) or demographically (minority- or women-owned) favored, his product or service may best jibe with or otherwise plug into what the agency already uses, and so on. These are perfectly legitimate and entirely appropriate reasons to forego competitive bids. Usually, a short memo describing the benefits is sufficient to justify such a purchase.

Other good reasons may underlie a purchase without competitive bidding, too. Sometimes they come down to paying off a favor. The payoff may be internal or external. It could involve the agency head personally or a board member or someone with heavy clout elsewhere in the agency's Prime Public—it really matters not which. The advertising budget at my first agency was divided, per agreement, between two advertising agencies, one with Republican, the other with Democratic ties, both turkeys (given the quality of the product they billed us for), as a reward for work they performed for someone else—which must have been of considerably higher quality than what they foisted off on us.

Many, probably most, agencies have a threshold sum above which all purchases must be competitively bid. A trick often used to bypass this procedure: dividing a purchase which exceeds the competitive bid threshold into bite-sized chunks, each of which falls beneath the threshold.

If a vendor for your project is a "sole-source" supplier, and his product or service is disturbingly sub-par, protest or question the arrangement with discretion and sensitivity lest you find your project (your turf) snatched away and given to a rival who's less inquisitive and more tolerant of shoddy work.

A friend was made responsible for purchasing a tract of land upon which we planned to construct a storehouse. When she was informed that the purchase was a matter of considerable sensitivity, she flippantly asked which board member was selling the land. Instantly, the project was snatched away from her and awarded to someone less inclined to speculate aloud over its ownership.

Later, she would learn that her flippant supposition was on target: its

SPECIAL INTERESTS,
THE IMMUTABLE LAW OF

This law is stated as follows, "Once an issue has acquired sufficient critical mass to become a special interest, it will require at least one agency to service its needs."

By way of explanation, two phenomena bear noting.

- First, if government resources are potentially to be gleaned from any business or other economic activity, the beneficiaries will ultimately coalesce into an interest group that requires, directly or indirectly, an agency to guarantee that their benefits flow uninterruptedly. If the stream of funds or goodies comes directly from a government agency, then the interest group has, for all practical purposes, already formed. Count on, or more accurately, bank on it.

- Second, every American holds dear to his heart a pet cause on which he'd gladly commit half the national debt. A sufficient number of like-minded citizens will eventually coalesce into an interest group. Once such a cause becomes agency turf, its public backers are sufficiently vocal and can muster sufficient clout such that if their cause is threatened, few politicians will have the *cajones* to buck them.

Reaching out to a prospective interest group, helping its backers coalesce, then retaining their backing is one of the major tasks confronting an agency. Some agencies perform this it better than others.

The implications of the law of special interests with respect to advancement and job security are well worth noting.

See also CAUSES, MARKETING, MISSIONARY WORK, PICKING WINNERS, PUBLICS, and SAFETY NETS.

---

the problem was fixed immediately, much to the surprise and bemusement—and mild annoyance—of her peers. After all, they each suffered, too, so why was the offending condition rectified for the obnoxious colleague but not for them? Hint: the colleague was the only person in the office who complained.

The squeaky wheel gets the grease. The person or party who squawks about a problem while others remain silent will usually find it taken care of. Why? Because squawks draw unwelcome attention from administrative quarters, attention which no administrator wants, because it could leave him open to criticism and liable for blame. So he ensures the problem gets resolved, and the squawking and squeaking end.

I think "Squawk Theory" explains the initial success of consumer advocates. When the movement started up, they squawked loudly, after what had previously been dead silence, and their strident squawking succeeded in forcing the passage of legislation which addressed their initial concerns. Continuous loud squawking, however, loses effectiveness, especially when others come to expect nothing but squawks and protests—remember the parable of the brat who cried wolf? So, one might say that selective, strategic (i.e.,carefully controlled) squawking produces a greater reward, a higher payoff, than continuous squawking.* Also, continuous squawking allows opposition to coalesce.

Alternatively, a department or agency head may take steps to remove a perpetual squawker; a squawker, by definition, makes waves. Even (perhaps especially) if he's right, it's far easier to remove a perpetual squawker than fix everything that he complains about—or, worse, be subjected to outsider inquiries regarding the cause of the squawking in the first place.

---

* Consumer advocates have learned, too, that the most effective squawk is a selective squawk. Their plaints are most effective following a disaster, which guarantees them and their views maximum media coverage—and public attention.

See also BLAME, DALEY, and PURGING.

STATISTICS, LIES, AND DAMNED LIES

Recognizing the timeless truth of the adage, *figures lie and liars figure*, it follows that no agency can call itself prepared this century (with all that *Information Age* stuff that seers keep telling us about) if it is unequipped to deal with either.

This brings us to statistics. Here, an historical note is in order. A branch of mathematics developed after World War II to help decision makers grapple with and reduce uncertainty, statistics is extensively used in industry, science, engineering, finance, even in government agencies. In fact, the only important relevant endeavors I can think of whose practitioners appear grossly and overwhelmingly ignorant of statistics are lawyers, politicians and the news media.

Statistical knowledge allows you to refute with ease the spurious or fraudulent claims of rivals, and (if done correctly) insulate the work of your staff from similar criticism. Alternatively, for claims you release (via the media) to the legislative oversight and the general public, few of whom are well equipped to analyze or counter them—you can make the numbers say anything you damn well please: together, your agency's lawyers and press relations officer can handle any required weasel-wording.

Many years ago, I attended an industry gathering where a corporate senior vice-president, talking about an operating problem with real-world data, noted disdainfully that his staff people had cautioned him that the numbers "weren't statistically significant." Today, such disdain would only underscore the ignorance of the speaker: in fact, it is highly unlikely such an utterance would occur—at that forum. I'm not so sure that this holds for the agency.

As agency head, my first decree would be that, henceforth, every professional and technical hire be conversant with statistics. *Asbestos!*

See also BACK UP THE NUMBERS, BLAME-FREEDOM FROM, INSULATION, THE MEDIA-SOME THOUGHTS, and MUZZLE THE TECHIES.

stealthy work is extra-legislative; it takes place despite, not because of, an agency's mandate. It is bootlegging by the whole agency.

Why is stealthy work undertaken? The simple answer: to grab turf and expand the agency's charter. Completed stealth work, and its resultant special interest group, ultimately confronts the legislators with a *fait accompli* and renders it more difficult for them to snatch turf away legislatively from an agency—turf is a property right, where possession is nine points of the law.

A more complex answer: all organizations naturally seek to extend and expand the portfolio of tasks they undertake, and agencies are no exception. It is perfectly normal to voice a sentiment along the lines of, "If we could just add this one task to our mandated portfolio, then we could really regulate/control/monitor/solve this activity/issue/problem more completely or effectively." A well-documented sociological phenomenon, this is classic organizational behavior, no more, no less. (As an aside, I suspect that private sector organizations are more likely to limit these urges than public ones. But their risk/reward structure differs markedly from that facing an agency.)

See also DOING SOMETHING, HIDDEN AGENDA, *IPSE DIXIT*, MANDATE, MOONLIGHTING, SPECIAL INTERESTS, THEORY OF THE AGENCY, and TURF.

SUCCESSION

When an agency or department head names a successor from within the ranks, one can be reasonably certain that the heir apparent will have the same weaknesses and blind spots and the same strengths, though in lesser quantities, as his predecessor. Why is the successor likely to be a man of less ability? Many, perhaps most, people in power are loath to promote anyone of equal or, God forbid, greater ability: the protégée might overshadow the Great One and cause him to lose face. This also applies to complementary strengths among leading subordinates, where these strengths could lead to the head being overshadowed.

I believe this a major, though by no means the only, cause for the degradation in agency capabilities over time.

When you assume any supervisory position, your first order of business is to determine (if you don't already know) whether any of your leading subordinates bid for your job. If any did so, watch them closely for signs of disloyalty; your interests may be best served by purging them.

Why? Almost certainly, they are bound to feel equally, if not more, qualified for the position than you. They may know the job technically and professionally better than you, especially if you came in from outside, and doubly so if you are a patronage placement. Because they have been around a lot longer, your senior staff will almost certainly have developed personal ties with your boss and maybe his boss—which you cannot break—and they will be watching you closely for signs of weakness or incompetence. If you prove weak or incompetent, many in their position will not hesitate to stick it to you over and over, as often as they can. And worst of all, if they're smooth, when lightning strikes you, you'll have no idea where it came from.

So save yourself a lot of heartburn, and eliminate any threat from this quarter at the outset.

On his first day at the office, a newly hired department head called a mid-morning staff meeting. His two most senior subordinates had applied for his job, and feeling themselves fully qualified, each felt he had a fair shot at it: certainly ~~~~~~ When all hands were

See also AGENCY LIFE-CYCLE, DEPUTIES, FACE, POLITICAL APPOINTMENTS, PURGING, and SHOWING UP THE BOSS.

SURPLUS WORK, DISPOSITION OF

This topic could more accurately be titled *Surplus Work, Disposal of*, or just *Deepsixing*.

When the work piles too high, staff at some agencies dispose of their in-box surplus by simply throwing it away.* This disposal takes place mostly in drips and drabs, but there have been exceptions: some years ago the Postal Service did so on an industrial scale. Trash dumpsters outside a District of Columbia Post Office were found crammed with undelivered (and mostly second-class and bulk) mail, and one cannot help but wonder whether the practice isn't more widespread.† Surely the Postal Service holds no monopoly in it.

And there is much to commend this practice. If you limit it to low priority work, its loss may well go unnoticed, especially in a department with no or unenforced follow-up. If anyone asks you, you can say that you never received the paperwork or, more accurately, perhaps it got lost (but never "I lost it").

Should you employ this method to reduce the paper inventory that clogs your in-basket, your best bet is to either shred it or, if you must throw it away, take it home and do so there. Never leave your unshredded work in an office wastebasket: it—and you—can be discovered all too easily.

Had the DC postal workers resorted to shredding to reduce their delivery backlog, their petty expediency would almost certainly have gone undetected. And they could have spared themselves much unfavorable publicity squarely under the eye of their legislative oversight. Alas, the use (and quality) of shredders would appear to vary directly with the degree to which confidentiality characterizes the prevailing work load.

---

* Naval jargon for this practice is most colorful, *shit-canning*. I suspect its use to be a function of the current life-cycle stage of the agency it occurs in, but this suspicion remains to be proved.

† The penalty one pays for paying below market rates for a service.

See also AGENCY LIFE-CYCLE, CUSTOMER SERVICE, IF YOU ARE BLAMED, PROMISES, PUBLICS, and SHREDDER.

disillusioning to others. And in truth, many come to understand, inchoately, more than explicitly, one suspects, where as employees they truly rank in the constellation of their agency's publics. Ultimately, many tire of the energy—and zeal-draining rules and procedures, or they lack the self-confidence to appear before, or can no longer stomach the prospect of getting beaten up by legislative overseers who are grandstanding for the media, or worse, getting beat up by the legislator's staff. Others lose zest for the incessant turf wars with other agencies or rivals. Or resent having their optimal solution to a pressing problem compromised by political reality, again and again. Or maybe that last random drug test, even though it came out negative, killed any remaining zeal for work, for their agency, for making a difference. What to do?

Some true believers leave for the non-profits, where they can continue in a drug test-free milieu their never ending struggle to *make a difference* or at least, differ; others depart for the private sector, hoping to cash in on their experience and the lure of real money. But most, who've patiently built up seniority, vested pension, four weeks of annual vacation time, and all the other perks that go with it, choose to stick around . . .

They stop out, but they don't drop out, and they join the ranks of the time-clock punchers. Here's how:

For the technique to work best, it is important to stop out at a level in the hierarchy where one knows his stuff cold, even as he forgoes further advancement. The pay remains more than adequate, perhaps most comfortable. In government, the salary differential between upper mid-level staff and those at the top-of-the-hierarchy, who must face and deal with the trials noted above, is extremely thin (with government pay scales, the spread in compensation is much narrower than that in the corporate world) and can't begin to compensate them for the cost (to their health) of holding a more senior, higher paying job. Many now award themselves a pay-raise by throttling back their efforts, easing up in intensity, turning it down a notch—maybe several notches.

As a stopped-out staffer, one ideally is one or more levels insulated from agency-wide game playing, yet still may be challenged by being called on when the competent network is activated. If the work no longer challenges or is not enough to keep him busy, there's always the possibility of moonlighting. But no migraines or ulcers, no burning the midnight oil, few (and then, most likely, routine) dealings with the Power Team, less haggling with unreasonable power grasping jerks, less kowtowing to threatened, insecure bosses whom he's smarter than, anyway. True, all the niggling, petty, procedures remain, but now he cares about them more than he does the real work. Unhurried, he accomplishes what he can during the day, and goes home happy to family and friends at quitting time. He threatens no one by his presence or activities, and because he knows the job and makes no waves, nobody in his right mind would even dream of firing him—because that *would* make waves. He thereby maximizes his chance to reach retirement with his reputation intact. And his health.

The pool of talent and expertise within an average agency varies between incredible and extraordinary. Many employees choose to remain here, even though their skills and knowledge could earn them two to three times as much in industry. But here, they are spared the worry attendant to unfriendly takeovers and layoffs or the secular economic slowdowns that elected officials blame on their predecessors, or perhaps some are afraid to venture forth after becoming settled where they are. Either way, it doesn't matter.

Many stop out. Their choice, be it implicit or explicit, conscious or intuitive, suggests Peter (Peter and Hull, *Ibid.*), is their way to enjoy work and life, and preserve their health and competence.

And for them, that's plenty.

See also AGENCY EMPLOYEES, BEHAVIORAL GAP, COMPETENCE, COMPROMISE, EXPEDITERS, GIVE YOURSELF A RAISE, HIERARCHY, OBJECTIVES, OPTIMIZATION, PUBLICS, and THEORY Y.

half of my department, and we were being mobilized to get something (when?) done. That evening, I went home and proudly told my wife about my appointment, and she was even more excited. Needlessly, it turned out.

The next day, the Task Force met twice—for the first time and the last time. And after a week or two, I realized that nothing had changed. Our effort had produced a lot of hot air but nothing tangible. I could see that our department's lack of output posed a problem, but the Task Force did not solve it.

This puzzled me, until I learned the purpose a Task Force serves.

As time went by, I saw more Task Forces, some of which I was named to, some not, and "Blue Ribbon Panels and Committees"—more Task Forces—convened, and came to understand that rarely, if ever, does a Task Force accomplish anything concrete. Why? Seldom is a Task Force opportunity-based: it is problem-based. However, it can still perform a great many useful and valuable services: it can, variously, assign blame, punish, obfuscate, whitewash and seek a working public consensus. Getting the work out is seldom one of these services. (My first Task Force failed because it was poorly conceived, involved only half the department, and nobody followed up our assignments. A competent, hands-on department head could easily have achieved what our Task Force failed to accomplish.)

Got a big problem? Convene a Task Force to look into it. Want to whitewash, block or kill a nettlesome issue? Then form a "Blue Ribbon Task Force," and hand the hot potato off to them.

Blue Ribbon Panels convened in the wake of a horrible disaster are exercises in public sado-masochism. They are constituted for one and only one reason: to grandstand to the media, though the process is intended to reassure the public that everything is hunky-dory and, most of all, to retain or restore all-important public confidence in government. If anything is seriously wrong, it will be aired only if it is already common knowledge. The only beneficiaries are elected politicians who can be expected to gain points with the media at the expense of the unfortunate agency or its head. And every member of the panel is chosen for his political reliability—no place for crusaders or mavericks here.

Why are Task Forces black holes into which issues disappear and never see the light of day? Perhaps a clue lies in the motivation of the members. The late George Stigler offered an academic's description of the motivation and behavior of Blue Ribbon Panels: Each member will tolerate the finished product, even when it misstates many (or even, perhaps, most) of his own views, as long as it contains the one piece which he wants included. This guarantees that nobody gets left out. The inevitable result is a mishmash of contradictory goals and aims that virtually guarantee nothing of consequence will ever happen. The greater the number of participants and the more varied their constituency, it follows that there's less chance anything meaningful will ensue.

See also BUCKPASSING, KILLING THINGS and THE MEDIA-SOME THOUGHTS.

Some employ legal and lawful means to avoid taxes; others cheat. Either way, it comes down to the same thing.

Those who duck taxes seek to enjoy the benefits of being governed without paying the bill.

For this reason, unlawful tax dodgers who get caught are to be viewed without pity.

See also THE PUBLIC, PUBLICS, and TAXES.

TAXES . . .

. . . are as certain as death itself.

You may not like to pay them, but they cover your salary. And fund your work program.

Now, aren't taxes wonderful?*

So when outsiders gripe about taxes, resist the urge to bitch along with them or gloat or, worse, to preach or counter-argue.

Best strategy: keep your mouth shut.

---

* "With taxes I buy civilization," Oliver Wendell Holmes told tax complainers. Doubtless DC-Area citizens would agree, though Distrik residents may wonder at this.

See also BELTWAY and THE PUBLIC.

teachings of their curriculum), the *Theory of the Agency* is equally critical to us.
And like the Theory of the Firm, which business students encounter midway
through their studies—they have to work up to it: it's not an introductory
topic—it probably is fitting that the Theory of the Agency lies near the end of
this manual.

The Theory of the Agency provides the underpinning for all agency activity.
It can be stated quite simply in the jargon of management science as the objective
function of the agency.[†]

"Maximize the number of people on the agency payroll."[‡]

Amplification is needed. First, the payroll in question is our agency's, not
that of a competitor.

Second, *employees* is broadly interpreted to include not only the good folk for
whom our agency cuts a paycheck, but direct recipients of our subsidies, goods
and services. It also includes vendors and contractors whom the agency pays for
goods and services. It includes, at slightly greater distance, the media, for whom the
agency buys meals and drinks, provides other favors, and performs for them work
by providing news releases, press conferences, exclusive interviews and the like. It
also includes true believers in our charter who ceaselessly lobby to have us do more,
and academics, to whom our agency pays for their consulting services and, in some
cases, who act as our advisors, an "accomplishment" that they proudly add to their

---

[*]   Lest we forget, the theory of the firm holds that the economic purpose of a firm is
       to "maximize the net present value of all its assets."

[†]   When paired with the two Daley laws, the theory of the agency forms an elegant,
       rigorous construct in constrained optimization.

[‡]   Since it is assumed to be axiomatic, a rigorous mathematical derivation of this
       proposition is omitted.

vitae and translates into pay and prestige. Note that anything this has to do with "serving the public" or "making a difference" is strictly coincidental.

If one believes that to pay someone is to control him, then this implies that one way or another, everyone the agency pays comes under its control. Control means power. And the more people the agency controls, the greater the power it wields. And that is the name of The Game.

An alternative explanation: at election time, each employee will vote for (versus against or not vote at all) politicians who support agency programs. The more votes an agency can count on, the lower the likelihood its programs will suffer cuts in authorization.

This theory can be expanded to include government as a whole, but to me, its beauty lies in its application to discrete branches of government and individual agencies.

The vigor with which an agency pursues this goal is believed to be a function of the stage in its life-cycle it currently occupies. I say *believed* because, to the best of my knowledge, this thesis rests unproven.

One final caution: never, never confuse control with loyalty. The two are mutually exclusive.

See also ACADEMICS, COMPETITION, CONTROL, GOVERNMENT-A BRIEF ESSAY, INDEPENDENCE, LOYALTY, NATIONAL INCOME ACCOUNTING, PRESS RELATIONS, TURF, UNDERSTANDING THE GAME, and VOTING.

Some years ago, MIT behavioral scientist Douglas MacGregor proposed a novel dichotomy between two diametrically opposed styles of management, which he termed Theory X and Theory Y (MacGregor, *The Human Side of Enterprise*, New York, McGraw-Hill, 1960). To oversimplify, Theory X presumes that work is anathema—workers hate it—and further, that they are lazy and cannot be trusted, and so if an organization is to accomplish anything, its employees must be closely monitored, even driven, to ensure that they work and that their work gets done. Theory Y'ers, on the other hand, believe that work is a natural, vital part of life, that people actually enjoy and, thus, they truly want to work. And so, if you really want to get things done, get the employees to commit themselves to organizational objectives, get off their backs and stay out of their way; their performance and output will astound you.

Theory Y organizations, when they have been put together, usually in the private sector, have enjoyed success. I suspect their biggest problem is that the guy who instills a Theory Y culture in the first place will ultimately, nay, inevitably be replaced by a control freak, someone who cannot let go, and back come the rules and their checkers, and out drains all the employees' zeal.

Theory Y management is almost unknown in government (the one Theory Y agency I know was temporary and got sunsetted), By the time an agency reaches full maturity, it has become so cumbered with rules, regulations and procedures that even thinking of Theory Y is a sick joke. With all the demeaning, energy draining regulations and procedures they face each day [I've worked at an agency where you signed in when you arrived for work in the morning and signed out at night; you signed a log (superseded by an automatic counter) to make photocopies; I've had $0.35—yup, thirty-five cents—knocked off a meal reimbursement; and I've even been advised not to consume gin-and-tonic the night before mandatory drug testing, because, I was informed, the test identifies traces of quinine (from the tonic), which junkies use to cut their heroin fix—all at the same agency], employees can be forgiven if they get the idea they are not trusted.

And indeed they aren't. The rules and procedures presume them *a priori* untrustworthy. The agency they work for seeks to eliminate uncertainty, and this means rules and procedures up the ying-yang. Remember, agencies, like pro football teams, pursue the most risk-averse behavior possible.

Whether the procedures always work as they are intended—or whether or how they were intended to work—is debatable. After I signed in on arrival, as the rules required, I headed downstairs to a café to breakfast with a friend who had also previously signed in. Before heading home in the evening, I joined my friends in the bowling alley bar for a couple of beers, and then returned to the office to sign out. When I wanted to photocopy personal material, I just photocopied it—nobody knew what I was copying, and even if someone knew or suspected I was running off personal stuff, the chances were slim that he really cared enough to stop me or report my act. Clearly the procedures didn't ensure compliance.

So why even promulgate them? Two possible answers come to mind. One, which assumes the rule makers truly expected or believe that their procedures would, simply by virtue of being implemented, guarantee compliance, implies the rule makers are either severely out of touch with reality or grossly ignorant, or both. The other, which I favor, is that the rules and procedures aren't expected to ensure compliance, far from it. However, in publishing these rules, the agency effectively insulates itself from the actions of rule violators: if a violation is reported, the senior staff can say, "We had a rule against what he did, and he broke it, so we will take action against him." Thus, their skirts are clean.

And that's why Theory Y will never and can never take hold in government. The private sector is all about taking risks, and that's where the risks are taken. Trusting employees entails some risk. So Theory Y is a private sector philosophy. The public sector is strictly Theory X territory—no risk takers here.

If you don't like the fact that from the outset you are presumed untrustworthy, stop whining and find a job outside government.

See also AGENCY LIFE-CYCLE, BLAME-FREEDOM FROM, BUREAUCRACY, COST ACCOUNTANTS, MANAGEMENT STYLES, and RULES AND PROCEDURES.

no longer on an agency payroll) professional appointed officials, high level personal appointees, who, when their party is out of office, would otherwise be out in the street.

A secondary reason for their existence is to mediate between the truly cutting edge ideas propounded by colleges and universities (which, I believe, enjoy a wide comparative advantage over think tanks), on the one hand, and their acceptance or ultimate implementation at an agency, on the other. Truly original, groundbreaking work seldom, if ever, originates at think tanks (if you don't believe me, then quickly tell me how many Nobel, Balzan, or Wolf Prizes have been awarded for work conducted at think tanks. I don't know either, but I suspect the number is few, if any; certainly far fewer than the number awarded for work at colleges and universities). Tank staffers, especially the transients, tend to be inbred (most have spent too much time on agency payrolls to come up with original thought), which leaves them ill-equipped to push conceptual envelopes or develop new paradigms. No, these tasks are best left to the universities.

So think tanks produce voluminous studies to provide "policy guidance," which is used in the platform of the party aligned with their think tank and whose fat cats sponsor their work, and usually pushes the envelope on, or justifies, future legislation. It may take years, even decades, before their agenda is enacted and implemented—which is as close to policy creation as think tanks come.

A tertiary reason they exist is to justify the policies espoused by their political party—and inoculate the public against objections. Sort of a CYA for future legislation.

In considering the role of the think tank, one would do well to recall that the power they exercise is indirect, only by influence, and, when their payrollers are out of office, declining influence at that. Nevertheless, think tanks are extremely well suited to carry out their activity. Success provides their guests the greatest incentive of all: return to office and real power.

See also ACADEMICS, INDOCTRINATION, INOCULATION, POLITICAL APPOINTMENTS, and RADICAL THOUGHT.

TIME, TWO THOUGHTS

Time, say psychologists, can be divided into two categories: distracted time, and non-distracted time. When you need to get someplace in a hurry and your ride is late, every passing minute feels like an hour (non-distracted time), but to someone immersed in a good book, an hour-long bus ride seems like five minutes (distracted time).

A good manager takes pains to ensure that as much of the time of his staff as possible is distracted time: that means they're heavily involved with work and don't have time for other, non-productive shenanigans. Come to think of it, sex in the office sure can make the time pass more quickly!

A good friend relates a story which deserves to be included here because it is so instructive. An outside expert, he had held a consultative position with the federal government for some twenty years. In annoyed detail, he told me that a few years ago new procedures required him to resubmit all his credentials (college and professional degrees, certificates and recommendations), redo his obligatory conflict of interest statement, and a lot more. It was as though he were applying for his current position all over again—which, in effect, he was.

An older man, he went to some difficulty to extract and pull together all the information he had tendered decades earlier, find a typist to help fill out the myriad forms, and finally resubmit the whole mess to the personnel office. Thinking the matter concluded, he then went back to work, having wasted (to his way of thinking) two days struggling to comply with this irksome new procedure.

The following year, he was once again informed he would have to resubmit everything—unearth his certificates, fill out the forms, the statements, the works. Wearily he repeated the process—perhaps unwisely (though as a mere consultant, not a staff insider, we can forgive him), because he had not thought to photocopy the paperwork he had submitted the prior year! This time, he got smart and photocopied all the forms without dating and signing them, so if it became necessary he could resubmit them again next year with much less effort.

Given that agency employees' time arguably constitutes the most valuable resource of an agency manager, then it follows that these procedures demonstrate that employee time is accorded almost no value, as though it were free. Conversely,

These procedures thoroughly and absolutely reflect the core values, not just of the agency my friend consults for, but of all government agencies.

See also CONSULTANTS, DOING SOMETHING, MORALE, PERSONNEL, RULES AND PROCEDURES, and SEX.

TITLES

The longer the title, and the more descriptors it contains, the less it means. And the less the turf and importance of the holder.

"Deputy-Under-Assistant-Secretary-of-State-for-Micronesian-and-Oceanic-Affairs" has little oompf and impresses only the outsider, the ignorant, and the mother of the appointee.

A senior manager's studied lack of involvement in office matters finally caught up with her, and a slow but steady erosion of her turf suddenly culminated in the loss of the two largest (of four) departments initially assigned her.

An unsympathetic subordinate characterized her loss: "Today Mavis had her title extended."

See also RITUAL and TURF.

this ploy is arguably the one most often seized on by ambitious underlings to bypass institutional reporting relationships and almost always to shorten the normal promotional process. If you think the practice would seem to counter the notion of hierarchical organization, you are correct.

Note the qualification *usually* in the introductory sentence. Triangulation can go both ways: a boss can triangulate around a subordinate to isolate him from some project. Possible motives for this ploy include punishing a troublesome subordinate or getting things done in a hurry.

If a subordinate is actively triangulating around you, it's a good bet that he's set his sights on your job. And if your supervisor condones this practice, it's a sure sign of his weakness and insecurity. Incidentally, by his action he unmistakably signals that he doesn't trust you—nor can you trust him to back you if push comes to shove.

One way to stop a subordinate from persisting in this practice is to sit down after work with your triangulator and inform him that you are aware of what he is practicing and make it unequivocally clear that if he persists, you'll trash his performance review. Better yet, have a letter, *dated today*, addressed to his personnel folder, stating his actions to be disloyal, disruptive to, and unsupportive of, established agency policy and procedures. One nice aspect of this missive is that everything in it will be factually correct! You can also restructure his responsibilities by reassigning to others any juicy, high-visibility assignments and load him up with dead-end, low status grunt work. Better yet, if he's still in his post-hiring probationary period, during which he can be terminated for cause, fire him on the spot and save yourself much future heartburn.

If, as a supervisor, you reward a triangulator by promoting him into the job of the triangulee, do so with full knowledge that your job—and your backside—are almost guaranteed to become the next bulls-eye, not only in the triangulator's target scope, but also in the sights of the triangulee, if you're foolish enough to keep him on the agency payroll. Stalin, who used this ploy more effectively than most, eliminated this distraction by having the purged subordinate shot, but this luxury may not be available to you.

From the foregoing, it clearly pays would-be triangulators and those who would play footsie with them to do so with extreme caution.

See also BUREAUCRACY, EXPEDITERS, HIERARCHY, LOYALTY, and PURGING.

appear, whether or not your presence has been requested, at all possible public gatherings—ribbon cuttings, speeches, interagency meetings, and the like. That way, even if you have nothing whatever to do with the event taking place, nothing but your winning smile to contribute to meetings, others will see you, and perhaps they will presume that you and your agency or department are playing an important role in things. It goes without saying that if your agency or department actually is taking part in the effort, then your presence at these events is mandatory. To reiterate, it's not what you do; it's what others think you do . . .

A brilliant variation on this theme is to appear in the place of your subordinates who have been invited to speak or make a presentation at outside conferences or symposia. That way, the spotlight shines on you, not them. Getting invited is simple: monitor their mail, and if they are invited to speak, you appear in their place. If they don't like it, hey, that's football.

On second thought, maybe this chapter should be entitled, "Trooping *Your* Colors."

See also THE CUTOUT, IMAGE, IN-BOXES, PURGING, and RESPONSIBILITY

TURF

In a real sense, turf doesn't just define the agency: turf *is* the agency, and so turf *is* power. To attack its turf—to (attempt to) grab or curb its power and annex it to another agency—is to attack the agency itself.

This explains why agencies that thrive in the earlier stages of their life-cycle attempt to seize more turf, either from the public at large (e.g., by regulating additional facets of hitherto public life) or from rival agencies which are perceived no longer able to defend turf or fulfill their charter. The successful conclusion of a turf incursion against another agency is marked by the legislative enlargement of the winner's mandate and (best of all) the concurrent and overlapping diminution of the loser's.

Regarding the former, one sure clue to possible new or expanded turf is a growing collection of callers or complainers who require more agency resources to be dealt with. The cultivation of this group constitutes a potentially rewarding marketing task that many agencies dismiss under the heading of pain-in-the-ass complainants.

The quest for turf seems as deeply ingrained into agency behavior as the fight or flight response is ingrained in animals. And for the same reason—survival. This makes one aspect of prognostication easy: bet that whatever policy initiative the staff favor will invariably be the one which maximizes the turf they can annex.

See also AGENCY LIFE-CYCLE, COMPETITION, COMPLAINTS, CONSULTANTS, GOVERNMENT—A BRIEF ESSAY, MANDATE, MARKETING, MISSIONARY WORK, OBJECTIVES, SPECIAL INTERESTS, and THEORY OF THE AGENCY.

year. Others retire; to some, opportunity outside beckons, and even as a few are drawn to greener pastures, so do others flee unfavorable job circumstances. Agencies and departments in the later life-cycle stages invariably fail to counter the negative impact of turnover, usually because the capability to do so has long since eroded away.

Consider turnover as a diagnostic tool. Like absenteeism, turnover rates provide an excellent barometer of agency or departmental health. Turnover (this excludes changeover in plum appointive or patronage jobs after an election) and, more important, the reasons it took place may afford an observer an excellent insight into an agency or department.

For an agency head to use turnover to measure the effectiveness of his subordinate managers is almost unheard of in government.

If the door to an agency's employment office is constantly revolving, or if a senior staffer or department head just can't retain anybody worth a damn, then that may signal an office well worth staying away from. And to a predatory department head, turnover in a rival department can signal it ripe for a turf grab.

See also ABSENTEEISM, MORALE, OBJECTIVES, PATRONAGE, and TAXES.

UNDERSTANDING THE GAME

Now that you have advanced this far in this manual, it should be apparent that to advance equally far up the agency's hierarchical ladder, you'd best bring considerably more to the table than just an overwhelming desire to improve the human condition or by acting on the premise that performance and promotability are determined solely by performing your work well, handing in assignments on time, comporting yourself as the personification of probity and grace, and being respectful to your boss, your peers, and even your subordinates. In fact, no single one of these, nor all of them together, will likely carry you anywhere close to the limits of your abilities. Not in an agency, anyway. In fact, they almost guarantee that your career will top out long before you come anywhere near the highest rung you could potentially ascend in the hierarchy.

Conversely, understanding and using the ploys and protocols listed herein have taken many far beyond the limits of their ability, or at least, the limits of their ability as others perceive them. It all comes down to playing The Game.

And that, playing The Agency Game, is the bottom line, the purpose of this manual. This Game is precisely the stuff that no one tells you about in high school civics or undergraduate government classes.

The Game is everything. But to play The Game competently you must first understand it.

See also ACADEMICS, BEHAVIORAL GAP, HIERARCHY, and PERFORMANCE.

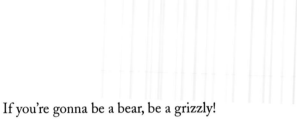

If you're gonna be a bear, be a grizzly!

Being a panda or a teddy just doesn't cut it.

This wisdom came to me in the military from a boss who practiced what he preached.

It gets into the fuzzy area of management style. Consider the tradeoff between being respected and being loved. If your congenital need to be loved overshadows your need to be respected, then by all means have—and do not hesitate to use—a Hatchet Man. If, on the other hand, you can put aside the need for your staff to love you, then by all means heed this.

It should be noted parenthetically that it is possible to be respected (feared) and not be hated.

To paraphrase Machiavelli, who several hundred years ago put it so much more elegantly, it is best for a prince (senior staffer) to be loved and respected (feared) by his subjects (staff), but *there is greater security in being respected (feared) than in being loved.*

Although I love and appreciate the elegance and classic timelessness of Machiavelli's wisdom, I find my old boss's paraphrasing more memorable.

See also HATCHET MAN and MANAGEMENT STYLE.

USING TEMPS

This practice comes from the hallowed halls of state government.

By using temps, I don't mean hiring temporary people to "help out," to fill in the gaps or do the grunt work on major projects. Nor do I refer to summer interns, whose presence in agency offices is an annual occurrence. Nor even to hourly or part-time clericals. All these folk can be found in agencies across the land, and their presence signifies nothing out of the ordinary. They are around to perform routine, entry level tasks or to complete boring busy work (data entry, for example) that must get done and that most employees neither want nor have time to do.

Instead, by using temps, I mean placing them in positions where they can take the blame if things sour, where they are (nominally) in charge of important projects, especially politically charged ones, where someone later may want to know who did that, anyway. Ditto, for decisions nobody want to commit himself to: get the temp to decide it. Best yet is before the temp goes back in school or won't be around that day.

And if any temp gets ideas of grandeur or starts to play games, he can be terminated instantly, since he's hourly.

Temps. God bless 'em! They do have their uses.

See also DECISIONS-MAKING AND AVOIDING, PERSONAL EMPIRE BUILDING, and SCAPEGOATS.

Occasionally, your agency must deal with another agency that becomes intransigent at the wrong time: your agency desperately needs funds or services or a signoff from the other, and no cooperation is forthcoming—and I'm not talking about replacing a lost passport in Timbuktu. When this occurs, it may be necessary to call your elected representative for help.

The use of the phrase *may be necessary* is deliberate: understand that summoning help from your congressman is an action never taken lightly. It should be an act of last resort. For run-of-the-mill, everyday services, exhaust all standard, procedural (and diplomatic) means to resolve a problem. Never inject your congressman into these proceedings. He serves as your fixer of last resort.

Why so? When you run (or cry out) to your congressman for help, three things can happen afterwards, none of them fortunate nor favorable:[*]

- First, after you lean on your congressman to help deal with an intransigent agency, don't expect it to bend over backwards to help you next time. Your action has effectively poisoned the water. Agencies at all levels of government share a pronounced dislike of one who summons help from elected representatives, because that casts them in a most unfavorable light and holds them up as an object of blame. In retaliation, you can count on that agency later on to throw as many obstacles (some proper and procedural, others not) in your path as possible.
- Second, calling for help may cast your agency, and maybe you, in a most unfavorable light: it implies you cannot resolve your own, everyday problems; even brands your agency incapable of performing its daily mission. No congressman or other legislator wants to burn political chips to support a loser.

---

[*]   *Lest we forget, Don't make no waves.*

- Finally, recall that everybody, including legislators, hates and nobody respects a stool pigeon.

This is not to denigrate the usefulness of having your congressman needle an agency that's supposed to help and is really dogging it, which occasionally happens. Or if a working relationship with a particular agency is antagonistic and adversary, it may take a threat from your congressman to move it off dead center, to get your just due.

See also IMAGE, LOBBYISTS, OFFICE STOOLPIGEON, REVENGE, and WHISTLEBLOWING.

Discovery of this gap can always be expected to occur swiftly after a vacuum comes into being, often instantaneously. This applies at the level of the branch of government, that of the agency, the department, the individual staffer.

In government as in physics, vacuums don't last long.

VOLUNTEERING

Volunteering means taking risks when success, when the desired outcome, is highly uncertain—in other words, when the odds favor failure, blame, or punishment. Volunteer only when the reward for success is high enough to justify the risk. Otherwise, forget it: a call for volunteers then becomes a disguised form of the Downward Buckpass.

Volunteers are called upon when a task cannot be routinely delegated or assigned without severe risk to the assignor and his career.

See also AGENCY EMPLOYEES, BLAME, BUCKPASSING, CREDIT, OBJECTIVES, and TURF.

across all walks of life and through all layers of society. Save one—government employees.

An agency employee who can vote is twice blessed: you, unlike your private sector peers, are constitutionally empowered to vote for your agency, for your program, for your job, and you can do so free from the conflict of interest restrictions that Americans have seen fit to impose more or less systematically on all of the other actions you may take (except for paying taxes) that relate to your employment.

It follows that to decline to vote when elections roll around amounts to more than merely neglecting yourself and your job and your security and your welfare; it is, in my mind, tantamount to betraying all of your colleagues, your agency, and your government.

As a government employee, I wish I could fire and then burn at the stake each and every co-worker who declines to vote when the opportunity presents itself.

See also INDEPENDENCE.

WASHINGTON, DEALING WITH

It is commonplace for municipal, county, regional or state agencies to apply to Washington for funds. Often, supplicants tend to place the feds on a pedestal, perhaps believing that since the feds control their purse strings, they are omnipotent and are constantly looking for niggling reasons to delay or preclude giving away funds for needed local programs.

This fear is misplaced and groundless. Assuming the paperwork is submitted to the feds in reasonably good order (worry not, dear supplicant: if your application isn't in order, the feds will let you know in detail where it is deficient), they will come across with the loot.* They have to.

Why this smug certainty?

Simple: the feds *have to* spend their authorization. And most of the funds they are slated to dispense are formulaic, not discretionary: a fixed percentage of their annual authorization *must* go to, or be spent on, *your* program—or *your* agency, or *your* state, or *your* region (of course, it's up to you to submit the request for funding). If the feds fail to spend it, either *they* face potential budgetary cuts or an unhappy federal agency head can count on being raked over the coals by his agency's appropriations committee. You can bet your last tax dollar that the chances of either taking place are about as favorable as those of a snowball in a blast furnace.

This tells you that anyone back home who is overly scared about, or makes too big a deal over, filling out and submitting this year's grant application is almost certainly in over his head.

---

* This is not to imply that, if your agency submits an off-the-wall grant request, the feds will fill it. Feds have guidelines, too.

See also BUDGETS and SAYING NO.

largesse, was talking on the phone when a visitor from another department came to see him. His greeting: "Just a minute, I'm talking to Washington."

"*I'm talking to Washington.*"* There's magic in these words. *Talking to Washington.* Plugged into the epicenter of government, connected and important, moving and shaking, pushing buttons and pulling levers, getting things done.

The visitor was duly impressed. Wow! Washington!

My reaction, on overhearing this exchange, was, "Which one, George, Martha, or Tyrone?"

The reason for the call in the first place was to determine the proper placement of a comma in an outstanding request for funds, or something equally meaningful. Whomever he was telephonically collaborating with was almost certainly a minion of equal or lower stature (i.e., a glorified clerk).

The point is that when someone says he's "talking to Washington," what he really means is that he's trying to impress others by exaggerating the trivial or the commonplace. He impresses only the easily impressionable.

You can, too—even if you're listening to nothing more than a phone sex line. If the telephoner is talking to someone in Washington who really counts, he'll name the person, not the city.

---

* This ploy works best when the conversation takes place outside the Capital Beltway.

See also BELTWAY, IMAGE, SEX, and WASHINGTON-DEALING WITH.

WHISTLEBLOWING

Blow the whistle only with extreme caution, because when you do so, you risk your job and a lot more. Here's why.

NOBODY LIKES A WHISTLE-BLOWER! You can bet the Power Team will view (and react to) a whistleblower in the same light that a schoolyard bully views a tattle-tale. In World War II, the Nazis executed not only traitors but also the person who fingered them, believing (correctly) that anyone who finks on a fellow countryman would rat them out in a heartbeat. Rightly or wrongly, whistleblowers are perceived as stool pigeons, rockers of the boat, makers of waves and, worst of all, public pointers of the Green Weenie of Blame.* The higher in an agency one ascends, the stronger this attitude.

It doesn't matter how noble a service one may perform when he blows the whistle. Others in the agency—one's peers, administrators, the Press Relations Officer, even military chaplains—have no sympathy for a whistleblower, because to toot is to cast blame; worse, cast it publicly and over all of us. A successful whistle ignominiously breaches the agency's defenses from within, results in widespread loss of face to the agency head, and of public confidence in the agency in particular and government in general.

So a whistleblower identified is a whistleblower who probably won't be around much longer. Administrators will take excessive zeal and special pleasure in running him out of the agency. From them, he can expect no quarter and no sympathy. If he toughs it out and sticks around, his friends may treat him as a pariah; certainly he can kiss off any chance for raises and promotions. And worse, if he does leave, he may encounter problems finding work in another agency. And even if they don't mobilize as many resources against him as the Department of Defense did against Daniel Ellsberg, an agency will nonetheless

---

* Before Glasnost, Communist party ideology permitted *Pravda*, the official party newspaper, to criticize individual incompetence or malfeasance. However, to criticize the party or any particular organization was a no-no, since doing so implied the system and, therefore, the party was flawed. Substitute government for the party and whistle blowing for criticism, and see the same phenomenon here, live.

go to extraordinary lengths to identify and purge itself of misguided idealistic activism.

So if you want to stop billions in waste and fraud, eliminate a troubling conflict of interest, or otherwise and

WHO'S IN CHARGE?

A weak agency head will tempt his board of directors to meddle actively in internal affairs, a sandbox that they properly have no business playing around in. A power vacuum. When this practice becomes advanced (i.e.—widespread and open), department or division heads may overtly work for, and report to, individual board members, usually the one to whom they owe their current cushy position, and they act as his highly paid errand boy. It is as if the agency head no longer exists, and in fact he does not—except in title. Certainly the agency is no longer his.

Once board members acquire this power, you can be sure that they will be most unwilling to choose a replacement head who exhibits the slightest amount of strength or independence.

When someone I don't report to, an outside department head, for instance, comes to me and gives me work without even the formality of asking my boss, much less me, for assistance, that angers me.

But that's nothing compared to how I feel about a boss, who, when I protest being given work by someone I don't report to, takes up for the outsider. His action tells me loudly that he values the favor (shrinks would call it the love) of a peer, who neither reports to him nor whom he reports to, over the time (and love) of his own staff. If something goes wrong, who takes the blame? Not the outsider, you can bet, only me. But if I do a good job, who gets the credit? Not I, I'd wager. Nor my boss.

More important, and more basic, who's in charge of the department, anyway? If outsiders are calling the shots for his staff, clearly not the nominal department head.

A boss who sells out his staff in this way ranks among the most infuriating men one can encounter in agency life. All things being equal, staff want their boss to act like an alpha male, not an omega wimp.

If you accept that his staff's time arguably constitutes a boss's most valuable resource, then one who fails to safeguard that resource from arrogant, demanding, alpha-esque marauders will keep neither his staff nor his department intact long. Nor, realistically, should he expect more than the most cursory support from his staff. His are the actions of a loser.

that need to be stuffed. They have to go out today, and I want your people to help." Her department, it must be added, never returned the favor.

It didn't take us long to learn her ways. Late one fine Friday afternoon, she came marching down the hall, yelling "McGillicuddy, McGillicuddy!" and disappeared into the boss's office. When the two emerged moments later to round up the work detail, not a soul was around. The whole crew had departed to the bowling alley until this threat to their leisure had safely passed.

We later heard that our PR colleague was royally annoyed at us. But she got the message: she never again tried to round up help from our shop that way.

See also AGENCY LIFE-CYCLE, ALPHA DEPARTMENT, CREDIT STRATEGIES, DALEY, GENDER DIFFERENCES, LEADERSHIP, LOYALTY, TITLES, TRIANGULATION, TURF, and VACUUM.

WILLIAMS' LAW

A cynical, free-spirited philosopher friend who left government service years ago left behind this memento, which I have correctly attributed to memorialize his contribution to my observations. I hope my friend forgives me for using his name. I find this body of philosophy to possess great descriptive and greater predictive power, especially as it relates to the actions of government agencies. Perhaps, on reflection, you may agree.

"Any system devised to perform a task whose completion can by represented by a universe of possible outcomes will ultimately be changed to suit a vested interest who will benefit from a constrained set of outcomes whose distribution will exhibit only incidental congruence with that produced by the unaltered system."

In other words, people—and agencies—will alter (subvert) any system to their advantage.

This can be accomplished in two ways:

- By controlling the process. To restrain competition, firms in regulated industries will put temporarily aside their rivalries to present a front so united against a prospective market entrant that the interloper can scarcely tell them apart at regulatory hearings that examine its "fitness" to enter the market. Government will vigorously prosecute all attempts by outsiders (i.e., non-government organizations) to supply or perform services that compete with services it provides.

- By altering the measurement system. Firms may change accounting methods to obscure unfavorable period-to-period earnings comparisons. In a like manner, government agencies change how they compute economic and other indicators when the incumbent administration stands to benefit by changing the computational methodology and, thus, render the outcome or output more favorable.

I suspect these alterations occur solely at the convenience of the incumbent administration, which is probably more frequent than one might suspect, and since they carry little news value, no reporter is likely to note them; in fact, nobody cares.

This leads to Williams Postulate: given that all systems lend themselves to being changed, it is to one's advantage to be first to alter a system to suit one's agenda.

Our agency was about to adopt the Hay Pay Plan. To ensure its proper implementation, every employee was directed to fill out a sheet that exhaustively detailed all the tasks he performed and all his assigned responsibilities. To each of these, the good folk at Hay Associates, a compensation consultant, would assign "Hay Points" which equated to salary dollars. For each employee, Hay Points were totaled to produce a "fair" imputed salary, and the more Points one amassed, the higher one's (supposed) salary. It follows that for each employee, there was a pretty clear incentive to perform this assignment as thoroughly as possible.

Afterwards, my friend Duane related that his department head, to make himself appear more important, crossed off from Duane's Hay Point tally sheet many tasks he (Duane) performed each day, and substituted them on his own sheet.

A classic case of the system being changed to suit those who control it—before it was even implemented.

A state government management information systems manger, who was charged with generating and providing data to support a major capital project, sought guidance in attacking the task before him in a manner that left little doubt as to his intent, to wit: "Tell me what you want the numbers to be."

A man who's easy to work with.

In seeking to revise the way the Consumer Price Index is calculated so as to slow its rate of increase—and thus the payout of benefits tied CPI changes—Congress demonstrates heightened awareness of Williams' timeless wisdom. A textbook example.

Williams must be chuckling over this.

See also COMPETITION.

decline, resentful of anyone and everyone who holds greater power than he does (not merely the man or men who deposed him), he visits bile and resentment on everyone around him, and seeks to obstruct or otherwise harm all with whom he interacts.

Few on an agency payroll pose a more negative, poisonous or corrosive influence than a wounded tiger.

It pays to identify wounded tigers, treat them with great care and keep them at arm's length. If a tiger actively pursues his agenda, it may be well worth the time and effort to purge him. Certainly I'd have no problem doing so.

One last note concerning wounded tigers: the severest wounds they cause are almost always self-inflicted.

---

*   This holds especially if the trappings of office were forcibly stripped away.

See also FORMER EMPLOYEES, MORALE, PICKING FIGHTS, PURGING, and REVENGE.

YES-MEN

When an agency head begins to believe all the great things the agency's news releases say about him—in other words, as he becomes increasingly oblivious to reality—he may seek to shut out of his life sayers of unpleasant truths and purveyors of discomfiting wisdom, and surround himself with staffers whose expressed views are far warmer and more congenial; subordinates and assistants who never say *no!* or, God forbid, *you're wrong!** Sycophants. Toadies. Yes-men.

A growing cluster of yes-men surrounding an agency head is a sure tip-off that the agency is highballing down the wrong track with no brakes and a blind engineer at the throttle. It also signifies that if you must oppose the Great Man on some issue, you need to exercise creativity or risk demotion—or having a yes-man inserted in the organization structure between you and him, which means you've been effectively demoted, anyway.

In dealing with a boss who dislikes hard truths, it pays the astute subordinate to assume the guise of a yes-man. This isn't as difficult as it sounds: it means feigning obsequious acquiescence: laughing at the boss's jokes, choosing areas of disagreement with great care (and loudly agreeing with him on non-issues, topics which, regardless of your true opinions, neither effect nor interest you). When you must disagree, refrain from using the second person singular: never employ the pronoun *you* in these conversations.

Instead, you might counter his latest manifesto with something on the order of, "Jeez, Mel, that's a great idea. But wait, I'm concerned it (make the idea the actor, not your insecure boss) could leave us/the agency (never "you") open to unfavorable/ hostile reactions or criticism from . . ." and go on to spell it out.

---

*   The head of my first agency employed this tactic with a slightly different slant: he insulated himself from reality (in the form of naysayers) by inserting women into the reporting relationships with subordinates who troubled him with the *N-word* or any similar message unfit for his ears.

or

"You know, they tried that in Brooklyn in 1968, and here's what happened . . .

Increasingly under siege over his prosecution of the Viet Nam War,

"... President Johnson continued to reach out for advice. For help in deciding what changes, if any, he should make in the conduct of the war, he solicited Mac Bundy's judgment. Mac replied [by] memo ... '*I think your position is as right as ever* . . .' [emphasis added]" (Robert S. MacNamara with Brian Van de Mark, *In Retrospect*, Random House, 1995.)

McGeorge Bundy, national security advisor to President Johnson, is described by David Halberstam, a John F. Kennedy booster and apologist, as among the very brightest of Kennedy's "brightest and best."

Clearly, yes-manship is unconstrained by individual brilliance and flourishes in the highest levels of government.

See also INSULATION, *IPSE DIXIT*, OFFICE HUMOR, PRESS RELATIONS, SAYING NO, and SENSORY DEPRIVATION.

be more accurate, since this ....

Friends in government who've read early drafts of this amateur foray into the sociology of government agencies have found this manual, in no particular order, entertaining, amusing, enlightening, insightful, elucidating, infuriating, even disturbing. And a handy reference—one friend claims to refer to it every day. Reading it brought into sharp focus many little things around their office that they had either noticed but paid little mind to or had simply taken for granted. In a few instances, it profoundly deepened their understanding of otherwise anomalous or aberrant behavior. In every case, it broadened and deepened their understanding of agency life.

I hope you find it equally useful.

One thing for sure: if you judiciously apply what you learn here, it's unlikely that you will get in trouble. And, as I hope you now understand, if supervisors, rivals and colleagues don't like what you've learned, there's not a damn thing they can do about it!

And, I hope, it will make playing The Agency Game infinitely more fun and rewarding. Just one last caution: beware of innocently parroting the ideas and theories propounded here with any colleagues, lest you be instantly and irreparably (for your career) be branded a free-thinker, or worse, a heretic; denial runs deep in the human psyche. and people will rationally strike out, especially at bearers of hard, uncongenial truths.

Additional readings for the serious student of enduring and prospering in agency employ. Plus what teachers never taught you.

Kotler, Philip H. *Marketing Management: Analysis, Planning and Control,* third edition, Prentice Hall, 1976. The definitive ABCs of marketing. The skills and body of knowledge so little known yet so important to the survival of the agency. Kotler deserves an economics Nobel for organizing that body of knowledge concerned with selling goods and services.

————, and Roberto, Eduardo L. *Social Marketing: Strategies for Changing Public Behavior,* Free Press, 1989. Sometimes authority alone is not enough: how to bend a suspicious, recalcitrant public to the agency's will.

Machiavelli, Niccolo. *The Prince.* New American Library, 1952. *The* timeless classic on running a public sector organization. Although it was written for a 15th Century Italian monarch, its message is as fresh and relevant today as it was in Renaissance Italy.

Parkinson, C. Northcote. *Parkinson's Law and Other Studies in Administration.* Houghton Mifflin, 1957. The precursor of the theory of agency life-cycle. Primitive by today's standards, yet for its day, a work of penetrating insight and wisdom.

Townsend, Robert. *Further Up the Organization: How to Stop the Corporation From Stifling People and Strangling Profit.* Alfred A. Knopf, 1984. The definitive "how to run a Theory Y Corporation" manual, and therefore, the ultimate compendium of don'ts and never for public sector management—the classic how not-to book of public administration.

Trattner, John H. *A Survivors' Guide for Government Executives.* University Press of America, 1989. Narrow in scope: Trattner writes expressly for incoming presidential appointees to federal positions, who comprise an infinitesimally small percentage of government staffers. Still he does a good job in enumerating and classifying the myriad factors and forces that can turn the head of senior staff. Since Trattner writes about the governmental

.ie (and the public) would like it to be—he presumes incoming
sition holders seek to *make a difference*—his treatment of the topic
. tad from mine.

1ax. *The Theory of Social and Economic Organization.* trans. by Talcott
;ons, the Free Press, 1947. Another timeless classic, ranks with Machiavelli.
;plains the hows and whys of bureaucracy. *The* work in its field.

.ams, Joseph M. Style: *Toward Clarity and Grace.* University of Chicago
Press, 1990. A masterful explanation of how to use the written word to your
advantage. His theory of agency, of actor, embedded among his how-to-write
explications, well repays the effort required to unearth it.